The Millennium Snark Trilogy

ALSO AVAILABLE FROM EVERTYPE

Snarkmaster, written and illustrated by Byron W. Sewell, 2012

In the Boojum Forest, written and illustrated by Byron W. Sewell, 2014

Murder by Boojum, written and illustrated by Byron W. Sewell, 2014

The Haunting of the Snarkasbord, by Alison Tannenbaum, Byron W. Sewell, Charlie Lovett, August A. Imholtz, Jr., 2012

Close Encounters of the Snarkian Kind, by Byron W. Sewell, 2016

The Annotated Alice in Nurseryland, by Byron W. Sewell, 2016

Sun-hee's Adventures Under the Land of Morning Calm, by Victoria J. Sewell & Byron W. Sewell, 2016

The Aventures of Alys in Wondyr Lond, Middle English verse by Brian S. Lee, illustrated by Byron W. Sewell, 2013

Alice's Bad Hair Day in Wonderland: A Tangled Tale, by Byron W. Sewell and Victoria J. Sewell, 2013

Alice's Adventures in an Appalachian Wonderland, written and illustrated by Byron W. Sewell, 2012

Álopk's Adventures in Goatland, by Byron W. Sewell, illustrated by Mahendra Singh, 2011

Alix's Adventures in Wonderland: Lewis Carroll's Nightmare, written and illustrated by Byron W. Sewell, 2011

The Carrollian Tales of Inspector Spectre, written and illustrated by Byron W. Sewell, 2011

The Millennium Snark Trilogy

SNARKMASTER
A DESTINY IN EIGHT FITS

ATCHAFALAYA BOOJUM

MURDER BY BOOJUM
A MYSTERY IN EIGHT FITS

Tales inspired by Lewis Carroll's
The Hunting of the Snark

by Byron W. Sewell

ILLUSTRATED AND WITH MAPS BY
THE AUTHOR

2024

Published by Evertype, 19A Corso Street, Dundee, DD2 1DR, Scotland. *www.evertype.com*.

Snarkmaster was first published by Evertype (ISBN 978-1-78201-002-9) having been previously issued privately in 2000 in an edition of fifteeen copies); *Atchafalaya Boojum* was first published by Evertype in *In the Boojum Forest* (ISBN 978-1-78201-078-4) having been previously issued privately in 2000 in an edition of ten copies); *Murder by Boojum* was first published by Evertype (ISBN 978-1-78201-079-1) having been previously issued privately under the title *Snark! A Murderous Agony in Eight Fits* in 2000 in an edition of ten copies);

A catalogue record for this book is available from the British Library.

ISBN-10 1-78201-329-6
ISBN-13 978-1-78201-329-7

Typeset in De Vinne Text, Mona Lisa, ENGRAVERS' ROMAN, and *Liberty* by Michael Everson.

Illustrations: Byron W. Sewell.

Cover: Michael Everson. "Bird and Bellman with Boojum cactus" was taken from *The Haunting of the Snarkasbord* (ISBN 978-1-904808-98-5); "Raven and Cactus" was taken from *Murder by Boojum* (ISBN 978-1-78201-078-4).

Preface

It has been my very great pleasure to put many of Byron W. Sewell's Snarkian and other works into print for a wider audience than the ten or fifteen copies the first editions could reach. As Snark Day approached this year, I tbought it would be nice to take three of Byron's tales, which he considered to be a trilogy, and issue them under one cover.

Snark Day was perfectly described on 18 July 2010 by Mahendra Singh:

> Today is Snark Day, that auspicious day 136 years ago when Lewis Carroll began composing *The Hunting of the Snark* and thus, in a semiotic and hypermetaphysical manner, began decomposing the non-existence of *The Hunting of the Snark*.

Thanks are due to Lewis Carroll, for that composition and decomposition, 150 years ago this year, as they are due to Byron for having given us such inspired and delightful tales. Byron's works stand out as an important part of the Carrollian canon. They deserve more attention.

Michael Everson
Dundee, 18 July 2024

Ocean of Sorrows

Snarkmaster

A Destiny in Eight Fits

SLAND

SNARKII ISLAND

ISLE OF SKARN

Boojum Strait

SNARK ISLAND

EQUATOR

ISLANDS

Byron W. Sewell

Illustrated by the Author

The Millennium Snark Trilogy

Snarkmaster

Foreword to the 2012 edition of *Snarkmaster*

Among the many unique Snarkian works written by Byron W. Sewell, *Snarkmaster* stands alone quite distinctly as a unique, gripping tale of a power struggle between good and evil, concluding with the development of an unusual intermediate state. Most of the story takes place prior to the traditional Snark voyage (described in verse in Lewis Carroll's *The Hunting of the Snark*), but becomes inextricably linked with it—unless it isn't…

The literary structure of *Snarkmaster* reveals some influence of Carroll's *Sylvie and Bruno* tales, as the characters (including the great Charles Dodgson himself) experience dream states and the appearance of at least one fairy. The comprehensive glossary and painstakingly hand-detailed maps of each of the islands in the archipelago may not be essential to follow the story, but they certainly enhance it. The meticulously hand-inked illustrations emphasize some of the important aspects of the story and provide a tropical ambiance for the text. While not necessarily a prerequisite, knowledge of Carroll's original poem is likely to make *Snarkmaster* more enjoyable for most readers.[1]

The Snark Archipelago is a remarkable place. Readers will discover there that features of the islands take their tones (either depressing or cheerful, respectively) from the nature of each island's inhabitants, either evil or good.

In this work, we learn more about the natural history of the Snark than we do from any other source—their habitats, body sizes, array of scale colours, personalities, and behaviour. We find here, for the first time, that snarks can be more or less domesticated and trained to do the bidding of man (well, at least, those humans who are Snarkmasters!). We learn also that snarks are omnivores: Who would have thought that one of the staple foods of these potentially lethal creatures would be a four-foot-tall species of watercress?

Alison Tannenbaum
May 2012

1 The publisher quite naturally recommends the Evertype edition, published in 2010 (ISBN 978-1-904808-36-7)

Contents

Fit I
The Sighting

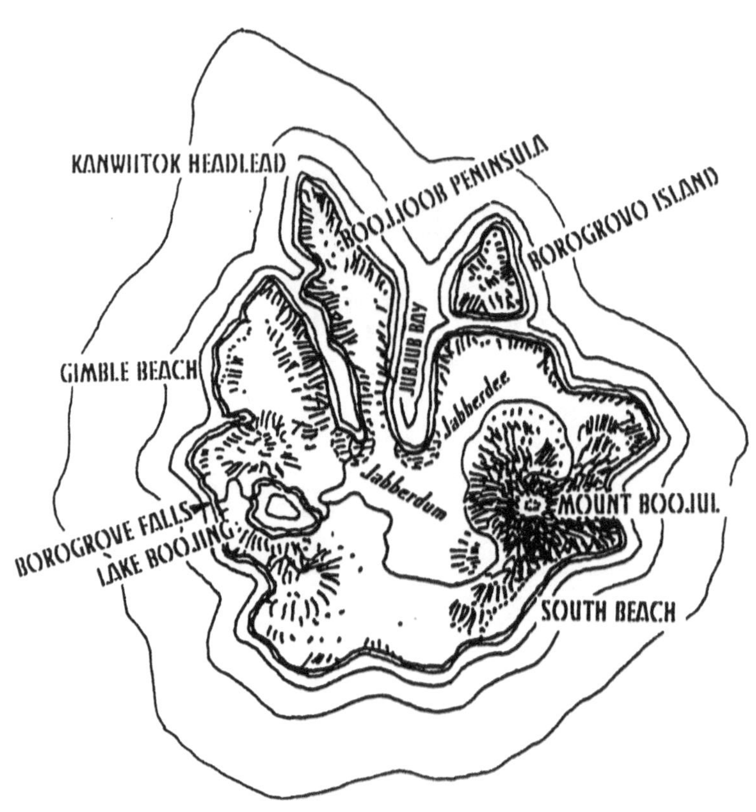
KANWHTOK HEADLEAD
BOOJOOB PENINSULA
BOROGROVO ISLAND
JUBJUB BAY
GIMBLE BEACH
Jabberdee
Jabberdum
MOUNT BOOJUL
BOROGROVE FALLS
LAKE BOOJING
SOUTH BEACH

KRANS

FIT THE FIRST

The Sighting

Twelve-year old Stobo stood as close to the edge of the rocky outcropping of Kanwiitok Headland as he dared and carefully peered over the sheer hundred-foot cliff at the surf crashing against the dark, jagged rocks. The water looked almost black in contrast to the white surf and the silvery-grey predawn sky. Thousands of sea birds swirled around the cliff's black volcanic face, squabbling like illegal immigrants for limited landing and nesting space on the narrow ledges. The stiff, humid wind blowing in from the sea carried their shrill cries over the sound of the crashing surf. The combination of height, the swirl of surf, and wheeling birds brought him a sense of vertigo, and he pulled back a few steps, suddenly afraid that he might tumble headfirst into the inky darkness of the Ocean of Sorrows.

He sat down and looked at the enormous arc of water at the horizon and then back at the dark green slopes of the jungle-covered foothills leading to the nearly vertical rise of Mount Boojul, six miles to the southeast, its three thousand-foot high summit perpetually obscured in clouds. As the sun began rising over the little offshore island of Borogrovo and across narrow Jubjub Bay the clouds surrounding Mount Boojul began to glow a neon-pink, as if the dormant volcano was coming back to life. It was breathtaking to see the sun emerge from beneath the sea, for a moment looking like it was floating on the surface of the ocean like a big luminous ball.

Kanwiitok Headland is the northern-most point of the chain of eight Snark Islands, an archipelago just south of the equator in the vast Ocean of Sorrows, as its residents call what Europeans had recently named The Pacific. The Snarkians hadn't gotten the word yet, since no European had ever visited the Snark Islands to set them straight on the matter and tell them what the *real* name is. In fact, as far as any Snarkian knew, *no* outsider had ever paid them a visit; not that Europeans hadn't been trying to find them, though. The problem is that a curious anomaly in the weather and ocean currents results in a persistent doughnut-shaped fog, which usually surrounds the archipelago. On several occasions, Dutch, Portuguese and English explorers had sailed by tantalizingly close, just missing the place by less than fifty leagues, though only God could see this, of course. Most of the maps of these early explorers show the area where the Snark Islands are located as perfectly blank. One Dutch map shows the area as a huge bank of fog and cautions the traveller to beware of shoals and sea monsters. The Snarkians believe that the gods had created their primeval forebears right there on one of the islands. They didn't call them "Adam and Eve", however; here they were "Snarl and Boob".

As Stobo stared at what he assumed to be the distant edge of the flat, circular world, he tried to imagine the waters of the ocean cascading over the edge in an enormous circular waterfall. That's what his grandfather, by far the smartest man he knew, believed and had taught him. "But where does the water come from that replenishes that flood?" he asked himself. "And what does it fall into?" He wasn't able to answer either question, which was okay, since no one else on the islands could answer them either. His grandfather simply said that the water fell into a bottomless abyss. At that particular instant of thought his eye suddenly caught site of a dark speck flying towards Krans from the northeast. It was either very small and close offshore or very large and far away; he couldn't tell which, though it would be very unusual to see something large coming from far out over the ocean. He finally decided that it didn't really fly like any bird he had ever seen and decided that it might be an aquatic god who had come up from out of the abyss. He watched its approach spellbound, having never seen a god before. However, when it finally got close enough for him to begin to make out its shape he decided that it was more likely a very large bird or a winged snark after all, though unlike any he had ever seen.

It occurred to Stobo that this winged creature might be hungry after its transoceanic flight from the abyss and that he might just be snack-size. He jumped up and bolted for the edge of the jungle, where he ducked behind the wide trunk of a towering tumtum tree, from where he peered out at the approaching monster.

It was the ugliest and largest animal that Stobo had ever seen and the hideous creature flew by just to the east of the canopy of his tumtum tree, so that he got a clear view as it glided by on gigantic leathery wings. Its huge, oversized head was attached to its very large body by a long, crane-like neck. Terrifyingly long, curved talons projected from the toes of all four of its feet, and its hind legs were so large and muscled that Stobo was sure it could easily jump over a coconut palm if it tried. But most wondrous of all was its long dragon-like tail that undulated like a sea serpent swimming through the air.

As Stobo watched, it flew straight for Mount Boojul, eventually disappearing into the clouds that hid the top of the mountain. Stobo emerged from behind the tree and danced wildly in a little circle, whooping and hollering at the top of his voice like a hallucinating savage high on blue mushrooms.

"I've seen the most amazing snark that ever lived!" he yelled at the soaring fleibinite birds and arguing gulls that swirled above him, but of course they could care less than nothing about what he had just told them. "I must tell Grandfather! I'm sure that it's an omen of good luck!" he thought (silly boy!), and he scampered off down the well-travelled jungle path that runs along the length of narrow Boojjoob Peninsula towards Jabberdee at the far end of Jubjub Bay.

It took him two hours to make the five mile trip back to Jabberdee, which was good time for scurrying along the path cluttered with logs, rocks and cut branches. When he finally emerged he sprinted the final one hundred yards to his grandfather's large snarkabana.

His grandfather, the hereditary Quarksnarkian High Priest of Krans, lived in a luxurious snarkabana second in size only to that of Krans' Snarkon, their island's sub-chief. The snarkabana was unusually long, with a towering swaybacked roof, which was thickly thatched with brown palm fronds. The northern end of the structure opened onto a wide verandah providing a breathtaking view directly northward across the length of Jubjub Bay. Enormous snarkaboodles that reached almost to the roofline guarded both sides of the verandah to ward off feral snarks and marauding Darksnarkian spirits.

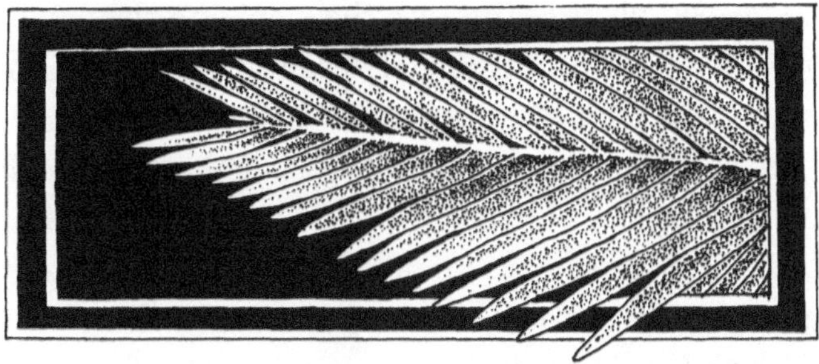

Stobo rushed into the snarkabana screaming at the top of his high pitched, pre-pubescent voice. “Grandfather! Grandfather!”

Stobo’s grandfather, Senbont, an ancient man of at least ninety years, was the oldest and most wrinkled man on Krans. In fact, he might have been the oldest man on all of the Snark Islands; no one was certain, since the only one who was allowed to celebrate his own birthday was the Snarkaiser, the unified archipelago’s Big Chief. Senbont was as thin and bent as a boojum tree, weighing no more than 80 pounds stark naked. He had lost most of his hair and teeth, and his eyes were beginning to cloud over with cataracts caused by years of looking at the bright sunlight reflecting off of the sparkling waters of Jubjub Bay. But in spite of his aging body he was as feisty as a two-month old snarkling.

He stopped chanting when he heard Stobo burst into the dimly lit snarkabana and looked up from his morning rituals. Pungent smoke from the altar on which he was offering his daily sacrifice of watercress to Quarksnark filled the room. Stobo’s eyes immediately filled with tears from the smoke and he couldn’t see much better than his grandfather.

“Yes, Stobo?” Senbont croaked in an ancient Skarnawakan dialect that was so thick that most of the younger generation found it to be almost unintelligible.

“What is it?”

Stobo groped his way through the smoke to the small altar and knelt before it on the floor. He bent forward, banging his forehead loudly on the timbered floor to get the god's attention. In the enveloping spirit world Quarksnark laughed at his impulsive behaviour. Stobo muttered a hurried, breathless prayer so as not to offend the god by not talking to him first: "Praise be to the Great Quarksnark, Giver of Life!" Having done this he turned to his grandfather. "I've seen the most amazing creature in the world! It was either a god or the grandfather of all snarks!"

Senbont squinted his eyes and looked hard at Stobo, trying to see his face through the opaque filter of cataracts and smoke, 'When and where did you see this creature?"

"It flew almost directly over me at Kanwiitok Headland this morning at sunrise!"

"What did it look like?"

"It was very big and savage looking, and had huge wings."

Grandfather held up his palm, 'Slow down, child. Think hard and try to describe it better than that. How big was it?"

"Almost as long as this snarkabana," he exaggerated, though not much.

Senbont laughed, then choked on the smoke, which made him cough for a minute. "Now, Stobo; do not exaggerate! Something as big as this dwelling could hardly fly."

"Honest, Grandfather! From the tip of its head to the tip of its long tail it was almost as long as this snarkabana!"

Senbont stood up on his creaking, arthritic joints with some effort. "Come, let's go out onto the beach and you can draw me a picture in the sand of what you saw." He headed for the door on thin, bandy legs, motioning Stobo to follow. They went out onto the beach and stopped above the tidemark. "Now, draw me the best picture you can," Senbont instructed. "Find a stick."

Stobo picked up a twig and sat down on the sand. His grandfather peered over his shoulder to watch him as he drew, able to see much better in the morning sunlight. "It had a big head," Stobo began, "with very big teeth, and bulging eyes. I thought they might pop right out of their sockets." He drew a circle and two smaller circles in the middle of it for eyes. Then he added some teeth to a mouth. "It had a long neck, like a crane or a pelican, and it had a very big body, with a funny fat stomach." He giggled as he drew a pear-shaped outline and connected it to the head with a long neck that looked insufficient to hold up such a large head.

"You said it flew over you," Senbont said. "What did its wings look like?"

"Like the wings of an enormous fruit bat. It didn't flap its wings very often though; mostly it just extended them and glided on the wind like an fleibinite bird." He drew two large bat-shaped wings attached at the shoulders. "It had very big hind legs and smaller front legs, rather like an emerald snark, and its toes and fingers had savage-looking claws." He drew two small legs in front and two large, very muscular legs on the back, then short curved lines to represent claws. "It had a very long tail that writhed like a sea serpent as it flew," he added, drawing a long, tapering tail. He stood up and looked down at the drawing he had made in the sand. "Yes, that's what it looked like," he said. "That's the best I can do. Oh, I almost forgot. I think its body was covered in feathers."

His grandfather stepped in front of him and erased the drawing with his foot. Stobo cried out, "Grandfather! Why did you do that?"

"We don't want anyone else to see it," he said and turned back to his snarkabana. "Come back inside," he croaked, and led the way. "I've got something to show you. Something I've never shown anyone else."

They stepped into the dimly lit snarkabana and Senbont felt his way over to a far comer. He came back with a snarkaddy, covered in iridescent purple snarkskin. He led the way back out to the verandah into the sunlight and sat down, placing the snarkaddy on the floor between them. He motioned for Stobo to sit down opposite him.

"Is there anyone nearby watching us?" he asked.

Stobo looked around. "No one, Grandfather. My brothers and sisters and our neighbours are on the beach, but they are all busy playing and fishing."

"Good," Senbont croaked, and proceeded to untie the leather thong that bound the snarkaddy. He removed the lid and pulled out a small flat bundle wrapped in costly white snark leather. He looked up, as if to see if anyone had approached them before going ahead and opening the wrap. "Is anyone looking now?" he asked.

"No, Grandfather. There is no one close by."

Assured, he unwrapped the bundle and handed Stobo a highly polished, dark wooden panel about six inches square, on which was engraved an outline drawing. "Grandfather!" Stobo exclaimed. "This is the same creature that I saw!"

"I know," he whispered. "It looks almost exactly like what you drew for me in the sand."

"Where did you get it?"

"I drew it myself, almost seventy years ago, when I was a young man, the first time that I saw the monster."

"Where did you see it?"

"I was on the slopes of Mount Boojul. It glided across the Ocean of Sorrows, approaching the mountain from the north."

"That's exactly where I saw it come from!" Stobo said, "from the Edge of the World."

Grandfather Senbont nodded. "From the Edge of the World, where the Ocean of Sorrows pours its infinite tears into the thirsty Abyss of Nothingness."

"Is it a snark?"

Senbont shook his head slowly. "No, I don't think so."

"Then is it a god?"

"Perhaps. I don't know; but I don't think so."

"How many times have you seen it, Grandfather?"

"Five times. Each time it was ten years since the time before."

"When was the last time?"

"Ten years ago. It's right on schedule."

"Where does it go?"

"Each time I saw it, it disappeared into the clouds at the summit of Mount Boojul. Perhaps it makes a nest there and raises its young, hidden in the mist."

"That doesn't sound like a god," observed Stobo. "Gods don't lay eggs and hatch godlings, do they?"

"Not that I know of, but who can say where gods come from? I suspect that the monster must be an animal or bird, though I've never seen a bird with four legs and wings. Perhaps you are right; it might be some strange sort of gigantic winged-snark."

"Has anyone else ever seen it?"

"I've never met anyone on Krans who ever said that he had. Perhaps someone on another island has seen it. I'm not sure. I suspect that no one would ever admit to having seen it, in any event."

"Why not?"

"They might fear that it is taboo. To admit to having seen it could bring a death sentence."

"Really?"

"Absolutely."

"Well, is it taboo, Grandfather?"

"I don't know."

"Couldn't you ask someone?"

"Yes, but I'm afraid to. Even a high priest can be put to death for violating a taboo."

"Even if you didn't know that it was taboo?"

"Ignorance of the taboo is no excuse. A taboo is a taboo, and there are no mitigating circumstances. In most cases, death is predetermined and certain. Once, many years ago, I even witnessed a Snarkon thrown into the mouth of Boojjum Volcano on Snarko Island for violating a sexual taboo."

"A Snarkon? The ruler of Snarko island?"

"No, he was the Snarkon of Ranks."

"Which sexual taboo did he violate?"

"I will leave the telling of that to your father."

Stobo was disappointed with that response, but knew better than to repeat himself. "So I should never tell anyone else that I've seen this creature?"

"As I said, I've never told anyone before telling you just now. Since you've seen it yourself I feel that I can talk with you about it. But my advice is to be *very* careful whom you tell. It's probably best for you to keep it secret, as I have done. This is why I have placed this tablet in the snarkaddy and marked it taboo, so no one will accidentally open it and come under punishment." He showed Stobo the taboo mark he had engraved into the snarkskin. Stobo handed the panel back to his grandfather, who carefully wrapped it back up in its white snarkskin, then returned it to the snarkaddy. He put the lid back on and tied it up securely. "When I die, this snarkaddy will be yours. I will inform your father."

"I don't want you to ever die, Grandfather," Stobo protested.

He smiled an almost-toothless smile at him. "My time is drawing near. I have lived longer than anyone else can even remember. Daily I thank Quarksnark, for granting me so many years and yet another day."

"Does the monster have a name?"

"I only know the name that I have given it myself, since I know of no one else who has ever seen it. It may have many secret names, each person having named it, but afraid to reveal it."

"What name have you given it, Grandfather?"

"I call it Jabberwok, after our twin towns of Jabberdum and Jabberdee, and the great Jabberbander River that flows from lofty Mount Boojul to the sparkling depths of Lake Boojing."

"Then I shall also call it by this name." Stobo thought for a moment. "I should like try to find the Jabberwok's nest," he said.

"That would be a very dangerous quest! You should wait until you are much older and stronger. You might have to fight with it for your life if it sees you."

"Have you searched for its nest?"

"Yes, but always in vain. The mist is so thick on the mountaintop that I could never find it"

"If I don't go and look for it now I would have to wait another ten years for its return!"

"Yes."

"And even then, I would have to be very lucky to see it again."

"That's true. You have been very blessed by Quarksnark to have seen it even this one time."

"I will go tomorrow and search for the Jabberwok," Stobo declared. "If I am eaten, then I am eaten. I don't want to miss this chance. And besides, I have wanted to climb to Boojul's summit for as long as I can remember. This is as good an excuse as I will ever have."

"You are a very brave boy, Stobo. I understand your desire. I can see that you are resolved to do this, so I will offer daily prayers to Quarksnark for your protection while you are gone, and plead for your safe return."

"If you do that then I will be fine." Stobo had great confidence in the effectiveness of his grandfather's prayers.

"Do not try to harm the creature," Senbont cautioned. "It could kill you in an instant! As you saw, it is *very* large and *very* powerful."

"I will bring you its egg," Stobo said with the confidence of youth.

"Don't disturb the egg under any circumstances! If the Jabberwok comes searching for it many of the villagers might be killed in its fury. It could easily destroy all of our dwellings. If you are lucky enough to find the egg just look at it; don't touch it! And be *very* careful! This is not worth the risk of dying for!"

"It *might* be," Stobo suggested. "Who knows what magic such an egg might hold?"

"Nor what *kind* of magic: either good *or* evil," his Grandfather added. "Be *very* careful!"

"I will," he assured him. "*Very* careful."

Fit II
The Feather

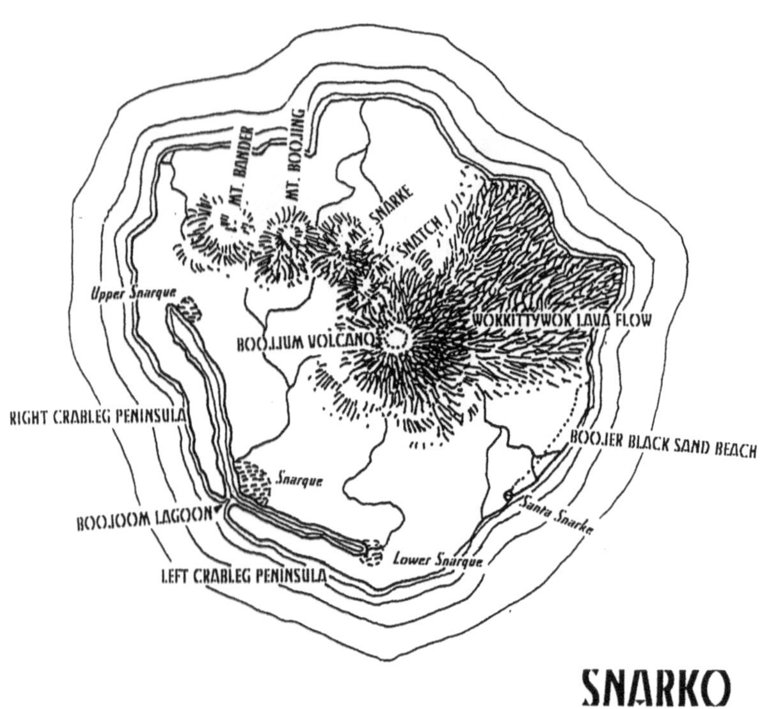
MT. BANDER
MT. BOOJING
MT. SNARKE
MT. SNATCH
Upper Snarque
WOKKITTYWOK LAVA FLOW
BOOJJUM VOLCANO
RIGHT CRABLEG PENINSULA
BOOJER BLACK SAND BEACH
Snarque
Santa Snarke
BOOJOOM LAGOON
Lower Snarque
LEFT CRABLEG PENINSULA

SNARKO

Fit the Second

The Feather

Stobo was up early the next morning, packing food into a soft basket with a shoulder strap for his trip: dried fish, snarkabbage and dried mingomangomingo fruit. His mother, hearing the noise in her cooking area, came in to investigate. "What are you doing?"

"I'm packing food. I will be climbing to the summit of Mount Boojul," he said.

"That's a very dangerous thing for a small boy to do," she responded. "Does your father know about this crazy plan of yours?"

"Yes, Mother," he said. "He gave me his permission last night after Grandfather talked with him, assuring him that this was something I should do. It's a spiritual quest."

"What is this necessary thing?"

"It has to do with my future as a priest," he said. "I can't tell you exactly; it's taboo. If I told you then you might feed the fires of a volcano."

His mother was silenced at this ominous announcement, and immediately backed off. "Do you promise to be careful?"

"Of course."

"There are wild snarks and poisonous snakes in the jungle; and horrid, biting insects and spiders as big as coconuts."

"I know. I'm not afraid."

"Such courage in a small heart!" she said, very proud of his spunk. "I will say prayers for you," she added, though still very apprehensive.

"Thank you, Mother. But you needn't worry about me. Grandfather will also be saying prayers. He has the ear of Quarksnark. I will be fine."

"I hope so," she said, then turned and left him to finish packing his lunch. "Be careful."

Stobo stopped by his grandfather's snarkabana before leaving. He knew he would be awake, out in Jubjub Bay offering the daily sacrifice of dried fish to Sharksnark, the God of the Sea. He found Senbont standing up to his skinny calves in the quiet, blue waters, sprinkling dried fish flakes all around him while chanting a song of praise. Hundreds of small fish repeatedly leapt from the mirror-flat surface of the water as he sang, as if the water was too hot for them to stay in. When Senbont had finished singing he clapped his hands loudly and two large fish beached themselves, sacrificing themselves for his breakfast.

"Good morning, Grandfather," he said as the old man shuffled ashore.

"Ah! Stobo!" he said, as he picked up the two fish that Sharksnark had sent him. "Are you still determined to hunt the Jabberwok?"

"Yes, Grandfather. I'm just now leaving."

"I have something for you to take on your dangerous trip," he said. "Come with me." He handed Stobo the fish. "Here; make yourself useful and carry these."

They walked up the beach to his snarkabana. "You can wait on the verandah," he said as he disappeared into the darkness of the door. In a moment he returned, carrying his vorpal sword in one hand and its sheath in the other. The sword's haft was fashioned from polished tumtum tree wood and was about as long as his arm. Embedded on opposite sides of the haft were rows of snark's teeth, forming two razor-sharp, serrated edges. It was a fearsome weapon that could cause great injury when sliced across an opponent or animal. In the hands of a strong man it could easily decapitate a person. Senbont put it in its emerald coloured snarkskin sheath and handed it to Stobo by the handle. "Take my sword with you, but be careful. It can also injure you badly if you mishandle it. Keep it in its sheath, so that you won't get cut on its sharp teeth. They have a terrible bite and if you cut yourself you might easily bleed to death before you can get help."

"Thank you, Grandfather. I shall take good care of it and return it to you. I promise to be careful with it."

"Go with Quarksnark," he told him, then patted his head as a way of blessing. "Remember; Darksnark likes to find small boys alone in the jungle, so be on your guard." Stobo bowed his head to show him respect, then turned away towards the path that led into the jungle. He felt proud to be trusted with such a dangerous weapon and the weight of the vorpal sword in his hand gave him a sense of invincibility. He felt ready for anything and pretended to be a professional snarker.

Mount Boojul was less than two miles distant as the snark flies, but there was no bridge across the Jabberbander River than ran between them. So the path to the mountain headed east, following the course of the river, circling the base and eventually going up the eastern slope near the headwaters. The result was that it was a difficult four-mile jungle trek. If he pressed hard it would probably take him at least four hours to get to the starting point for the ascent. The climb to the summit could take a full day, and he would likely have to spend the night in a tree to be out of the reach of foraging feral snarks and hungry jubjub birds.

The jungle soon closed in around him on both sides of the narrow pathway that had been laboriously hacked through the trees and brush over the years. Every few months a work party from Jabberdee and Jabberdum would spend a few days clearing the path of recent growth to keep it open. Felled saplings and branches littered the path, and there was even an occasional felled tree across the path that he would have to clamber over. The air along the path was as still as a basking lizard and was heavy with the sickly sweet aroma of the yellow dongbingodong flower, which was in perpetual bloom.

Stobo walked as quietly as he could along the path in hopes of seeing a snark, but they were elusive, and in spite of his best efforts he never caught sight of anything other than the brightly-coloured birds that flitted through the trees, sounding alarm calls at his approach. But he could easily hear the snarks scurrying through the underbrush to the side of the path or charging up ahead of him.

Occasionally there would be a sharp snarkbark, followed by the crashing sounds of snarks bolting through the undergrowth. And there was certainly no shortage of snarksign on the path. Small footprints could be seen in the mud and there were innumerable small piles of snarkscat. He even found a tree whose bark had been shredded on one side by the fearsome claws of a mature snark, and the leaves around it reeked of the distinctive odor of snarkpee where the animal had marked its territorial boundary. The penetrating odor of snarkpee even overwhelmed the strong perfume of the dongbingodong. He hoped and prayed that he would not meet up with such a snark, knowing full well that if he did he likely would not survive the encounter.

By the time he finally broke out of the dense river bottom jungle onto the sparser Eastern Highlands it was well after noon. He stopped at a clear pool, fed by a noisy waterfall from one of the numerous streams that cascaded down the steep mountain slope, continuously fed by incessant rainfall at the high, cool summit. While sitting on a large rock at the edge of the pool he heard the rustling of bushes on the other side of the pool and froze to watch. A few minutes later a troop of six small lime-green snarks, the largest a male about eighteen inches high, emerged, cautiously sniffing the air. Stobo watched as they foraged for small clumps of wild snarkabbage that grew along the banks. The male suddenly smelled Stobo and snarkbarked, sending the whole troop into panicked flight, scattering into the undergrowth. One small hysterical snark fell off of the bank into the pool. It was comical to watch as it frantically swam to the bank and clambered out, squealing as it went.

These brightly coloured, intricately patterned little snarks were harmless unless you tried to hold them, in which case they would invariably nip you. They were probably recent feral descendants of escaped snarkattle, with a justified and innate fear of man, their parents no doubt having told them about cooking pots. Many would be captured in nets and find themselves unwilling new residents in snarkfarms, and still others would be preyed upon by larger, carnivorous snarks. Mature wild snarks were a very real and lethal danger to anything they met, including their own offspring. Unless Stobo could find an appropriate tree to scurry up he would likely be snarkmeal for any that he encountered, vorpal sword or not. They were highly intelligent and quite capable of successfully stalking and preying upon men, even a well-armed and experienced snarker.

Stobo finished his lunch and got a drink from the dark pool whose water was stained with the tannin from leaves that had fallen into it. Satisfied, he began the climb up the steep mountain slope. There was no path to the summit so he followed the course of the stream that fed the pool where he had lunched, as it cut through the often dense and thorny undergrowth. He encountered frequent snarksign along the stream's banks, but didn't actually see any more of them for the rest of the afternoon. Towards dusk, exhausted from the climb and still a few hundred feet below the cloud shrouded summit, he spotted a large tammoo tree, festooned with a spaghetti of vines that he could climb.

He was a good climber, adept at scurrying up a coconut palm, and was soon ensconced on a large limb, high above the ground where he would have been easy snarkprey. He ate a meager supper, disciplining himself to save some of his food for tomorrow, and being exhausted from the day's hike decided to go right to sleep, even though there was still an hour or more of daylight. Afraid that he might fall out of the tree in his sleep, he used his vorpal sword to hack down a few vines and used them to tie himself to a large limb in a sitting position, where he would sleep, safe from all but slithy toves, bandersnatches, and winged snarks.

He went to sleep immediately, but was woken in the middle of the night by the low frequency sounds of snark growls and loud sniffing at the base of the tree. A full moon had risen and Stobo could see the ground distinctly, though colours were not discernible. He carefully peered over the edge of the limb and looked straight down into the face of a large snark, standing about six feet tall on his large hind legs. It either saw him or smelled him, because it stared up very intently at him, as if trying to judge whether or not he was within reach. Stobo pulled back and unsheathed his vorpal sword. He had no sooner done this than the snark leapt at his perch, its mouth agape and ready to snatch him away. Stobo struck it on its nose with a downward blow from his sword and the snark screamed in agony as it fell back to earth and went crashing noisily through the undergrowth. The snark's cry was nearly deafening, and Senbont, asleep in his hammock in his snarkabana back in Jabberjee, distinctly heard its high pitched sound, carried by the night winds that reversed themselves and returned north to the ocean. He was suddenly awake, knowing in his spirit that a snark had attacked his grandson.

Senbont lowered himself from his hammock and went to the small altar in the comer of his sleeping room, where he lit a burnt offering of watercress and prayed for the next hour, interceding with Quarksnark for his grandson's safety.

Back in the tammoo tree, Stobo was wide awake and shaking like he had contracted a snarkovirus fever. He had never faced a snark as vicious and as large as this one that had been intent on eating him. It had quite unnerved him, and he continued to hold the vorpal sword at the ready, just in case the snark should return to try again. Two hours later he was still awake, studying the jungle to try to see anything that might approach his tree. He gradually tired as the adrenaline rush receded and he managed to get a few more hours of sleep before he was woken once again by the calls of birds anticipating the dawn.

He untied the vines that had secured him in the tree and lowered himself to the ground. The leaves of the plants at the base of the tree were splattered with snark blood. Somewhere in a snarkave the snark would be nursing a very sore snout. Stobo looked up at Boojul's summit and saw it still obscured by the enveloping clouds. He had no idea if he would be able to see anything in those mists and began to worry that he might get lost as well. But he was determined to find the Jabberwok's nest and set off up the steep slope once again. He found an occasional patch of snarkabbage and plucked some of the newer, tender shoots to have a vegetarian breakfast on the move.

An hour later he was at the base of the clouds and with a gulp to swallow his fears he began to climb into the mist. He soon found himself enveloped and able to see only a few feet ahead. He climbed, rock to rock, tree to the next tree, in as straight a line as he could manage and always trying to go uphill. After another hour of this he finally reached a level area which he assumed to be the summit. Still unable to see more than a few feet in front of him he groped his way around on it for several more hours, but found nothing. He was now hopelessly lost, though he could see a faint light in the dense clouds that indicated the sun's position.

It was very frustrating to be so close yet so far, unable to find anything he had been searching for. He sat down on a rock and fought back unmanly tears of disappointment that tried to spill over chubby baby cheeks. He looked up and tried to decide which way was north, based on the position of the faint glow of the sun behind the clouds, intending to start back down the mountain. Then he heard what sounded like a loud cackle off to his left and he whirled around, raising his vorpal sword to defend himself from whatever might emerge from the mists. But nothing came. Then another loud cackle. This time he crept towards the strange sound as quietly as he could manage, straining his eyes to try to see through the opaque, glowing mist.

Suddenly a very large black shape loomed up in the mist and he froze, no more than four feet away from whatever it was. He could smell it now, a strange sweetish, sulphurous stench that was quite repellent, unlike anything he had ever smelled before. Then he sneezed.

The result was electric. The black form lifted off into the air with a sudden leap and screamed a hideous, terrifying noise. The downward stroke of enormous wings sent a gust of wind rushing into his face. Stobo bolted back into the mists in the direction he had come from, stumbling and leaping over rocks and brush until he came upon the enormous log of a fallen tumtum tree. He scurried frantically along its length until he found a depression beneath it into which he could squeeze. He slithered in and jammed himself as far back into the space as he could go.

The foul smelling monster pursued him and was soon at the entrance to his hiding place beneath the log. Another terrible scream, perhaps of frustration at having missed its quarry, rent the mists. A long talon suddenly emerged into Stobo's hiding space and clawed haphazardly about, as if blindly trying to snag a larvae. Stobo sucked in his stomach and tried to force himself even further back. The claw missed him by only inches, then finally withdrew. Stobo held his breath.

After fifteen minutes, that seemed like an hour, the stench retreated and Stobo knew that the monster had gone. He slowly emerged from his hiding place and listened carefully and smelled the mist to try to assure himself that it was indeed gone. Then he heard and felt a rush of wind as whatever it was took flight, and he finally realized that it had been the Jabberwok.

Stobo imagined that he must have inadvertently stumbled upon its nest in the impenetrable mist and was lucky to be alive. His natural inclination was to hurry off of the mountain as quickly as he could, but he wasn't about to leave without some hard evidence of the monster to show his grandfather. Assuming that the monster had indeed flown away, at least for the moment, he retraced his steps to where he thought its nest must be, and finally bumped up against an enormous pile of palm fronds and tree branches. He quickly checked the huge nest, expecting to find an egg, but to his great disappointment there was none. He wasn't sure if the monster had carried it away when it flew or if it simply hadn't laid it yet.

Then he saw the feather, on the opposite edge of the huge nest. He scrambled over and snagged it, then clambered back to the ground and headed for the descent. He didn't care where he emerged. He just wanted out of the obscuring clouds as soon as he could manage.

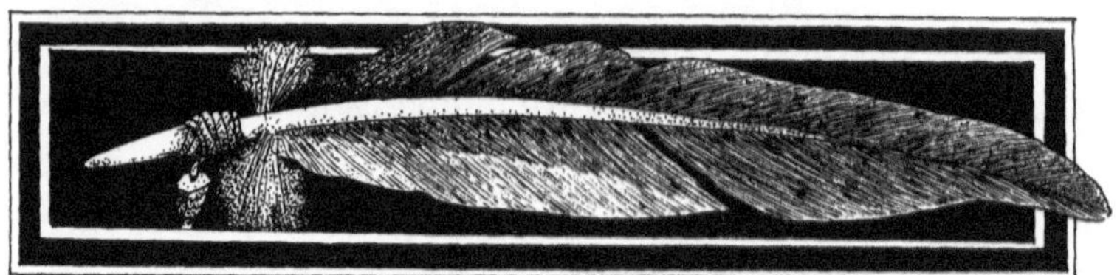

It only took him twenty minutes to scramble down the mountainside and back into the sunlight, which was his first real opportunity to study the feather. It was about a foot long, and reminded him of a parrot's tail feather. Depending upon how he turned the feather to catch the light it would be iridescent blue, or purple or black. There was even one position that revealed a hint of green. He could hardly wait to show his grandfather and father. He looked down the mountain at Krans spread below him. He quickly saw that he had emerged from the clouds on the northern slope. He could clearly see Boojjoob Peninsula and Jubjub Bay to the northwest, though he was much too far away to be able to make out his little hometown of Jabberjee

He had to circle around Mount Boojul to the east so as to come down on the north side of the curving Jabberbander River, and then descend, essentially retracing his steps of the previous day. It was near dusk before he finally entered the outskirts of town and made for his grandfather's dwelling. He found his grandfather standing up to his knees in the now darkening waters of the bay, praying to Quarksnark, pleading for protection for the village during the coming night. A stiff breeze was blowing and the normally placid waters of Jubjub Bay were rough, with even an occasional small white cap out in the midst of the bay. Stobo stood at the edge of the surf, shouting, "Grandfather! Grandfather! I've found a feather!"

Senbont turned around, interrupting his devotions and saw a small blurry shape that resembled his grandson Stobo, jumping up and down on the beach, excitedly waving something. He sloshed towards him to see exactly who it was with his poor eyesight. "Stobo! It's you!" He opened his arms and Stobo rushed to him and gave him a small hug. "What have you found?"

Stobo held the dark feather up close to his grandfather's face so he could see it in the dim light with his even dimmer eyesight. "It's one of the Jabberwok's feathers! Look! Isn't it beautiful?"

Senbont reached out to take it in his right hand, then screamed. A bolt of bright blue static arced between his hand and the feather's tip, even coiling up his bare arm to his shoulder. Stobo dropped the feather when Senbont lurched backward into the surf, his eyes wide in fear and astonishment.

Stobo was as stunned as his grandfather, but reached down to retrieve the feather. It did nothing when *he* picked it up. "What happened, Grandfather?" he asked, looking at the ancient man standing in the water, his long grey hair frizzled and standing strangely on end.

"Demons!" he croaked. "Darksnarkian demons!" He took a few more steps out into the bay to distance himself even further from the feather. The water was up to his skinny thighs.

Stobo glanced around to see if he could see the demons his grandfather was describing, but saw nothing except the normal beach activity of children playing in the surf and men casting nets. "What demons?" he asked.

"They're on the feather! Be careful! They may attack you too!"

Stobo looked at the dark feather, not understanding. "But nothing is attacking me!" he said, looking back up at his frightened grandfather. "Look, there's nothing on it." He held it up for his grandfather to see better, but Senbont refused to get closer.

"What was that bluish light that danced up your arm?" Stobo asked

"Spirit fire!" his grandfather said.

"From the feather?"

"From demons *on* the feather!"

Stobo looked at it again, this time examining it very closely to see if perhaps the demons were as small as mites and he just hadn't noticed them; but the quill and vanes looked quite normal. "I don't see them," he responded. "There's nothing here." He turned the feather over to see if something was lurking on the underside. Nothing. He shook it just in case something was hiding in the barbs. "Can you see them?"

"No, but they're there. Just because you can't see a demon doesn't mean that it's not there. Where did you find the feather?"

"On top of Mount Boojul, in the Jabberwok's nest."

"In its nest? You found its nest?"

"Yes. It was very cloudy up on top of the mountain and I could only see a few feet in front of me. I accidentally stumbled into the nest where the Jabberwok was sitting. It smelled terrible, like something dead. The stench made me sneeze, which startled it. I guess it couldn't see me any better than I could see it. It lifted off its nest with a terrible scream and flew up into the clouds. I knew that I was in trouble and ran away, but it chased me. Luckily I came upon a fallen tumtum tree and I crawled underneath its huge trunk into a small depression in the earth. It tried to drag me out with its enormous claws, but fortunately it couldn't quite reach me. I was sure that I would be eaten, but it eventually left when it couldn't drag me out. Later, I returned to its nest, to see if there was an egg. But all I found was this beautiful feather."

"You shouldn't have brought it back," Senbont said. "It's evil."

"Evil?"

"Yes."

"I didn't know," Stobo said. "I just thought it was special and beautiful. I thought you would be excited to see it."

"I didn't know either. I've never seen one. However, I now declare it taboo," he said. "You must take it back to the nest. Show it to no one."

"Take it back?" Stobo asked in dismay. He was bone tired from his long hike and couldn't bear the thought of parting with his new treasure.

"Yes; the sooner the better."

"Tonight?"

"No, that would be much too dangerous. You'd likely be a quick meal for a foraging snark. But you must take it back first thing in the morning."

"Yes, Grandfather," Stobo agreed reluctantly. "I will take it back tomorrow if you insist."

"Take it!" Senbont said, then turned to face the bay again to finish his evening prayers and to invoke protection from the evil that he perceived having touched. Stobo turned and headed up the beach to his parent's snarkabana.

Because of the faint light at dusk and his poor eyesight Senbont didn't see the large dark dorsal fin slicing through the water towards him at high speed. The shark struck his right leg, severing it at the thigh. The impact knocked him off of his feet and drug him underwater. He resurfaced, screaming. Stobo heard him and turned just in time to see his grandfather struggling in the water. He watched in helpless horror as the huge tiger shark hit him again.

Stobo ran to his parent's snarkabana, screaming about the attack. Everyone in the family rushed out to the beach, but by the time they arrived at the scene of the attack there was no sign of Senbont.

The next morning an ocean-going twenty-man canoe, equipped with outriggers, was dispatched to the capitol city of Snarkadelphia on the main island of Snark to advise the Quarksnarkaiser of Senbont's death, and to set in motion the inauguration of Stobo's father, Tebnons, as the new Quarksnarkian High Priest for Krans. All of the inhabitants of Krans would spend the next three days and nights mourning, each family performing the requisite burnt offering of a snarkow to send Senbont's spirit well-provisioned on his journey to the afterlife beyond the Edge of the World, where the Ocean of Sorrows falls into the void.

The night of the attack Stobo was too upset to quickly go to sleep. His trip to return the Jabberwok's feather to Mount Boojul would obviously have to be delayed for at least a week because of the mourning and funeral and the ceremonies for installation of his father as the new High Priest of Krans. Clasping the Jabberwok's feather tightly in his hand he finally managed to nod off just an hour before sunrise, and the moment he was asleep he was caught up in a dream so vivid that he thought he was awake.

He was walking along the broad, deserted beach of Jubjub Bay when a sudden wind of typhoon intensity sucked him straight

up towards the bright full moon suspended in a cloudless nighttime sky amid thousands of brilliant stars of every colour. He felt exhilarated by the sense of flying as he soared through the warm tropical air, leveling out at the same height of distant Mount Boojul's summit, high enough to see the entire island but not low enough to distinguish manmade objects. The dark stingrey-shape of Krans floated in the vast ocean, the moonlight reflected from the water's surface making it look like liquid metal. The Jabberbander River wound across the island like a silver thread attached to bright, balloon-like Lake Boojing. He flew east, past cloud-enshrouded Mount Boojul, and then banked southeast like an albatross, out over the open ocean. Shortly he could see the dark, jagged line of what he assumed to be Snarko Island on the horizon, though he wasn't certain since he had never visited it nor any of the other islands in the archipelago.

High above Snarko he could clearly discern its crab-like shape, the two crab-leg shaped peninsulas forming Boojoom Lagoon. To his astonishment he watched Boojjum Volcano's thin white plume of ash and smoke, thankful that the fire gods weren't very active tonight. He was soon out over the open ocean again and it wasn't long until he could see two-peaked Ranks Island on the eastern horizon. As he overflew the island he was struck by its odd shape, which reminded him of the head of a giant ant, it's fearsome jaws forming Jabberjabber Bay. The twin peaks of Mounts Jabber and Woky on opposite sides of Boojoojum Harbour resembled stalk-like eyes on the ant's head.

Banking to the southeast he was soon out over the ocean again and quickly saw the low dark line of Snarkadia Island, by far the largest and flattest island he had ever seen. As he overflew the island he thought how much it's shape resembled the head of a sea turtle, with Wabjab Bay forming the turtle's open mouth. He could see the white line of Snarkadian Beach along the northeastern coast and the Great Jabberwabber Reef not far offshore. His route took him directly over the small offshore island of Snarkania before once again passing out over the Ocean of Sorrows.

The flight to Snarkawaak Island was by far the longest and for awhile all he could see was water. As he overflew the odd-shaped island he was amazed by Jabbersnatcher Volcano, which towered well above the height of Mount Boojul. He counted the small offshore islands known as the Eight Sisters. Banking northeast for another long flight he eventually approached Snarkii Island, about the same size as Krans. He was enthralled by Lake Boojump, by far the largest freshwater lake on the archipelago.

Crossing the open ocean again he was quickly in sight of the huge island of Snark, which was larger than all of the other Snark Islands combined. He had never imagined that there could be so much land in one place. Snark Island had a shape, which appropriately resembled a snark's head, with Jabbaj Bay forming the mouth. He turned northeast and flew between two of the tall peaks that formed the Snarkian Range and could see towering Mount Boojum, also now dormant. He flew low over the northern beach and across Satona Island, one of the Boojabooja Barrier Islands.

Crossing the ocean again he soon saw the dark line of the sparsely inhabited Isle of Skarn on the horizon. The island was a jumble of towering peaks, with a scattering of offshore islands on the southwest coast. Flying at an altitude of no more than a hundred feet he skimmed across Dreadful and Gloom Islands at treetop height, passing through the Gates of Hell with its towering cliffs to either side. Looking to his left he saw the temple that was the island's only man-made structure, huddled against the foreboding base of Mount Darksnark. He followed the curving cliffs until they opened up into the mirrored blackness the Night Lagoon, surrounded on the north by the Wasting Mountains and the south by the curiously shaped Three Sisters. Skirting around Mount Ominous he overflew Massacre Marsh and to his astonishment saw huge grazing herds of snarks feeding directly below him on the wild watercress and snarkabbage that grew there in abundance. Circling to the north he flew around the perimeter of the marsh, against the dark backdrop of the Craggy Mountains, past Death Mountain and Mount Vanish, then finally made a pinpoint landing on the nipple-like rock that was the summit of Mount Snickersnack. As he looked to the east, down into the black depths of Phantasm Chasm he heard the piercing screams and wails of a boojum snark, that sounded eerily like, 'Wa–a–a–ake u–u–u–up!"

Fit III
Taboo

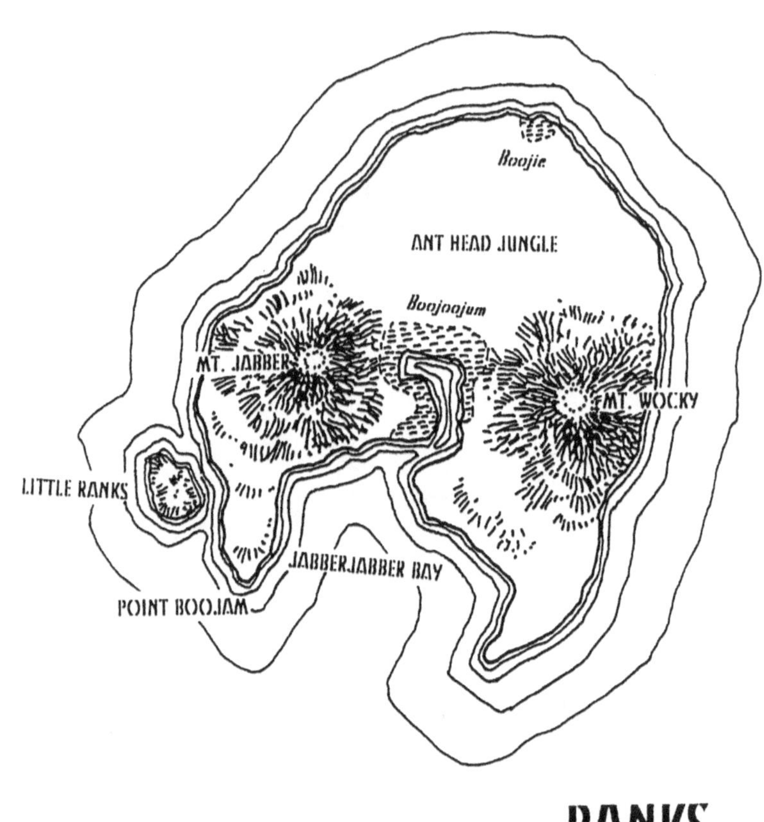
Boojie
ANT HEAD JUNGLE
Boojoojum
MT. JABBER
MT. WOCKY
LITTLE RANKS
JABBERJABBER BAY
POINT BOOJAM

RANKS

Fit the Third

Taboo

Tebnons tried to wake up his son by shaking his shoulders. "Wake up!" his father repeated.

Stobo sat up, then rubbed his eyes. "Where am I?"

"You're home. In bed. You were having a bad dream."

"Oh, it wasn't a *bad* dream, Father. It was wonderful!"

"What did you see?"

"I was flying like a bird. I visited all of the Snark Islands, and came to rest on a tall mountain on what must have been the Isle of Skarn. I could see everything vividly. I know exactly what the islands look like now."

"I'm sure that you think you do, but you have never visited any of those islands and could not possibly know what they look like. I have visited them all during my life and even I could not draw an accurate map."

"But Father, I could easily draw a map. I will do it for you."

Tebnons stared at his son for a minute, then decided to humour him. "Very well. Let's go out to the beach and you can draw me a map of your dream-islands in the sand."

Stobo stood up, forgetting in his drowsiness that he was still holding the feather.

"What's in your hand?"

Stobo looked down at the feather, then quickly put it behind his back to hide it. "Grandfather told me not show it to anyone. He said it was taboo."

"Why would he say that? I've never heard of a feather being taboo! Where did you find it?" He reached out. "Give it to me."

Stobo pulled back. "It may harm you," he warned.

"What do you mean? How could a feather harm anyone?"

"When Grandfather touched it he was burned by bluish devil-fire. That was just minutes before the huge shark attacked him."

Tebnons ignored the warning. "Give it to me!" he demanded.

Stobo reluctantly handed it to him.

Bolts of blue electricity hit his father's hand when he touched it. It knocked him backwards, flat onto his back, and briefly lit up the interior of the snarkabana in a bright bluish flash. The feather floated to the floor at Stobo's feet. He bent over and picked it up. His stunned father lay still on the flooring for a few moments to collect his wits, then slowly sat up, his eyes as wide and round as a nocturnal tove. His arm and shoulder were numb. He began to chant a Quarksnarkian mantra for divine protection.

"I warned you it might hurt you, Father," Stobo said. "Are you all right?"

Tebnons quit chanting. "Did the feather hit your grandfather with such force?" he asked in a hushed voice.

"No, not nearly as hard as that. Though it made his hair stand on its end. He looked like a wild man."

"Were you holding the feather as you slept?"

"Yes, I think so. I must have been."

"Perhaps it was the source of your dream. Come, draw me your map." He got to his feet and led the way out onto the deserted beach. He found a stick and handed it to Stobo. "Draw the map here," he instructed, standing well back from the feather Stobo was now holding in his left hand.

Stobo drew the islands as he could see them in his mind's eye. "This is Krans," he said. "It looks like a stingrey. This is the next island, which would be Snarko. It's shaped like a crab. You can see it's front legs. This is the next one, which must be Ranks. It looks like an ant's head with its eyes on stalks. This is the next one, which must be Snarkadia. It looks like the head of a turtle. This is the next one, which must be Snarkawaak. It has eight little islands offshore. And this is the next one, which must be Snarkii, with its big lake. And this is the big island of Snark, which looks like a snark's head. And the last island I saw must be the Isle of Skarn. It is covered with tall, dark mountains, and has a vast marsh in the center. I saw a temple there and vast herds of grazing snarks." He stood back and looked at the line of island shapes he had scratched into the sand, then up at his father.

Tebnons stared at the drawing in astonishment. Everything he knew about the islands, which was far from complete, was accurately depicted. He knew the names of the offshore islands and barrier reefs; the names of many of the mountains and the bays. He looked at Stobo again. "Only a god could have revealed this to you! No such map of the islands exists anywhere, not even in the Quarksnarkaiser's library."

"It's what I saw. I could show more detail, but I don't know the names of things. I will never forget it. It is engraved in my mind."

"The question is *which* god has revealed these things to you," his father said with a very serious tone.

"If it was a god, then surely it would have been Quarksnark," Stobo said.

"I'm not so sure. You hold that feather in your hands as harmlessly as you would the feather from a gull. When your grandfather, the Quarksnarkian High Priest of Krans, and I, his heir, touch the feather it attacks us. Your grandfather died moments after having touched it. Perhaps I will be next." He glanced at the bay to see if there was a fin, then up at the sky to see if a huge rock would fall out of the aether and crush him.

"What are you saying? That the feather is from some other god?"

"Perhaps. Where *exactly* did you find it?"

"In the nest of a monstrous bird that Grandfather told me he called the Jabberwok. I saw it fly to the top of Mount Boojul and I told him about it. I went there to search for it; perhaps to find its egg. Grandfather had seen the Jabberwok several times, when he was younger. He showed me a drawing he had made of it when he was a young man. He keeps it in a snarkaddy, which he has sealed as taboo. He said that if he died I was to have it."

"I see. Yes, he told me yesterday that when he died that I should give it to you as your inheritance, but he didn't tell me what was inside; only that it was taboo."

"Have you ever seen the Jabberwok, Father?"

"Never."

"Grandfather said that it comes to Krans every ten years to nest on the top of Mount Boojul."

"It is odd that he would not have shared this knowledge with me." Tebnons was growing steadily more and more jealous of his own son's revelations.

"Which god do you think would have revealed the dream to me?"

"It had to be Darksnark."

Stobo was shocked. "But he's evil!"

"Yes. The *embodiment* of evil."

"And he is the enemy of Quarksnark."

"Yes; his sworn foe."

"But I am to be a Quarksnarkian priest someday. I don't understand. Why would Darksnark reveal these things to me?"

"I wonder the same thing." His father's voice sounded ominous and cold. "You must return the feather to the Jabberwok's nest."

"Grandfather also told me to do that, just before the shark attacked him. He told me to do it that day. I was going to, but then he was killed, so I decided that I should wait, until after his funeral ceremonies were over."

"Don't wait."

"Go now? Right now?"

"Yes. Go right now!"

"But I'm hungry; it's a long trek to the top of Mount Boojul!"

His father relented. "Let's go back home. I'll have your mother fix food for you to take. You get a pouch and hide that infernal feather inside it. Don't let anyone touch it, especially any of your brothers or sisters. It might kill them."

They returned to their snarkabana and Stobo went to get a pouch. His father arranged for his wife to fix the food for Stobo's trek. His mother had everything ready in fifteen minutes. She had packed it in a palm basket, affixed to a shoulder strap to make it easy to carry.

"Your grandfather said that he had given you his vorpal sword," his father said. "Do you still have it?"

"Yes. It's there in the corner." He pointed to it.

His father went over and retrieved it. His father handed him the sword. "Take it with you."

"Can I have the snarkaddy that Grandfather promised me?"

"No. It will be burned today at his funeral."

"But—"

Tebnons held up a hand to silence him. "It will be burned. It is taboo. Even to you. His vorpal sword will be your inheritance. It's a valuable gift that I had always hoped would be mine one day, but you shall have it instead. Now go!"

Stobo lowered his head and reluctantly left through the rear door, between the towering snarkaboodles that guarded that entrance. As he passed between them the two skulls perched at the pinnacles suddenly rolled down and landed at his feet, their rows of sharp teeth grinning up at him. It was as if they had been knocked off of the piles by an invisible hand. Spooked, he ran to the edge of the forest and hid behind a tumtum tree to consider what to do. He was angry that his father had decided to burn the engraving of the Jabberwok. He started talking to himself.

"The snarkaddy and Jabberwok's picture were to be mine! He has no right to burn them! And I'm *not* taking the feather back!" He thought for a moment. "All right. I'll go to the mountain and find a hiding place for it. I can always go back and get it someday."

He got up and set off down the jungle trail towards Mount Boojul. As soon as he was well into the jungle he began to hear snarks in the undergrowth, obviously following him. If he picked up his pace they would too. If he stopped they would stop. He began to worry that the snarks might be stalking him and he rushed ahead, trying not to panic. Eventually he located the same waterfall where he had stopped on his previous trip up the mountain, and scrambled up into a large tree and watched to see if whatever had been following him would reveal themselves.

He didn't have long to wait. Within a few minutes a large blue-scaled snark emerged on the jungle trail, walking on all fours and sniffing the air. It was four feet high at the shoulder and would easily be strong enough to kill an adult man. It was a beautiful, but terrifying sight. To his horror it casually walked directly over to his tree and sat down on its haunches and stared up at him. Then another snark emerged from the jungle, this one a slender yellow one, about three feet long. It also walked over to his tree and sat down, beside the first one, and stared up at him. Other snarks emerged over the next half-hour, of various species, sizes and colours, until finally Stobo counted exactly forty-two of them sitting quietly around the base of the tree. It was as if they expected him to make an announcement or sing a song to entertain them.

The snarks were *very* patient, evidently prepared to wait as long as it took. After an hour Stobo finally decided to say something. “Hello,” he said, feeling very foolish to be talking to them.

The effect was electric. The snarks started howling and screaming, many of them running in circles like mad things, and some of them chasing their lizard-like tails. After a few minutes they settled back down and stared up at him again in rapt attention.

“My name is Stobo,” he said. This caused even more feverish activity among the snarks, some rushing wildly into the undergrowth and then rushing back and others leaping into the air. “Perhaps it’s the feather,” he thought. He pulled it out of its pouch and held it up for them to see. The snarks exploded into wild abandon. Rushing in circles, grabbing each other and rolling around or engaging in mock battles. The sound of their screaming was deafening. “It’s *definitely* the feather,” Stobo decided. He waved the feather and yelled, ‘Quiet!” in the most authoritative tone a small boy could manage.

They stopped instantly, sat down where they were and looked up at him expectantly. Stobo decided that he was in no danger and lowered himself to the ground. The snarks immediately rushed him and he thought he would be tom to pieces. But all they did was press in to get near him, licking his legs, body and face. “Snarkisses!” he thought, laughing at the touch of their wet, rough tongues.

"Stop!" he pleaded, and they did. Stobo spent the afternoon playing with the snarkpack. Chasing them, riding on the backs of the larger ones, swimming with them in the pool at the base of the waterfall. By the end of the day he was exhausted and hungry, but the happiest he had ever been in his life. He retrieved his lunch basket and climbed up onto a rock to eat his supper. When he had finished he stood up on the rock and addressed them, most of which were lounging around the bank of the pool. "You should all go back to your snarkaves now. I hope to see some of you tomorrow. But now I want to sleep."

Having said this, all except the large blue-scaled snark got up and slipped silently back into the jungle, disappearing without a trace, like apparitions. Stobo looked into the large eyes of the remaining snark. "You can go, too," he said. But it didn't move. Stobo repeated himself several times, but the snark would have none of it and lay down at his feet. Stobo gave up and lay down with it, propping himself against its back. He was soon fast asleep, the pouch containing the Jabberwok's feather hung from a lanyard around his neck and his sword rested beside him.

Thick white smoke rose up and engulfed him. His ears throbbed with the sound of loud drumming directly beneath him. Many male voices chanted strange words in ancient Skarnawakan in time with the drumbeats.

The smoke gradually cleared and he could see his father, Tebnons, as if he was watching him from a hiding place high in the rafters of his grandfather's snarkabana. His father was dressed in the ceremonial regalia of a Quarksnarkian High Priest, which he thought was odd because it would be weeks before he would be ordained. He was sitting cross-legged in front of an altar formed from a huge snark skull. The top of the cranium had been removed and live coals had been placed inside the cavity. Tebnons' tall conical hat was bedecked with layers of fresh small white orchids. The long golden tail feathers of a jacksprat bird protruded from the top of the hat in a long graceful arc, their tips sweeping back almost to the floor. Tebnons' white robe, made from the pounded bark of the bois bois tree, was decorated in bold geometric patterns, which had been painted with dark blue dye. As Tebnons chanted he dropped small clusters of watercress onto the hot coals, sending up thin plumes of acrid smoke. Some of the smoke emerged eerily from the snark skull's nasal cavities, making it look like a fire-breathing dragon.

The forty-two tribal elders were sitting four-deep in a semicircle in front of his father, accompanying Tebnons on snarkskin drums. He recognized almost every one of the elders. Three were his uncles and many of the others were cousins. Every few moments one of the elders would mimic the loud snarkbark of alarm, or a high pitched snarkaw; their singing was a snarkophony set to percussive music.

His father held up his hand and the elders and drums went silent. "A few weeks ago my eldest son, Stobo, found a magical feather on Mount Boojul. He brought it home to show my father, Stenbont, who was performing his ceremonial duties in the bay. Just minutes after touching the feather my father was attacked and eaten by a large shark. As you know, man-eating sharks have never been known to enter Jubjub Bay. The next day, when Stobo showed me the feather I was almost killed by it as well. When I touched it a lightning bolt of devilish-fire came from its tip, knocking me across the room, injuring my arm and shoulder. They are still numb and almost useless. Strangely, the feather has no impact on Stobo. Obviously, a malevolent, murderous spirit has charmed my son. It could only be Darksnark himself." A collective gasp came out from the elders as they contemplated this shocking possibility. Tebnons paused and sprinkled watercress onto the altar, sending up more plumes of white smoke. The elders pounded their drums furiously and emitted snarkbarks. It was dramatic and deafening.

"I sent Stobo to return the feather to Mount Boojul where he found it, but he never returned. At first we were fearful that he had been killed by wild snarks or jubjubs, and an armed party was sent out to search for him. They found him two days later, in the company of a large blue-scaled snark, which has apparently adopted him. No one has seen a large blue-scaled snark on Krans in over fifty years. As far as anyone knew, they had thankfully been hunted into extinction. Legend tells us that they were vicious man-eaters. Strangely, Stobo refused to return with the search party, and when they tried to force him to return with them they were set upon by a pack of wild snarks, which suddenly emerged from hiding places in the jungle. They were forced to retreat for their lives. As many of you know, several of the search party were badly injured, though none were killed, thank Quarksnark!

"It has been a difficult decision for a father to make, but I declare today that Stobo must die. There is no other recourse. I declare him taboo. Anyone who aids, feeds or shelters him will be put to death. Attempts will be made to lure him back to Jabberjee for capture. When he is caught he will be taken to Snarko and cast alive into the mouth of the Boojjum Volcano as a propitiatory sacrifice to Darksnark. Hopefully this will appease him and he will leave the rest of us alone.

"In the event that we are unable to lure Stobo to Jabberjee it will be necessary to capture him in some other manner. You are to tell everyone in your villages to be on the lookout for him and to report his location if sighted. If necessary we will send out an army to deal with his guardsnarks. He MUST be captured. However, he is not to be killed on the spot. He is to be reserved

for sacrifice. Anyone who slays him will be cast into the volcano in his place.

"Caution your people not to touch any feather he might have on him, since touching it will likely result in their death. Today I declare the feather and the creature it came from taboo. Touching the feather carries an automatic sentence of death if the person should happen to survive." He took a cluster of watercress and dropped it onto the coals, sending, up another dense plume of pungent smoke.

*   *   *   *

*   *   *

*   *   *   *

A loud nearby snarkbark woke Stobo. He bolted upright to see what was wrong. Blue, the name by which he now called his snark, was crouched in an attack posture, snarling menacingly at something coming along the jungle path. A moment later a child emerged, and Stobo recognized that it was his younger sister. "It's all right, Blue," he said. The snark relaxed, and slunk away into the jungle.

Stobo waived to his sister. "Lilibard! Over here!"

She turned at the sound of his voice and ran towards him. Blue snarled from his hiding place in the underbrush. "It's all right, Blue," he quietly assured the snark again, and the snarling stopped.

"Stobo! Who were you talking to?"

"No one."

"Are you all right? Are you lost?"

The dream he had just had came vividly back to him. "No, I'm not lost; I'm fine. I'm on my way to Mount Boojul. I got tired and took a nap. What are you doing out here? It's not safe for someone as young as you to be out alone. A snark might attack you."

"Oh, I'm not afraid of snarks."

"You should be. You'd make tasty snarkmeal. Why are *you* out here?" he asked again.

"I'm searching for feathers," she said. "I want to make a necklace. Sometimes you can find pretty ones along this path. How long will it take you to go to the mountain?"

"Perhaps two days." He looked up at the sun and saw that it was early morning. He had slept soundly all night, practically without moving. "I think you should go back to the village, before something bad happens to you. Do you want me to take you back?"

"No, I'll be fine. I'm a big girl. I don't need you to take me."

"Is father the high priest now?" he asked, remembering the dream.

"Of course not, silly. That won't happen for weeks. They haven't even held Grandfather's funeral ceremony yet. But I don't really see the point, anyway; there's nothing left of him to bury."

"All right. Just be careful. I'm going on to the mountain. Good-bye."

"See you in a few days," she responded. "You be careful, too."

He nodded, then set off. Blue rejoined him about a hundred yards up the path. He kept thinking about his vivid dream. "It showed me the future. It must be a warning from someone; perhaps even from Darksnark himself! I can't believe that Father would tell them to kill me! I thought he loved me! Well, they won't lure me back to be tossed into a volcano! I'd rather stay out here on the mountain with the snarks, even if I starve to death. The snarks seem to like me. And someday I'll escape from this island. If Darksnark really is my protector then I'll go to Skarn and live in his temple that I saw in my dream. But I'll need a boat to get to Skarn, and no one's going to let me on any of the inter-island boats; they'll be looking for me.

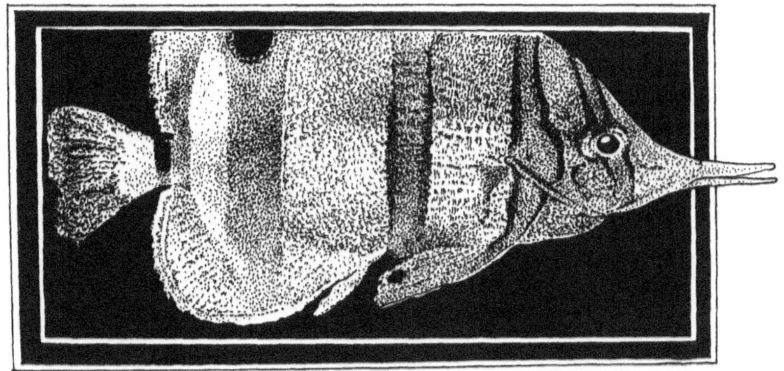

"Perhaps I'll just have to wait until I have grown up and no one will recognize me," he decided. "I can hunt and fish as well as anyone, and there's plenty of watercress and mustard greens. I'll live like a snark! After they've forgotten about me I'll sneak back into to the village some night and take a few things; a casting net, a few fish hooks, a spear or two."

"Well, Blue, I may have to depend on you. My lunch basket will be empty in a day or two."

Blue bolted and ran into the jungle. "Wait!" Stobo called after him, but he was gone in a moment.

"Now what?" he said, and sat down on a fallen tree. He looked in his lunch pack and pulled out a small dried fish and a ripe mingomango, which he ate for his breakfast while contemplating his sad situation.

As he was finishing his breakfast Blue suddenly reappeared, with a small fish in his mouth. It came over to Stobo and dropped the fish at his feet. "For me?" Stobo asked in surprise. "Did you catch this for me? This is amazing!" He reached over and patted Blue hard on the ribs. The snark was all wet. "Thank you! So you've been told to feed me as well, have you?" Blue looked up at him with big, liquid eyes. "Good Blue," Stobo said. "Good Blue! Well, Lilibard will be sure to tell my father where she last saw me, and he will send a search party. We'd better find a new place to camp. Do you know of any good caves up on Mount Boojul?"

Blue swished his long tail back and forth, as if he actually understood his question. Stobo considered this possibility for a moment. "All right, Blue. Let's go, boy!"

Blue led the way up the side of the mountain.

Fit IV
Darksnark

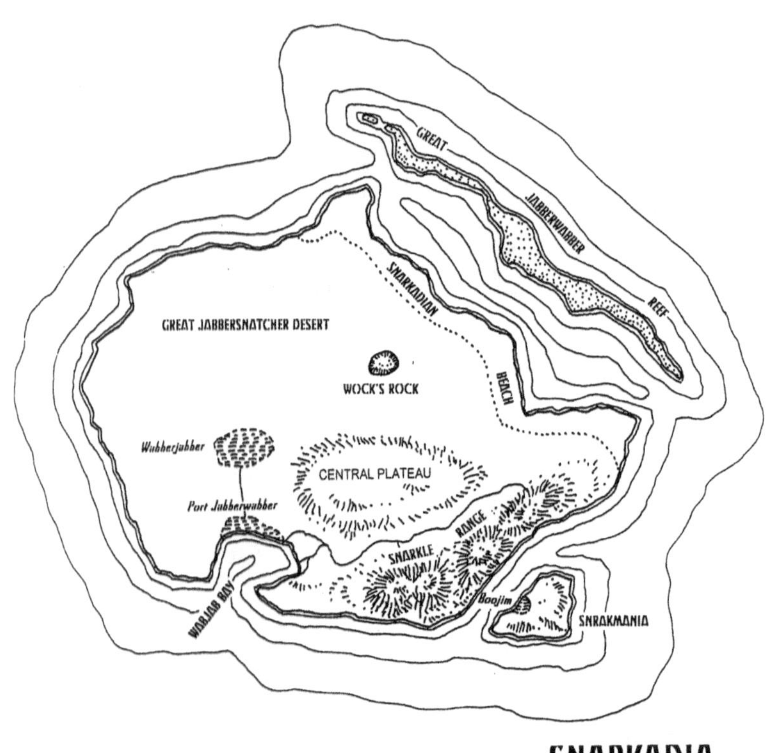
GREAT
JABBERWABBER
REEF
SNARKADIAN
BEACH
GREAT JABBERSNATCHER DESERT
WOCK'S ROCK
Wabberjabber
CENTRAL PLATEAU
Port Jabberwabber
SNARKLE
RANGE
WARJAB BAY
Boojim
SNRAKMANIA
SNARKADIA

Fit the Fourth

Darksnark

By Stobo's seventeenth birthday he had matured into a strong and athletic young man. His family had given him up for dead years ago and none of them would have recognized him if they had seen him. His five years of life with the snarks on Mount Boojul had been a combination of harshness, difficulty and loneliness, but he had survived with the help of Blue, who was ever faithful and protective. Strangely, there wasn't a snark on the island that didn't adore him, and his only real threats were from snakes, spiders, insects, and *humans.* Blue was absolutely fearless and, best of all, was skilled at catching fish in the pools near the base of the mountain. Stobo had learned to enjoy eating them raw. And there was always an abundance of mingomangos, watercress and mustard greens, so he never went hungry, though he did miss his mother's cooking.

They had lived in a snarkave close to the cloud-line at the summit, whose entrance was often obscured by the mist. Over the years a few hunting parties had come close to discovering their cave, but a determined attack by Blue had sent them scurrying and tumbling down the mountainside in terror. Stobo had acquired only a few possessions, most of which he had stolen from snarkabanas in nighttime forays to Jabberjee or Jabberjum. He had found that he could make most of the things he needed, except clothing, and these were usually what he took.

He still wore the Jabberwok's feather around his neck and protected it with his life, realizing that it was the mystical source of his power over the snarks and the reason for his very survival.

He had eventually located the Jabberwok's nest again after months of searching, though the monster had long since departed. The only evidence for its having been there was a fragment of light-blue eggshell, the size of his palm. The fragment's curvature indicated that the egg had probably been the size of a melon. He had taken it back to the cave and hidden it on a high ledge, where only he would ever find it.

Shortly after his seventeenth birthday, and after a supper of raw fish and overripe mingomango, Stobo went to bed early. Blue stretched out across the entrance to the cave where he normally slept. No sooner had he fallen asleep than

*   *   *   *
  *   *   *
*   *   *   *

he was flying through the air at high speed, his trajectory taking him out over the Ocean of Sorrows. The moon was full and high in a cloudless sky. He soon passed high over Snarko and Ranks, which he recognized from their distinctive crab-like and ant-head shapes, then descended steeply as he approached Snarkadia. He came screaming to earth like a falling meteor, landing unhurt in the midst of the Great Jabbersnatcher Desert. He rolled to a stop at the fat base of an ancient boojum tree, towering over sixty feet into the starry sky, its thin top bent over in a bizarre arc from the weight of the flowering cluster of small yellow blossoms festooned at the tip. Its stubby leaves and thorns were silvery in the bright moonlight. He stood up and found himself in the midst of a forest of hundreds of such boojums, the strange trees bent over and swaying in response to the wind blowing in from the sea, wonderfully fragrant from the trees' sweet blossoms. Small bats swirled around every cluster, searching for nectar. He turned back and looked at where he had landed, amazed that he could have landed where he did without crashing into one of the trees.

He circled the base of the tree he had rolled up against, feeling the hard texture of its bark. He plucked a leaf and bit it to see what it tasted like, then spit out the bitter pulp. He recognized the trees as boojums from the descriptions his grandfather had given him many years ago. The swaying trees made an eerie whiffling noise in the fragrant wind.

The moon suddenly dimmed, as if a cloud had passed by, though a quick glance at the moon confirmed that it was still a cloudless sky. His eye caught a movement to his left and he whirled around to face a dark, winged figure, at least eight foot tall. He couldn't see the details of its face or body; it resembled the flat, dark figure one might see in a very dimly lit room. Stobo, suddenly terrified, turned to flee.

"Stobo!" said a deep, commanding voice, which he was powerless to resist. Stobo turned slowly around to face it. "Who are you?" he asked in a tremulous voice. "How do you know my name?"

"I am Darksnark and I know EVERYTHING about you."

"The god?" Stobo asked in utter disbelief.

"Who else could have brought you here?"

Stobo didn't try to answer his question, but simply fell on his face, trembling and certain that he would be killed momentarily.

Darksnark let him lay there in the dirt for a minute, relishing his power over humans like this one. "Get up!" he finally commanded. "I have no intention of harming you—tonight, anyway."

Stobo looked up at him from ground level, his worm's eye-view perspective making Darksnark appear to be twice as tall as he actually was. He got slowly to his feet, still trembling. It was strange that from even a mere five feet away, the only features that he could make out were the demon's bright red eyes, which seemed to be back-lit with fire; his darkness seemed to absorb light from the surroundings, making him look two dimensional and flat. Stobo simply stood there in awe in front of him, not knowing what to say. Stobo noticed that a swarm of dozens of bats hovered and swirled in the air directly behind the demon's head.

"Do you know where you are?" Darksnark asked.

"In a dream, I imagine; though it seems very real!"

"I would call it a vision," Darksnark corrected him. "Something between wakefulness and dreaming. Do you know which island you are on?"

"I believe it to be Snarkadia, though I've never been here before."

"Snarkadia it is. You have a good memory."

"Pardon?"

"I showed it to you years ago in another vision."

"The only person that I told about my vision was my grandfather."

"I know. As I said, I know everything about you. I'm the one who warned you in a vision that your father would plot to kill you. And it's my servants the snarks who have cared for you."

"Thank you," Stobo said. "I had no way of knowing it was you."

"I brought you here to tell you these things and to tell you that it is time for you to leave Krans."

"But how can I leave? It is an island and I have no boat. If I try to catch a ride on a boat they will capture me and sacrifice me to the volcano!"

"Do you know the small beach on the southeast corner of the island?"

"Yes. I go there some times. It is largely deserted."

"Go there two nights from tonight. Wait on the beach. An oceangoing canoe will pick you up."

"How will I know it is the correct canoe?"

"This canoe will be black and manned by twenty oarsmen. The moon will be very nearly full, so will you will be able to see it clearly."

"May I bring Blue, my snark?"

"Of course."

"Where will I be going?"

"You will know when you get there. Do not fail to be on the beach at the appointed time. I will not send the canoe a second time, and if you miss the canoe I will abandon my protection."

"What if someone is on the beach?"

"Kill them."

"Kill them?"

"Kill them."

"But I have never killed anyone before."

"You will likely have to kill many times to stay alive. You are a marked man. It will either be them or you; it's your choice. I would think it would be an easy one."

Stobo didn't know what to say, unsure exactly which choice he might make.

"Would you like to see Wock's Rock while you're here?"

"I don't know what it is."

"It's a very big rock, the only thing that sticks up out of this desert higher than these boojum trees."

"Yes, thanks; I'd like to see it."

The last syllable was barely out of Stobo 's mouth when he shot through the air in a gut-wrenching parabolic arc, eastward across the vast landscape of innumerable boojums. On his descent he saw the monolithic outcropping of rock that rose out of the flat, forested landscape. He came crashing to earth a few minutes later, rolling through the dirt and coming to a crunching stop against the sheer face of the enormous rock.

Strangely it was suddenly mid-day, with a scorching sun directly overhead. The monolithic rock was composed of black basalt, and curved away from where he stood, so *that it was impossible for him to see the summit. He imagined that it might be as much as five hundred feet high. He decided to circle the rock to see if there was any sort of fissure or cleft that might afford a climbing pathway to the top. As a precaution, he first stacked five stones to mark his place of beginning. The rock was totally surrounded by the vast boojum tree forest, the towering trees growing right up to the face of the rock. Interspersed between them and covering almost all available ground-space, were a variety of snarkacti, some entirely covered with thick, six-inch long, needle-sharp spines. Most were in bloom, their bright yellows, oranges, pinks, and reds creating a festive display, but swarming with wasps and bees. Every fifty to a hundred feet he would come upon snarkaic pictographs chiseled into the rock. Most were enormous, possibly life-sized, and depicted at least one snarkaeopteryx, the extinct prehistoric winged snarks that once ruled the archipelago, and known to the Islanders only from a few fossil remains. Judging from the relative size of the pictographs of men being chased or devoured by them, they would have had wingspreads of twenty or more feet.*

It took him two hours before locating a cleft in the rock that afforded a possible route to the summit. He was a practiced climber, having explored all of the cliffs on Mount Boojul. After twenty minutes of climbing he managed to reach a very narrow ledge about one hundred feet above the desert floor, where he stopped to let his aching muscles rest. It was a breathtaking view of the boojum forest, whose innumerable blossom bedecked trees swayed back and forth in the sea breeze, making the forest appear strangely alive with constant movement, not unlike waves on the Ocean of Sorrows.

Having recovered his breath he began again and had only gone up a few feet when reaching for a handhold his hand grabbed a large spider the size of his fist that was sitting on the ledge. It bit him instantly and he jerked backwards in agony, losing his footing and falling back from the rock face towards certain death on the ice pick sharp spines of the snarkacti that covered the ground…

Stobo awoke in the midst of his dreamt free fall, screaming at the burning pain in his hand. He jumped to his feet, looking for a huge spider, but saw only a column of red ants. He set about stomping them to bits, while sucking on his bitten finger.

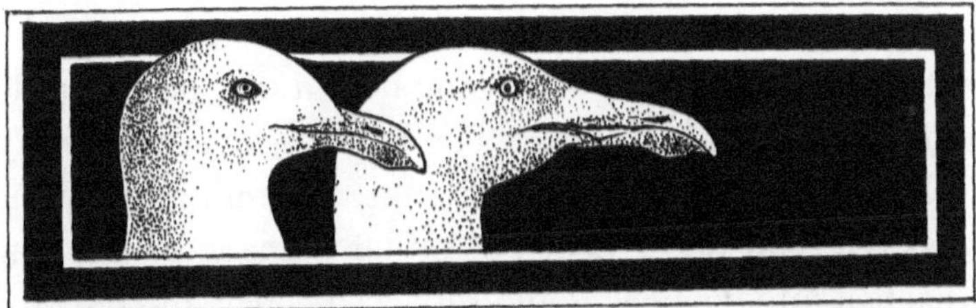

Charles Dodgson awoke with a start, aware that he had just had a nightmare, though uncertain exactly what it had been about. He hadn't slept well in weeks, which in itself wasn't all that unusual; he had been tortured by insomnia for as long as he could remember. He tried to clear his mind, which was fuzzy because of a mild fever. He felt ill; his muscles ached and he had a headache, though fortunately not one of his migraines; he was thankful for that at least.

The bedroom room was still dark, so he lit a candle to check the clock. It would be at least another hour before sunrise. He decided to get up and dress anyway. His lungs didn't feel congested, so he felt it would be safe enough to take a long walk; he had found that this often helped him to feel better when he was mildly ill. The fresh air and sunshine usually helped to clear his mind and alleviate his symptoms. As he dressed, his mind kept searching for a thread of memory about what he had dreamt, but his sudden awakening had driven it down into some recess and he couldn't quite call it up. He knew that it had been terrifying in some way, because he felt a residual dread. He finally decided that he would likely just have to wait until evening to find out what it was. His mind had a way of starting right back in on the previous night's dream, wherever he had left off; as if it had simply paused while he spent the day on conscious tasks, waiting for him to finish up so it could get back to the dream. This was wonderful if it happened to be a pleasant dream, but awful if it wasn't.

It was a fine day and he set off just as the sun was rising, at as brisk a pace as his headache would allow, striving to purge the aches and illness with vigorous exercise. About an hour into the walk, just as he was going over a hill, he had a flash of memory about his dream: "The Snark *was* a Boojum, you see!" his brain announced. Just that. A single line, without context. He had never heard of either a snark or a boojum. He reached into his pocket and retrieved pencil and paper and recorded the line. He found that his mind and muse often worked in this inexplicable way. He would suddenly think of a line of poetry, which would serve to focus his imagination. Over the following hours, days or weeks his mind would then dwell on the poem, almost as if it had an independent, parallel pattern of thought. He could go about his normal daily routine—teaching, writing letters, proofing galleys, solving a mathematical problem, or whatever—but his mind would spontaneously generate another line, or sometimes even an entire verse. It was exhilarating when it happened; a gift from God ("*Every good and every perfect gift cometh from above*," he would remind himself). Eventually he would stop whatever else he was doing and focus on the poem in a conscious way, carried along by the thread of an idea or theme.

"For the Snark was a Boojum, you see!" he repeated to himself, over and over as he finished his walk. He might not know exactly what a snark or a boojum was, but he liked the sound of the words as he said them aloud; they had a certain inexplicability to them; an inherent mysteriousness.

What Dodgson couldn't see was the terrifying winged demon striding the pathway beside him. Darksnark would say, "For the Snark was a Boojum, you see." The message would penetrate the veil separating the spiritual and natural dimensions, then a moment later it would register in Dodgson's subconscious. He would respond by repeating it, as if he had just heard it, which he unconsciously had. All of this was possible because Dodgson had spent a lifetime listening for the small, high-pitched voices of fairies in woodland and meadow, in portico and bedroom, beside streams and in barnyards. It was beginning to pay off; but he would have been very surprised at the fairy he was tuned into: Darksnark, Prince of the Snark Islands, half a world away. For, you see, there's no distance in the spirit.

There was an almost tangible creativity in the air; like the accumulation of electrical charge just before lightning strikes.

Fit V
The Isle of Skarn

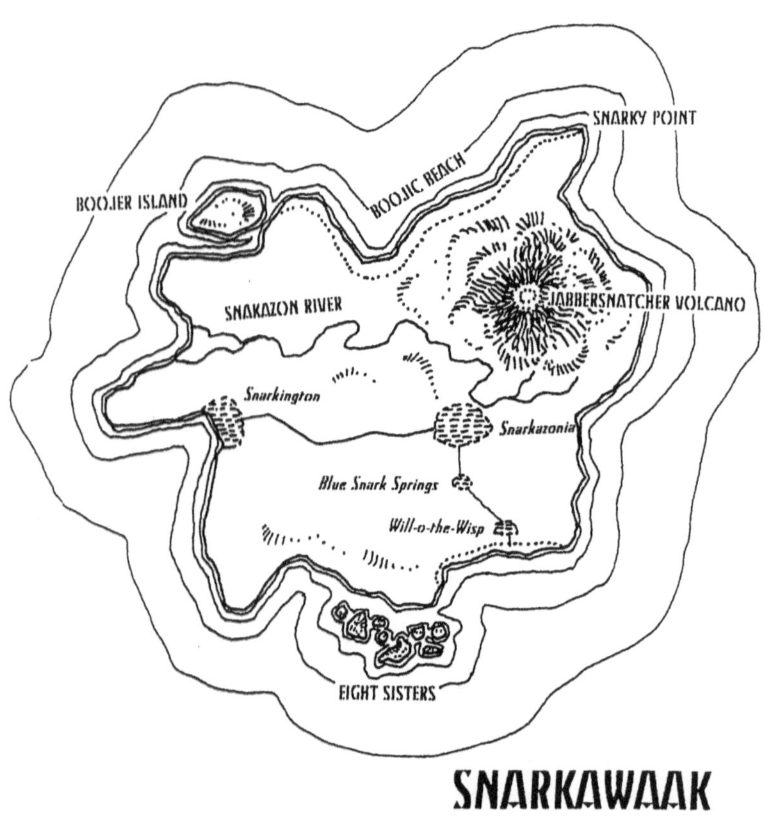
SNARKY POINT
BOOJIC BEACH
BOOJER ISLAND
SNAKAZON RIVER
JABBERSNATCHER VOLCANO
Snarkington
Snarkazonia
Blue Snark Springs
Will-o-the-Wisp
EIGHT SISTERS
SNARKAWAAK

FIT THE FIFTH

The Isle of Skarn

Two days later Stobo was waiting for nightfall at the appointed beach on the southeast coast of Krans. Blue was beside him, unaware of what was happening. He had selected a spot behind the tree line, out of sight from anyone who might happen to come along the beach. He was hoping that no one would; he had no desire to kill anyone. "If anyone comes along, Blue, I'm going to leave it up to you to chase them away." Blue wagged his long tail, as if anticipating the fun. "Don't kill them though! Just give them a good chase and frighten them away." Blue's tail stopped wagging, as if disappointed.

An hour later the sky had darkened and filled with stars. The deserted beach was bright in the white light of the full moon. The sea was calm, with gentle surf. Stobo scanned the horizon for any sign of a boat, but could see nothing on the shiny metallic-looking surface. He was considering the pleasure of wading out into the surf when his eye caught the movement of three figures emerging from the jungle at the northern end of the beach. Three men, heavily armed. The man at the back was carrying a small snark by its tail, limp and obviously dead.

Blue growled, focusing a stare on the figures and crouching into an attack position. "Easy, Blue," Stobo said. "Not yet. We'll give them a few minutes and see if they will wander off on their own." He patted Blue's head.

The hunting party wandered up the length of the beach, searching the surf for whatever the ocean might have deposited. This took them over an hour and was beginning to make Stobo nervous. The hunting party slowly made their way back up the beach and sat down on some driftwood just in front of where they were hiding, and began to act like they might be planning to spend the night.

"All right, Blue. We can't wait any longer. Our ride may arrive at any time. When I tell you, then you attack. If you have to kill them, then so be it. They're armed, so I will be right behind you." He unsheathed his vorpal sword. "Go!" he commanded.

Blue charged, and the men never saw him coming. He hit the back of the man standing and looking out to sea, savaging the back of his neck. He was dead by the time he hit the sand, his neck broken and bleeding profusely. By that time his companions had reacted by grabbing their weapons. Blue whirled and charged the larger of the two, just as Stobo ran up, yelling at the top of his voice. The third man wheeled to meet Stobo's attack, taking a wild swipe at him with his own sword. Stobo stepped harmlessly aside and then brought his own sword down at an angle across the man's face. He fell to the sand in agony, holding his face, with blood gushing through his fingers.

Almost simultaneously, Blue tore a gash into the other man's thigh. His victim grabbed his leg and fell backward, pleading for his life, and trying to stem the flow of blood.

Stobo raised his left hand to stop Blue, who was ready to finish him off. Blue snarled viciously. Stobo recognized the man, from his childhood. “This is a private beach,” he said.

“We didn’t know! You could have just told us!”

“You wouldn’t have left. You have a choice, Chozo. You can leave for Jabberjee now, or I’ll set this snark on you. Your wound is ragged and you might not bleed to death; I’m not sure. But if you stay here, you have just moments to live.”

“I’ll leave! Immediately. But, who are you? How do you know my name and village?”

“I’m Stobo. We used to be neighbours.”

“Stobo? I don’t recognize you. We thought you were dead!”

“I’m sure that’s what you hoped. But as you can see, I’m not.”

The man got up, holding his leg to staunch the flow of blood.

“You can take your sword,” Stobo told him. “You’ll need it. The snarks will smell your blood for miles. I’d advise you to spend the rest of the night in as high a tree as you can climb into.” He turned to Blue. “Guard him.” Blue assumed an attack posture and growled threateningly. Chozo froze.

Stobo went over to one of the dead men and pulled off his loin cloth, which he handed to Chozo. “Wrap this around your leg as a bandage. It might keep you from bleeding to death.”

Chozo took the cloth and did as he suggested.

“When you get back into the jungle find a pool of fresh water and wash the wound. Then make a compress with snarkabbage leaves. They will help the wound to heal. Now leave. I want you off of the beach at the northern end in fifteen minutes. If you’re still in sight I’ll send Blue to finish you off. And belive me, your sword will do you no good against this particular snark.”

“I believe you. I’ve never seen such a snark. Nor have I ever met anyone who could control a snark as you do.”

“Go! You have only a short time to get off of the beach.”

"Thank you," Chozo said.

"For what?"

"For not killing me."

"Go!"

Chozo turned and painfully headed north up the beach as fast as he could manage. Stobo once again scanned the horizon for the boat. Chozo managed to make the end of the beach before Stobo lost patience.

"Good boy!" he told Blue, patting him on the flat of his head.

They waited another hour without sign of the boat. "Blue, go and check on Chozo; see if he's really gone, or just hiding in the bushes. Don't kill him. Just drive him away."

Blue leapt to his feet and charged up the beach, following the scent of Chozo's blood. He found him perched high in a tammoo tree about a hundred yards back in the jungle. He raced back to Stobo.

A few minutes later the wind suddenly picked up and in just another few minutes was blowing steadily from the east. White caps had begun to form and there was now a four-foot high surf. About twenty minutes later Stobo spotted the boat approaching from out of the east with the wind. It was a huge canoe, with outriggers on both sides. As it got closer to shore Stobo counted twenty men rowing. The prow of the canoe was unlike anything Stobo had ever seen. It came up sharply to form a stylized snark's head, with fearsome teeth bared. The entire canoe was pitch black.

Blue got very excited when he spotted the canoe. He raced a short distance up the beach, then raced back, then 'leapt into the air, and then spun in circles.

"Someone you know?" Stobo asked.

Blue's tail wagged excitedly.

"This must be our ride."

The canoe came straight into the beach. The twenty rowers jumped out and held the canoe steady. The lead rower made his way through the surf and came up to Stobo. Blue seemed to recognize him and rubbed against his muscular legs.

"Are you Stobo?" he asked in a stern, humourless voice.

"Yes."

"Into the canoe quickly," he ordered, then turned and led the way into the boat.

There was space for him and for Blue in the stern. When he had seated himself one of the rowers handed him a paddle. Remarkably, the wind suddenly shifted and began blowing out of the southwest.

The crew pushed the boat back through the surf and made their way back out to sea. Stobo had never ridden in an ocean-going canoe and it took him a minute of watching the others to get the hang of how to row. He was soon into the rhythm. They headed due east, skimming along the moonlit water at a remarkably fast pace, the muscular rowers stroking tirelessly.

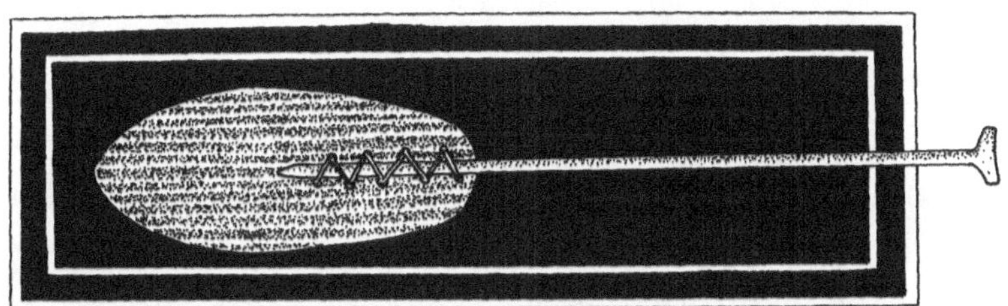

It took Chozo two days to painfully make his way back to Jabberjee and by then he had developed a high fever and serious inflammation from the nasty bite on his leg. It took his wife and extended family three days to nurse him back to the point that his fever receded. He was lucky to have survived.

On the third day after his return Tebnons came to see him. He sat down on the floor beside his mat. "What happened?

You have been talking deliriously about a blue snark and my dead son, Stobo."

"He isn't dead."

"Nonsense! Of course he's dead. No one can live alone in the jungle for five yeas."

"But I saw him. I tell you he is alive! I didn't recognize him at first. He's grown into a man. But he knew me, and told me his name. It was him all right. I'm certain of it."

"Tell me exactly what happened."

"Nam, Chul, and I were on a hunting expedition. It was approaching evening and we decided to spend the night on the beach on the southeast shore. The beach was deserted and we settled down on some driftwood watching the surf. Suddenly, out of nowhere, a large blue snark attacked us. It hit Nam from behind, biting him savagely in the neck. He was probably dead when he hit the sand. We grabbed our weapons and turned to face the snark, which attacked me next. He bit me here in the leg, knocking me on my back. At the same time a young man, armed with a vorpal sword, attacked Chul. I never saw where he came from, but he must have been hiding with the snark back in the palms. Chul took one swipe at him, but was immediately cut down with a blow to his face. He bled to death in minutes. I was sure that the snark would finish me off, but the man raised his hand and the snark stopped. He seemed to have authority over the animal. I've never seen anything like it! A genuine Snarkmaster! I asked him to spare my life, and who he was. That's when he told me that he was your son, Stobo."

"And he let you go. Just like that. After killing Nam and Chul?"

"Yes; he recognized me. He even knew my name and that I lived here in Jabberjee."

"Did he explain why he had attacked you?"

"He only said that it was his private beach. He obviously wanted us off of it."

"Enough to kill you? Odd. That seems a bit extreme, don't you think?"

"That's what I thought. I asked him why he didn't just tell us that he considered it to be his private beach. He said that he didn't think we would leave just because he said that, which was probably true. We were three heavily armed men."

"So you left and made your way back here?"

"I spent the night in a tree, then slowly made my way back. The pain in my leg wound was terrible, and I began to think that I wouldn't make it. I'm lucky to be alive."

Tebnons nodded, then stood up. "We will see if he is still there," he said, then left the snarkabana.

Within an hour Tebnons had organized and provisioned a party of one hundred heavily armed warriors. They set out at once for the beach where Stobo had last been seen. Two hours later they entered the deserted beach and fanned out to scour the surrounding jungle and hillside.

They found what remained of Nam and Chul in the middle of the beach. Their bodies had been scavenged by snarks, who left little but their skulls, femurs and swords. They searched for two hours before concluding that Stobo was no longer there. The elders met back at the beach, where Tebnons addressed them. "Well, he has to be on the island somewhere. He doesn't have access to an inter-island canoe. Repeat warnings to everyone who owns a canoe that he may try to take their canoe or disguise himself and catch a ride. We will set up routine patrols here on the beach. Twenty warriors should be adequate, even if he does have a pet snark. Leave a patrol here for the next few days and the rest will return to get provisions for replacements. Stobo *must* be captured. You can all see how dangerous he has become."

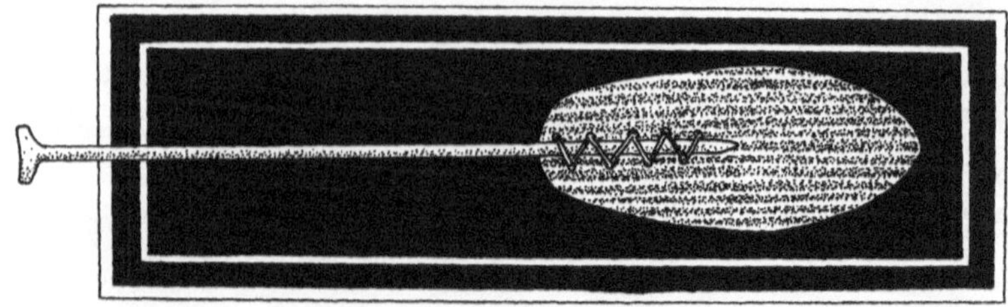

The rowers split into two teams, each team alternately rowing for two hours then resting for two. Thirty hours into the trip an island appeared on the horizon. It looked rather like a sea urchin because of its numerous peaks.

Stobo tapped the shoulder of the rower in front of him, and he turned to see what he wanted. "What's the name of the island?"

"The Isle of Skarn," he replied. "Our destination, thank Darksnark. I'm exhausted. I'm sure the others are as well. Who are you, anyway?"

"My name is Stobo. My father is the Quarksnarkian High Priest on Krans."

"Quarksnark?" he asked, with amazement in his voice.

"Yes."

"Why would Darksnark send us all the way over there to pick you up?"

"I have no idea. He told me that you would be coming to get me in a vision I had several days ago."

"Why were you on the deserted side of the island?"

"I have been hiding in the jungle for five years. I've been declared taboo. They have sentenced me to be sacrificed to Boojjum Volcano."

"Who has?"

"My father."

"Your father?" he asked, amazed at his answer.

"Yes. He somehow feels threatened by me."

"Why?"

"Because of a feather."

The rower laughed at his answer, which seemed totally preposterous. "Indeed."

"It's true. The feather has bestowed special powers on me."

"Like what?"

"Snarks adore me. They will do anything I bid them do."

"Very well. I suppose that blue snark there behind you will do whatever you say, then?"

"Instantly. He's very obedient; and vicious."

"I've never seen a blue one. Doesn't look too *vicious* to me; rather more like *cute*, I'd say."

Stobo turned to Blue. "Growl for the man."

Blue emitted a deep and very threatening growl that startled everyone on the boat. They all looked over their shoulders to see what had happened. The rower he had been talking to practically jumped overboard.

Stobo waived to them. "It's all right. Nothing's wrong." They looked at him sceptically, but turned and resumed rowing. "Very impressive," he said

"What's your name?"

"Dag."

"Where will we land on the island, Dag?"

"There's only one way on to the island. Through the Gates of Hell."

"Sounds ominous."

"Very. It's a narrow inlet on the southwest side of the island. It leads into the Night Lagoon. The Temple of Darksnark in on the northern shore, not far into the lagoon."

"Yes, I've seen it. At the base of the tallest mountain on the island."

"What do you mean? How could you have ever seen it?"

"In a vision."

"I suppose your feather grants you visions as well?"

"Exactly. I saw the entire island from a great height, but I was not told the names of the peaks or other physical features."

Dag was sceptical. "Where's the tallest peak?"

"Just north of the entrance to the Gates of Hell."

"Someone could have just told you that. What's in the centre of the island?"

"A vast wabe. There are enormous herds of snarks living there."

"What's on the south side of the Night Lagoon?"

"Three peaks of about the same elevation. I don't know what they are called."

"The Three Sisters," Dag told him. "What distinctive features are on the northeast side?"

"There are three very large craters there. Is that what you are referring to?"

"Fear, Care, and Woe," Dag told him. "I believe you."

"Thank you."

"Can I see your feather?"

"No. It's taboo. It carries a sentence of death."

"Maybe on Krans; not here. Darksnark makes the rules here. Let me see it."

"It would kill you to touch it."

"Touching a feather would kill me?"

"Exactly."

Dag yelled to the other rowers. "Stobo back here says that he has a magic feather, and if I touch it that it will kill me!"

This caused the entire crew, except for their leader in the prow, to burst into laughter. Stobo wasn't smiling. "Don't tempt me," he warned.

Dag laid his oar down in the bottom of the canoe and stood up. "Give me your best shot!"

Stobo stared at him for a moment, then opened the pouch he wore around his neck and pulled out the feather. He handed it towards Dag.

"Oooo, very scary!" Dag mocked, then reached over to take the feather, which he intended to throw overboard.

A bolt of blue lighting came out of the tip of the feather and struck him in the chest, knocking him backwards overboard. The canoe sailed on, quickly leaving him behind, waving his hands frantically, and yelling for help. The crew stopped paddling and looked back. One of them started to leap over the side to attempt his rescue, but the man in the prow held up his hand and he stopped. "A shark has been following us for the last ten miles. Look there; you can see his fin."

The crew looked where he was pointing and saw a terrifying fin protruding several feet out of the water, making a direct attack on Dag, who was still waiving frantically at them. The shark hit him a few seconds later and he was gone.

The crew looked back at Stobo in astonishment, then up towards their leader.

"I trust that you will now appreciate exactly whom we have on board. He is protected by Darksnark and that blue snark sitting there behind him. If I were you I would treat him with the appropriate respect. Now row."

The crew looked back at Stobo again, then put their oars back in the water.

They sailed along the west coast of the island and approached the Gates of Hell on the channel between Dismal and Gloom Islands, taking a hard turn to the north at the entrance to the Gates. It was only a short row to the landing that served the Temple of Darksnark. The canoe ran ashore and the crew got out. Stobo and Blue were the last off. When they came ashore the crew moved back a respectful distance, now very leery of their mysterious passenger and his guardsnark.

The leader of the crew motioned to Stobo to follow, and they walked up to the sarkabana that served as the Temple to Darksnark. Stobo told Blue to stay, and he settled down in the shade of a large palm. A broad veranda faced the Night Lagoon. Eight-foot high kaboodles were positioned at both ends of the veranda, but these were not the typical snarkaboodles made of snark skulls found elsewhere on the islands—these were pyramidal stacks of human skulls.

A Darksnarkian priest emerged from the entrance to the temple, wearing a black headband and loincloth, but nothing else. His arms, chest and back were heavily tattooed with elaborate designs based on ancient Skarnawakan pictographs. Stobo noticed that there was no sparkle of life in his eyes. He looked dazed or drugged.

"Are you Stobo, the Snarkmaster we have been awaiting?"

"I am Stobo," he replied. "Whether or not I am who you are looking for I can not say."

"Stay here," he commanded, then went back into the temple. A few minutes later a prisoner was led out from the back of the temple, his hands tied behind him, and led by two very muscular guards. The priest returned to the veranda. "That is a Quarksnarkian priest that was captured recently on the island. We are uncertain what he was doing, but it doesn't matter; he has been sentenced to death. I will tell his guards to release him in a moment and give him the opportunity to flee. You are to command your snark to track him down and bring him back alive. Do you understand?"

"Yes. That will be no problem."

"It won't if you are truly a snarkmaster. If the snark fails to do as you tell him you will be immediately executed alongside this prisoner." He signalled the guards to release their prisoner, whom he then addressed. "You have a slim chance to survive. You can flee into the jungle. You will be given a five-minute head start. If you are brought back here you will be killed, and your skull added to one of those kaboodles." He pointed to them. "Go! Now!"

The prisoner bolted for the jungle behind the temple, heading for Mount Darksnark. He was gone in a few moments, obviously terrified at what might happen. They waited a short while. "Send your snark to fetch him back; alive."

"Is injured all right?"

"As long as he's still alive."

"Blue!" he said to the snark, who immediately ran up to him, wagging his tail. "Fetch that man that just ran away from here. But don't kill him. I need him back here alive. Go!"

Blue was off in a flash, running at full tilt. Ten minutes later they heard screams from the mountainside. The priest stared at Stobo with a raised, questioning eyebrow. Stobo ignored him.

Another ten minutes later the prisoner reemerged from behind the temple, his face registering terror. His legs were badly bitten, with blood streaming down his calves where Blue had nipped at him. The guards grabbed him as he tried to run past them into the lagoon.

"Blue!" Stobo yelled, bringing him to a sudden stop. He loped over to Stobo, wagging his tail. "Good boy!" he said, patting his broad head. "Good boy!"

"I'm impressed," the priest acknowledged. "But I'm not sure that he wouldn't have done that for me had I told him."

"Try it," Stobo said.

"Release the prisoner again," he commanded. The guards let him go and once again he bolted for the mountainside. The priest waited a few minutes then commanded, "Blue! Fetch that man back! Go!"

Blue didn't budge an inch.

"Go!" he commanded. Blue was impassive. The priest strode across the veranda and picked up a club, prepared to strike the snark.

"Kill the priest," Stobo said calmly. Blue instantly leapt through the air and caught the priest by the throat, shaking him viciously and snapping his neck. He dropped the limp body on the veranda in a bloody heap.

"Good, boy!" Stobo said. "Now, fetch the prisoner back, but don't bite him again."

Blue responded instantly, and twenty minutes later the prisoner reemerged from the jungle, running again. The guards grabbed him.

Stobo addressed them. "Take him to the canoe. Ten of you man the canoe and take him to Snark. Drop him off on one of the beaches on the northeast coast. Then come back. He is to be set free. Go!"

There was no hesitation or lack of volunteers to row. In less than five minutes they were in the canoe heading west.

Stobo turned to the remaining men standing in front of the temple. "Who's in charge here?"

"I am," said a deep voice from someone standing in the doorway to the temple.

Stobo turned to face him. A moment later an elderly man stepped out of the darkness onto the veranda. Everyone except Stobo went down on one knee and bowed their head.

"What have you done to my priest?"

"He committed suicide," Stobo said.

"In a way, I suppose," he agreed. "He acted foolishly."

"Only an insane person would try to beat that snark with a stick," Stobo said.

"Do you have control of all snarks or just that one?"

"I don't know. He is faithful. I believe he is a gift from Darksnark. The other snarks on Krans seem to like me as well. Those are the only ones I have ever encountered."

"We will soon see," he said.

"Who are you?" Stobo asked.

"I am the Darksnarkian High Priest."

"Of the Isle of Skarn?"

"Of all of the islands; there are no others. And what's more, you've had my heir apparent killed, so that leaves a rather large gap in the hierarchy. But it may be just as well. He probably wasn't cut out for the position."

"He did seem to lack common sense."

"And apparently little power over snarks."

"Apparently."

"Come inside. Your guardsnark can come along if you like, though you'll be perfectly safe."

They sat down in a dark corner, in front of a small altar made from a human skull, with the cranium cut away. The priest transferred a few live coals from a hearth to the skull, then sprinkled a handful of dried watercress onto the coals, sending up a thin column of acrid smoke.

"Whose skull serves as your altar?"

"It used to belong to an old Quarksnarkian priest I had some trouble with. He lived on Krans; where you've come from. I've forgotten his name."

Stobo stared at the priest for a minute. "Was it Senbont?"

"That's it! Did you know him?"

"Very well; he was my grandfather."

"Oh. I see. A pity. But he was very old; he had a good life."

"Where did you get his skull?"

"A tiger shark deposited it on the shore in front of this temple. I watched it. It had a very distinctive fin. A chunk had been bitten out of it by some other shark, near the tip."

"How could you possibly know that's my grandfather's skull?"

"I saw this same fish in a vision. I see that you were in it as well, though I hadn't realized it until just now."

"Exactly what did you see in your vision?"

"Old Senbont here was standing up to his waist in Jubjub Bay, feeding the fish. A young boy came up carrying a feather and handed it to him. That would have been you I imagine. The feather sent a bolt of lighting up his shoulder and the old priest fell back into the water. That's when the shark attacked. The shark in this vision had the same fin."

"Do you have a name?"

"Of course; but I don't tell it to just *anyone.* If you know a person's name it gives you a measure of power over him. I try not to let that happen to me."

"Are you afraid of me?" Stobo asked.

"Not in the least. I have no fear of you nor anything; except Darksnark. It is wise to have a very healthy fear of him."

"Not even of Blue?"

The priest looked at the snark, sitting on its haunches a few feet away. "He looks like a rather *sweet* snark to me."

"Kill him, Blue!" Stobo said, deciding to avenge his grandfather's death while he had the opportunity.

To Stobo's shock, Blue didn't budge.

"I seem to have overstepped my authority," Stobo observed.

"A bit. Show Stobo how sweet you are, Blue. Knock him to the floor!"

Blue was to his feet in an instant and Stobo was flat on his back almost as quickly.

"He is loyal to you, but within limits. That's something you need to remember. I too am a snarkmaster, and senior to you. He will always obey me rather than you. I have authority here; you don't."

"I will remember that."

"You had better," he said, a distinct threat in his voice. "Back off, Blue," he said. Blue returned to his earlier place and sat down again.

"We will tour the island tomorrow. Be here at sunrise. Someone will be waiting for you on the veranda to show you to your quarters. You can go now."

Stobo stood up and left. The priest gave Blue a small nod and the snark followed Stobo out the door.

Fit VI
Forks and Hope

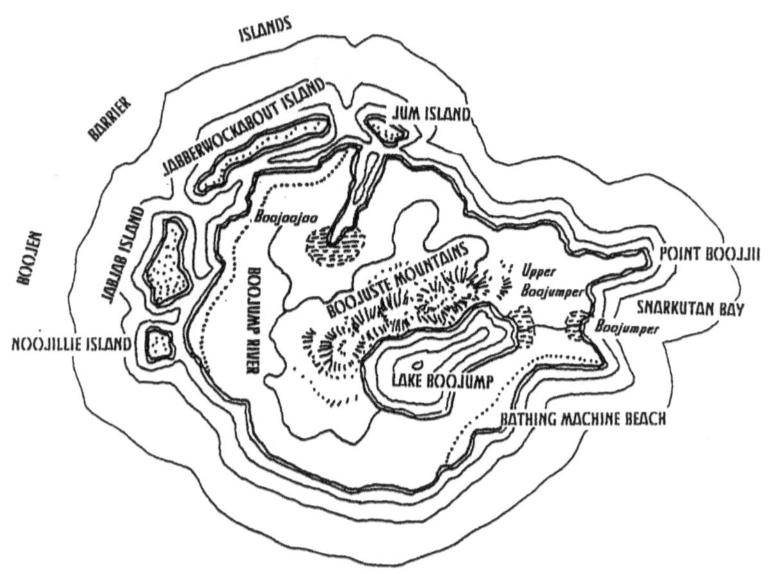
ISLANDS
BARRIER
BOOJEN
JABBERWOCKABOUT ISLAND
JUM ISLAND
JABJAB ISLAND
NOOJILLIE ISLAND
Boojoojoo
BOOJUMP RIVER
BOOJUSTE MOUNTAINS
Upper Boojumper
POINT BOOJJII
SNARKUTAN BAY
Boojumper
LAKE BOOJUMP
BATHING MACHINE BEACH

SNARKII

FIT THE SIXTH

Forks and Hope

The schooner FORKS AND HOPE *had been crisscrossing a particularly empty stretch of the south Pacific for weeks, having put out from Papeete, Tahiti. They hadn't seen so much as a flying fish or a sea bird in weeks. The crew of eight men, along with Captain Imholtz and his pet beaver, Éclair (named after his favorite pastry), were intent on searching for a mysterious creature that the Captain had dreamt of, which he curiously referred to as a "snark". The Captain was both eccentric and extremely wealthy (an oft times dangerous combination), having made a fabulous fortune shipping triple-virgin olive oil from Greece to Washington, D.C., to supply the burgeoning Italian restaurant business that had sprung up in the nation's capitol and surrounding areas. He had also made a great deal of money selling ancient Greek antiquities (plundered from tombs by Greek peasants in his employ) to the American nouveau-riche commercial pirates. He had spent a good bit of his profits buying old ship's maps and captain's logs of the South Pacific from retired ship's captains, bankrupt shipping fleet owners, antiquarian book dealers, and other such rascals. He had spent an entire year pouring over these documents, comparing them, and looking at them under a powerful magnifying glass, searching for some hint or anomaly that might indicate the location of "The Snark Islands", as he had heard them referred to in his feverish dreams.*

He had eventually focussed his attentions on a doughnut-shaped grey smudge on an ancient Dutch map, deciding that it might represent a circular fog-bank large enough to hide a small archipelago, though he admitted to himself that it might only be an ancient gravy stain. Typhoons and the sloppy table manners of sea captains had a way of soiling maps. However, he had been encouraged in his conclusion by a French map dating from the 1750s, which had a beautiful and elaborate border (though the rest was almost entirely blank). However, this map had a depiction of a strange feathered-and-scaled creature perched on a small island in almost the exact latitude and longitude as the Dutch gravy smudge. He had concluded that it just might represent some rare species of snark. Based on this meager evidence, he decided to purchase a suitable boat. To finance this, he had sold off his valuable antiquities collections (Persian gold pieces, Median signet scrolls, Philistine fertility objects—which his wife detested—and Japanese ear cleaning-scoops), as well as twelve copies of first editions of ALICE'S ADVENTURES IN WONDERLAND (these to Justine Thriller of New York City, an eccentric bibliomaniac and ex-vaudeville entertainer). He used the money to purchase a schooner by the somewhat foreboding name of DESPAIR.

He had undertaken significant repairs to the boat, including the purchase of replacement jibs, forestaysail and mainsail. He had even taken the precautions of having the boat pulled out of the water to have its hull scraped and painted, and its keel plated with copper. At the last minute he also had it fitted with a spare rudder in the bow (for backing out of tight situations, he had said), over the strenuous objections of the shipwrights. When the repairs were complete he had christened the refurbished boat as the FORKS AND HOPE, *and backed out of the flooded dry dock with his spare rudder, to the amazement and cheers of his sceptical detractors.*

He had experienced considerable difficulty in obtaining his crew. The majority of the seasoned sailors he had approached in bars and dives in the Eastend along the Thames had simply laughed in his face when he told them the nature of his planned expedition. He had eventually signed a crew of landlubbers, many of whom had never even been on a boat, but were enthusiastic about the idea of a Pacific cruise and the promise of culinary delights (snark sandwiches, and so on). He had taught them the fundamentals of sailing by circumnavigating the Isle of Wight forty-two times in all sorts of weather.

The Captain had provisioned his quarters to accommodate his quarrelsome wife of thirty-plus years, including lace curtains (which Éclair had knitted) on the portals, for privacy from the prying eyes of leaping dolphins and swooping sea birds. But when it was time to set sail her lawyer had met him at the dock in her stead, with papers suing for divorce. "Such is the price for pursuing a dream," he informed her lawyer without bitterness. "I didn't really like the curtains anyway; and besides, Éclair is rather better looking and has a more agreeable temper, to boot!" He had been forced to delay their departure for a day to go to the bank and withdraw funds to pay her off. When they eventually sailed out of the harbor he hung over the railing and declared, "I divorce thee, I divorce thee, I divorce theeee!" (in the Arab manner). Then he added, "What I tell you three times is true!" He departed a happier, if poorer, man.

On the forty-second day out of Papeete, Maurice McQheturer (a maker of bonnets and hoods, who had prehensile toes and taken a liking to climbing the rigging in his bare feet, and perching atop the masts like an escaped langur avoiding his pursuers) yelled out that there was an enormous fog-bank to the north-northeast.

"Gravy, at last!" cried the Captain as he rang his bell loudly to inform the rest of the crew. He immediately adjusted the helm and laughed all the way to the bank. It wasn't long before they were in the thick of it, unable to see any further than their long English noses. Captain Imholtz could do little else but tie down the helm to hold a steady course and hope for the best. He was either extremely brave or a foolhardy idiot, a matter of considerable dispute among his crew.

Several hours later they suddenly emerged from the fog into bright weather, to the cheers of the entire crew. Éclair smacked the deck loudly and repeatedly with her tail, like a true Canadian at a hockey game.

Charles Dodgson sat up in his bed with a start. The knocking continued. "My word! There's a Beaver at the door!" he said aloud, still half-asleep. Then he regained his senses and corrected himself, 'I mean I must have overslept!" Since he had suffered from virulent insomnia, this was indeed a rare occasion (which he would later note in his diaries with a white stone).

He scrambled out of bed and pulled on his housecoat (which he got on backwards in his haste) to answer the door. One of his students was standing there with a quizzical look on his face.

Dodgson recognized the blighter by his short hair and unwashed neck. "Yes? What is it, Winston?"

"Are you all right, Mr Dodgson?"

"Yes, of course."

"We were worried when you didn't show up at class; which was very unlike you. We thought, perhaps, that you might have fallen ill. I was dispatched to see if I might be of any assistance."

"That was very thoughtful of you, Winston. No, I'm fine. I'm sorry to have missed the class. I shall be there tomorrow for sure!"

"Good day then, Mr Dodgson."

"Good day."

Dodgson closed the heavy door, then reopened it. "And wash your neck!" he yelled after Winston.

"Yes, Sir. I will, Sir!"

Dodgson closed the door again and then stood there with his back to it for a moment. "What a curious dream I've had," he said aloud to himself. "Curiouser and curiouser!"

He didn't notice Darksnark perched on top of his high headboard, grinning from pointy ear to pointy ear, quite enjoying himself.

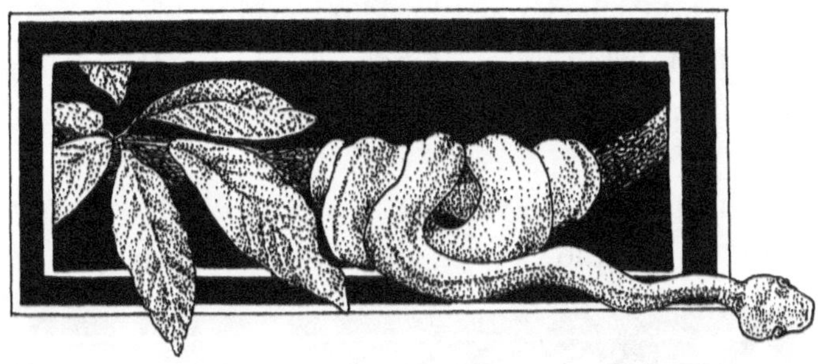

The *Forks and Hope* had entered the Ocean of Sorrows too far north of the Snark Archipelago to see any of the islands. They sailed due east all day long until they came upon the opposite side of the circular fog-bank on the eastern horizon. "Ninety degrees to starboard!" yelled Captain Imholtz, as he turned his boat due south. They sailed on this southerly course for the next two hours, when Maurice again let out a cry from atop the foremast: "Land ho! Land ho! Land ho!" (he cried this three times so that the Captain would believe him). Maurice had no way of knowing that he had just been the first European to have ever espied the tall peaks of the Isle of Skarn (a dubious honour).

"It looks like a bloody sea urchin!" Maurice said (his exact words!). The gull sitting next to him on the rigging screamed three times, then pooped on the poop deck, missing the Captain by mere inches.

Pandemonium broke out amongst the crew when they heard this long-awaited good news. Some of them took to climbing madly up and down the rigging, while others ran back and forth the length of the deck like schoolboys at recess. To celebrate the occasion, Sandy Beerstein, the ship's cook and barkeep, obtained one of his famous bride cakes from the larder and set about decorating it with a festive red star fish they had netted that morning (though this wasn't particularly successful, as the starfish kept trying to escape, no matter how much icing Beerstein applied). Selwig Bonhectare, a banker by trade, who had suffered miserably from seasickness the entire trip, lifted his tired head from over the railing and actually managed a greenish smile. "Are we there yet?" he asked.

To which the Captain yelled, "Yes! Yes! Yes!"

"Thank, God!" said Selwig, then heaved again.

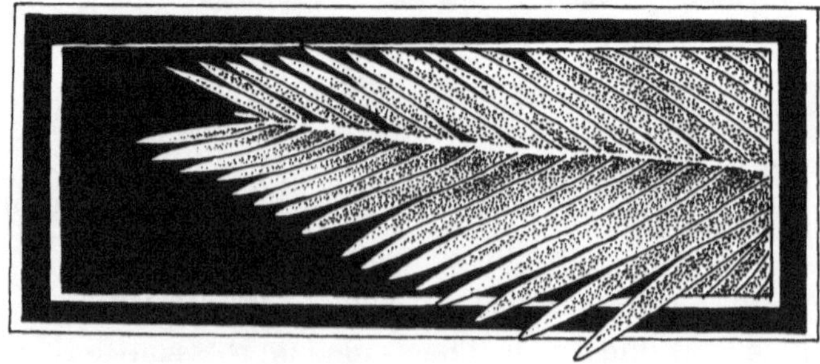

Stobo had risen early to meet the High Priest at sunrise as instructed. When he walked up to the veranda the priest was standing there waiting for him, with a scowl that made him look like an unhappy *tiki*.

"Am I late?" he asked.

"No; but you're not early *either,*" he replied as a way of rebuke. Stobo decided to ignore him. "Come on!" the priest said. "The canoe's waiting for us." He led the way down to the shore of the lagoon. The canoe had only ten oarsmen, so Stobo concluded that they wouldn't be heading out to sea.

"Good morning!" he said brightly to the crew, who ignored him. "They must have missed breakfast," Stobo thought.

"You and your snark sit up front," the high priest instructed. "I'll sit right behind you. We'll take a spin around the lagoon and I'll tell you the names of the prominent peaks. Shove off!" he instructed the sour-faced crew.

Within minutes they were gliding across the mirrored surface of the lagoon.

"As you know, the tallest peak back there behind the temple is Mount Darksnark. I'd advise against climbing that one. Darksnark himself often frequents the peak and he isn't always happy at being disturbed. The range of mountains that stretch from there to Mount Ominous at the eastern end of the lagoon is called The Wasting Mountains. The three tall peaks on the south side of the lagoon over there," he said, pointing starboard with his arm, "are known as The Three Sisters."

"What are their names?" Stobo asked.

"El-see, Lai-see, and Til-lee."

A shoal of mullet suddenly leapt out of the water fifty yards ahead of them. The dorsal fin of a shark sliced through the water three yards behind them, the fish obviously pursuing its breakfast. A few minutes later three rainbow-hued parrots swept across their bow, intent on crossing from one side of the lagoon to the other, screaming the entire way, their cries echoing back and forth across the lagoon from mountain to mountain.

"It's very beautiful here," Stobo remarked, quite taken by the landscape.

"It's deceptive," the priest said.

"How's that?"

"The lagoon is extremely deep. No one knows how deep; perhaps half a mile. It is more like an underwater canyon, and teems with sharks and barracuda. They come here to mate, hough not with each other," he said. "Your chances of survival if you fall in are negligible. The pregnant females are ravenous. You might make it to shore if you're a strong swimmer, but snarks will be waiting for you when you come ashore; either way you likely wouldn't survive for long."

"I doubt the snarks would harm me," Stobo remarked.

"Not you, perhaps; but they certainly would most men."

They sailed on for awhile towards the end of the lagoon, only disturbed now and then by the shriek of a snark hidden in the jungle lining the shores or the flight of birds skimming along just above the surface of the black water.

As they approached the eastern shore the priest resumed his descriptions. "There is a large marsh that occupies much of the interior, fed by almost continuous rain on the tall peaks on the eastern half of the island."

"What's the name of the marsh?"

"It's called Massacre Marsh."

"Why?"

"There is an ancient legend of an attempt by humans who lived on Snark Island to the west to colonize this island. They were intent on exploiting the enormous quantities of watercress that grow in the wabe. But they didn't appreciate the fact that the marsh was inhabited by a vast heard of very inhospitable and protective snarks. The snarks waited until the immigrants had set up camp, then swept in and killed all but a handful, who fled back to Snark Island in a canoe, with tales of the massacre."

"That sounds plausible," Stobo agreed. "I've seen the snark herds."

"Impossible. No one dares enter the wabe; not even me!"

"Such a thing is possible in a vision," Stobo remarked.

The priest was silent for a moment. "You've been given such a vision?"

"Yes; when I was twelve."

"What else did you see in this vision?"

"I was given a bird's eye tour of all of the islands. Skarn was the final destination. I flew around the island, and skimmed just over the heads of the herds of snark in the marsh. I know what the mountains look like; I just wasn't told their names. For example, east of the marsh there are three very prominent peaks. What are they called?"

"Death Mountain, Mount Vanish, and Mount Snickersnack," the priest informed him in a very subdued voice.

"I landed on the top of the southern of the three, which I assume was Mount Snickersnack," Stobo continued, "and on the eastern side there was a deep canyon, separating Mount Vanish from Mount Snickersnack."

"Yes, I have also been there, though not in a vision."

"What is that called? It must have a name."

"Phantasm Chasm," the priest informed him.

"I heard a very piercing scream come up from the depths of the chasm. I assume that it was some sort of snark, though I've never heard anything quite like it."

"You're lucky you were just in a vision. Had you been alive you would likely have vanished had it appeared."

"Vanished?"

"Vanished."

"Don't you mean 'eaten'?"

"No, I mean 'vanished'. It was indeed a snark that you heard," he explained. "A very peculiar type. It has a name."

"Which is?"

The priest hesitated, almost as if he was reluctant to even speak its name. "It's called a Boojum."

"I see!" said Stobo. "That explains a *lot* of things!"

"Like what?"

"Why they call the odd trees in the Great Jabbersnatcher Desert 'Boojum' trees. Why so many things on the islands have incorporated the name: like Mount Boojul and Boojjoob Bay, back on my home island of Krans."

"Yes; it's undoubtedly the reason for such names. There are many, on all of the islands."

"You've obviously never seen a Boojum," Stobo said.

"Obviously; I'm still here."

"Not even from a great distance?"

"Perhaps, but I'm not certain about that. One time, years ago, I saw a strange apparition near the Chasm. A sort of golden glow; a tiny ball of light in the far distance, entering the trees. That might have been it; I'm not sure. It did make me feel very peculiar, even from that distance."

"In what way was it 'peculiar'?"

"It's hard to describe. There was a temporary loss of memory; a deep depression that took several weeks to lift; a strong sense of dread; all of those things, rolled up together. Only worse."

"Did you have the feeling you might vanish?"

"Well, no; it was more a fear of extinction; a dread of dying. Perhaps the distance was enough to prevent that fear from actually happening."

"Interesting." Then Stobo thought of something. "Do you know the legend about Snarl and Boob, the first man and woman Quarksnark created?"

"Of course. Every child over the age of three knows that myth."

"Why do you call it a myth? Don't you believe it?"

"No; they were created by Darksnark, whose dominion was later usurped by Quarksnark."

"How could you possibly know that?"

"Darksnark has told me this."

"And you believe him?"

"Of course."

"Do you think that Boob was named after the Boojum?"

"Perhaps. Who knows? But I'd have thought she would have been named Booj, if that was the case."

"*Boob* has a better *sound* to it. Perhaps it got altered in the retelling over the millennia."

"Perhaps."

"The next time you talk with Darksnark, would you please ask him about this? I'm very curious about it."

The canoe jolted to a sudden stop, interrupting their theological discussion, the prow resting against a small island of watercress. "Are we getting out?"

"No, *we* aren't; *you* are."

"What?"

"Get out!"

"Never! Not after what you've just told me about this place!"

"Blue," the priest said. The snark turned to see what was needed. "If he doesn't get out in less than a minute, kill him."

Blue got a very puzzled look on his snout, his eyes glancing back and forth between Stobo and the priest, as if uncertain what to do. Then he turned to Stobo and growled a very threatening growl. Stobo got out.

"You and I are going to have to have a long talk, Blue," he said.

"There is a clearing with a small sandy beach about a mile back on the northern side of the lagoon. A canoe will be sent there to wait for you tomorrow morning. If you aren't there it will be sent again the next morning. If you miss the second one you will be on your own."

"I take it that I'm being tested for some purpose."

"You can assume that. Remember to avoid the Boojum at all costs; even a snarkmaster is not immune." The priest commanded the crew to pull back.

"Be sure to ask Darksnark about Boob!" Stobo called out as they paddled off across the lagoon, leaving him stranded atop the clump of watercress. He didn't want the old priest to think he was afraid; actually, terrified was more like it. "What a jerk!" Stobo said, as he watched the canoe grow smaller and smaller. He nervously reached up and checked to be sure that he still had his feather, which he did. He was relieved that they hadn't confiscated his vorpal sword. It wouldn't do him much good against a mass snark attack, but would be useful against slithy toves, which undoubtedly inhabited the island. "Where there's snarks, there's toves!" he told himself, repeating the old adage.

"Well, I had better make for a big tree while there's still light," he said aloud, and struck out across the marsh, trying to go from watercress clump to watercress clump, but having to occasionally swim for it. After an hour of effort he was getting close to the edge of the jungle, which held the promise of towering tumtum and tammoo trees. He spotted an ancient one, festooned with a thick tangle of vines and decided to try to get to that one if he could.

Fifty yards from the tree he saw that he had a reception committee: a bevy of very large snarks, who had obviously anticipated his intentions. He changed course to the northwest, towards another large tree, but the snarks understood his plan and he could see from the movement of the head-high watercress that several snarks had fanned out to cover that tree as well. He was obviously being stalked by highly intelligent creatures.

He decided to retreat and head east, but when he turned in that direction he could see movement in the cress in that direction as well. Soon he realized that he had been encircled and that he had no way of escape from their ever-decreasing perimeter, which was closing like a noose around him. He unsheathed his vorpal sword, though he realized his situation was hopeless if they attacked in a pack, which they were sure to do.

A few minutes later the snarkangel emerged from the cress, teeth bared and indicating every intention of attacking. He was an enormous creature six feet high at the shoulder, a dark-blue in colour. Stobo imagined he might easily weigh a ton. Deciding that his sword was worse than useless he pulled out his feather and waved it just as the snarkangel charged, mouth agape and drool spraying to both sides.

The snarkangel pulled up as soon as his massive weight would allow, stopping a mere foot in front of Stobo, and looking him right in the eye. His fierce countenance melted and he eased his huge head forward, as if to smell and taste him. Stobo extended his hand, which the snarkangel licked with an incredibly raspy tongue.

"Good boy!" Stobo said.

Twelve other mature snarks emerged from the cress in a circle, all with puzzled expressions. They came forward a few at a time and smelled him to see what this strange creature was.

"My name is Stobo," he said, as if the snarks could understand him, which, of course, they could. He turned to the snarkangel. "I'll call you Twilight, if that's all right with you." The snarkangel tossed its head, which Stobo took to mean that it was acceptable. "I could use a ride. This marsh is very difficult to manage."

One of the snarks, a dark-green mature male that was not quite as large as the pack's alpha-male, stepped forward and lowered his head, as if inviting Stobo to climb aboard. "I'll call you Mingomango," he said, and climbed up onto his scaly back. "How about a tour of the marsh?"

Twilight wheeled around, surprisingly nimble for such an enormous animal, and led the way. The pack followed at a respectful distance as they set off at a trot, effortlessly crossing the cress.

Fit VII
Jabberwoky

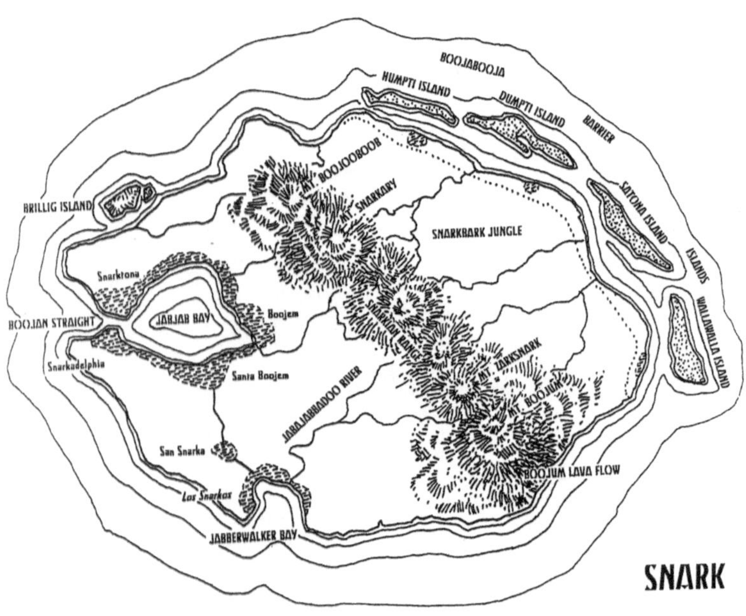

BOOJABOOJA
HUMPTI ISLAND
DUMPTI ISLAND
BARRIER
SATONA ISLAND
ISLANDS
WALLAWALLA ISLAND
BRILLIG ISLAND
MT. BOOJOOBOOB
MT. SNARKARY
SNARKBARK JUNGLE
Snarktona
BOOJAN STRAIGHT
JABJAB BAY
Boojem
SNARKIAN RANGE
Snarkadelphia
Santa Boojem
JABAJABBADOO RIVER
MT. ZARKSNARK
MT. BOOJUM
San Snarka
BOOJUM LAVA FLOW
Las Snarkas
JABBERWALKER BAY
SNARK

Fit the Seventh

Jabberwoky

Stobo spent his first night with the Skarn snarks resting beneath the enormous canopy of an ancient tumtum tree, with Mingomango sleeping beside him. He missed Blue, but realized that he had already changed allegiances and it was unlikely that he would be seeing him again as long as the Darksnarkian high priest was still alive. Mingomango, or Mingo as he called him for short, was quite an acceptable new companion. He felt confident that he would be as safe as a person could be with him at his side, and he readily drifted off to sleep, exhausted by the eventful day.

Sometime in the middle of the night he was jolted awake when Mingo stood up and turned to stare through the trees at the edge of the marsh. A low growl came from deep in the snark's chest. Stobo stood up to try and see what it was, trying to imagine what this powerful snark could possibly fear. Then it occurred to him that it was possibly a Boojum. A minute later Mingo bolted and ran into the jungle, leaving Stobo standing alone in the dark to face whatever it was.

*   *   *   *
    *   *   *
*   *   *   *

Stobo unsheathed his vorpal sword and took a defensive stance, hopeful that it wasn't a Boojum, as he was in no mood for vanishing. Then he smelled it; the unmistakably foul, sulphurous odor of a Jabberwok.

Stobo at first panicked as the memories of his earlier childhood encounter with the monster rushed back in a flood. He had an almost irresistible urge to run, but decided to stand his ground. A few minutes later he heard the whiffling of the Jabberwock's enormous wings and then saw the monster in the moonlight as it swooped down to attack low across the wabe. As it came, only a few feet above the head-high cress and above the smaller trees at the marsh's edge, he could clearly see its huge eyes, glowing blood-red as they caught the light of the full moon.

Moments later it was upon him, and he ducked at the last moment, the monster's mouth snapping at him as it flew past, just inches away. Stobo extended his vorpal sword, which ripped through a leathery wing flap, spaying him with blood. The monster enraged by its wounded wing, screamed in fury as it banked sharply to miss the huge overhanging branches of the tumtum tree. It flapped its enormous wings (not damaged enough to ground it) a few times to gain altitude and speed and then came sweeping back to the attack.

Once again Stobo waited until the last moment and then jumped to miss extended claws, while striking out with all his might as it flew past, this time leaving a deep gash along the length of the Jabberwock's right leg. After a dozen passes, each resulting in another slashing wound across some portion of the Jabberwok's body, the monster changed tactics and landed a short distance from where Stobo stood, foolishly deciding to attack on foot. It was a fatal mistake. Though immensely powerful it was also slow and Stobo had little trouble in darting out of harm's way at every attempt by the monster to bite him with yellowed teeth or catch him on pointed claw. After every thrust or charge Stobo's sword went snickersnack and left its bloody mark.

After half an hour of this one-sided combat the Jabberwock was eventually cut to ribbons and collapsed from loss of blood. Stobo moved in for the kill and chopped off its enormous head.

Covered in gore and triumphant, Stobo raised his vorpal sword to the moon and shouted a victory cry, "Ka-LOO-ka-lay!" his cry echoing back and forth across the Night Lagoon, disturbing snoozing snarks and dozing Oxford dons.

* * * *
* * *
* * * *

Dodgson's eyes popped open, half expecting to see the Jabberwok's severed head lying in the middle of his bedroom on the well-worn oriental carpet. He pulled himself up into a sitting position in his bed, his eyes wide open. The room was pitch black, so he fumbled around for a match and lit the candle by his bed. He was relieved to see that there was no massive head at the foot of his bed.

"Such a dream!" he exclaimed, talking aloud to himself. "It was as if my poem had come to life! I wonder if I'm losing my sanity? It all seemed so real!"

Darksnark manifested into the natural realm as a fairy, seated at the end of the bed. "Did you enjoy that?" he asked in the tiny voice of a very small girl. His manifestation was as a scantily clad fairy about six inches high, with the wings of a butterfly attached at her shoulders.

Dodgson gasped. He had never actually *seen* a fairy before. "Wh–wh–who are y–y–y–you?" he stammered.

"My name is Sylvie," the fairy replied. "Did you enjoy your dream?" she asked again.

"Well, yes and no," he said truthfully. "It was *very* exciting. It was as if my poem '*Jabberwocky*' had come to life in a strange way, though in some jungle."

"That was on the Isle of Skarn."

Dodgson wracked his brain. "I don't recall ever hearing of such an island."

"It's one of the eight islands in the Snark Archipelago in the Ocean of Sorrows."

"I don't recall any of those either," he said. "Where is the Ocean of Sorrows?"

"Most people refer to it as the Pacific Ocean, but that's not its real name."

"I see," he said. "Who was the young man who slew the Jabberwock?"

"That was Stobo. He's a snarkmaster."

"A snarkmaster?"

"One who has mystical power over snarks."

"And what *is* a snark?"

"There are numerous kinds of this wonderful beast. Some have feathers and scratch; others have teeth and bite. They're very delicious."

"Are they good for anything except food?"

"Some are useful for striking a light."

"I see."

"Oh, yes," the fairy added; 'and some are Boojums. But I think you knew that already, didn't you?"

"I wrote a line of poetry to that effect. It goes, "For the snark *was* a Boojum, you see." I've been considering the possibility of writing a comic poem about snarks. It occurred to me that it might be fun to see if a poem could be written backwards. I would use that line as the final line of the poem."

"That *would* be interesting. I guess you could call it the 'Looking-Glass' style of composition."

"Exactly; ending first, beginning last."

"There's one thing you need to know about Boojums," the fairy said. "What's that?"

"If you encounter a Boojum you softly and silently vanish away; like this." The fairy vanished in a spray of pixie dust.

"Wait!" Dodgson called after her. "Don't go!" But the manifestation had ended.

Dodgson sat there for a few minutes, hoping that the fairy would reappear like a Cheshire Cat. He couldn't see Darksnark standing at the foot of his bed, towering almost to the ceiling, behind the veil separating their dimensions. The demon enjoyed tormenting this peculiar Anglican minister who was so confused about things of the spirit. He flexed his enormous bat-like wings and stroked them, blowing out Dodgson's candle, then left. Dodgson, suddenly chilled by the inexplicable draft, went to the windows and adjusted the heavy curtains then crawled back under the covers, where he thought about some day writing a book about a fairy named Sylvie.

Stobo stood by the Jabberwock's carcass, studying the bloodied monster. As he was doing this Mingomango sheepishly returned, dragging his tail in the dirt. He took a few sniffs of the Jabberwock and then licked it to see how it tasted. Satisfied that it was edible it proceeded to have a late supper.

"How can you *stand* to eat that thing?" Stobo asked.

Mingo stopped, then hung its head.

"It's all right. If you really want to eat it, go ahead. But I wouldn't be surprised if it gives you a stomach ache!"

Mingo perked up and commenced eating again, tearing off huge chunks of flesh and gulping it down without bothering to chew it.

"When you've finished gorging yourself why don't you fetch Twilight and the rest of his pack and see if they're hungry, too? But don't eat the head! I have plans for that."

Mingo finished his sixty-pound meal and then bounded off into the marsh, returning a short while later with twenty other snarks of various sizes, both male and female, and even a few snarklings. They set upon the Jabberwock with relish and very little bickering, and in very little time there was little left but a few feathers, some large hollow leg bones, the breastbone, and a set of sixteen extremely sharp talons.

"Are you guys all done?" Stobo inquired when they were all just sitting around on their haunches and cleaning themselves with their long, slithy tongues. They all looked up briefly, then resumed cleaning. "I'll take that as a 'yes'," he said, then picked up the dozen or so feathers that the snarks hadn't consumed, placing them in his feather pouch. He didn't want them falling into the wrong hands. Next he gathered up the talons and large (apparently inedible) bones one by one, and tossed them as far out into the lagoon as he could. He wasn't sure if these remains held any magical powers, but wasn't going to run the risk of their falling into the wrong hands either.

Stobo went over to the nearest tammoo tree and hacked off several lengths of pliable vines that hung from its branches, and used them to weave a carry cradle for the Jabberwok's head. The Jabberwok's once luminous eyes were now bluish-grey and opaque in death, and it's long purplish tongue hung out of its mouth in the dirt. "I'll need several of you to carry this head," he told the pack, and several large males stepped forward. "It weighs several hundred pounds." One of the snarks grasped the cradle firmly in it teeth and easily picked it up.

"Come on. We're going to church," Stobo told them. "Bring that thing along."

They set out at once for the Temple of Darksnark, making their way slowly around the northern shore of the lagoon, stealthily bypassing the little beach where there was a canoe waiting patiently for Stobo in the unlikely event he had survived the night. "We'll just let them sit and cook in the sun," Stobo told Twilight. "I'd rather show up unannounced this time. Let them think I'm dead or that I've vanished."

By that afternoon they were in the jungle well out of sight behind the temple. They sat down to rest for awhile before making their entrance.

Captain Imholtz had sailed the *Forks and Hope* clockwise around the Isle of Skarn, looking for somewhere to come ashore, and while he was at it, giving the various mountains they saw proper English names (all duly entered into his log).

They first passed by Mount Ruin (which they named Mount Britannia), then back out to sea to skirt around Boojum Point (which they name George III's Disaster, because of its dangerous rocks well off shore of the crumbling headland). They named the higher peaks of the Craggy Mountain Range after various English kings and queens (Mount Perish became The Virgin Queen's Peak; Mount Vorpal they dubbed Mount Charlie, after the two of them; Mount Despair they named Victoria Peak, because of its massive rounded twin peaks; Mount Slaughter became Mount Henry, after all eight of them; and, Mount Destruction became Queen Anne's Peak). The enormous twin peaks of Death Mountain and Mount Vanish the Captain named after himself and his pet: Mount Imholtz and Mount Clare (his affectionate diminutive for the semiaquatic herbivorous rodent). Mount Decimate he named Mount Mum after his dear departed mother. Butcher Mountain was renamed Mount Derbyshire, after his home county.

When they came around Doom Island they dropped anchor and gazed at the splendor of towering Mount Darksnark, which rose like a space needle into the clouds. They drew lots for the right to name it, and Éclair won, so they named it Mount Canada in her honor (the Beaver being unable to communicate in any manner other than slamming her flat tail on the deck).

Captain Imholtz decided that it would be prudent to spend the night aboard ship and then enter through the maze of small islands that guarded the Gates of Hell in a dinghy.

Spirits were high amongst the crew, and to reward their bravery and persistence the Captain ordered extra rounds of grog after their typical meal of bride cake and salted pork, a most welcome culinary diversion. "It's snark meat tomorrow, me lads!" the Captain declared, and the crew all cheered (except the beaver, of course, who was a vegan).

After Stobo and the snarks had rested awhile Stobo stood up and addressed the pack. "We're going down there with the Jabberwock's head and kick butt!" he declared. "But before we go we need to take some precautions. The High Priest will undoubtedly try to control you, even though I've got the feathers. So, I'm going to have to stuff all of your ears so you can't hear him. We will depend upon hand signals. When I hold up one finger you should kill the High Priest. If I hold up two fingers you should kill everyone in sight, except me, of course. If I hold up three fingers you should tear down the temple. Four fingers will mean to fight off any snarks he might have on his side of the equation. Five fingers will mean to stop whatever you're doing. If I waive my arms madly and jump and down that will mean that he has a pet Boojum and we should all run for our lives. When I raise my right hand that will mean to follow me. Is all of that clear?" All of the snarks wagged their long scaly tails. "All right. Twilight, it will be your job to carry the head. Now I realize that most of you won't have ever had watercress stuffed in your ears, but don't worry. When we're all done I will clean them out for you." He went over to a stand of watercress and pulled off a large clump, then went from snark to snark, plugging their small auditory canals. When he was done he stepped back to see how they were coping. Some of them were shaking their heads, others were scratching their ears. Almost all of them had quizzical expressions.

Stobo raised his right hand. Twilight picked up the ghastly head. Then they all paraded down the mountainside and entered the Temple courtyard, which resulted in a riot, with Darksnarkian priests, acolytes, guards, and slaves running for their lives. Most climbed trees. A few dove under the veranda. A dozen clambered into a canoe, pushed off, tipped it over in their panic, and were promptly eaten by sharks.

They marched up to the Temple entrance, where the High Priest was standing, his arms folded across his chest. Twilight dumped the Jabberwock's head on the polished floorboards at his feet with a loud thud. Stobo went up and cut away the vines to reveal the thing in all of its gory. Strangely, its eyes had comically crossed.

Charles Dodgson had been suffering all day from one of his persistent migraines. He saw bright sparkling lights in his peripheral vision and kept thinking that he had just seen a fairy. His neck was as stiff as a poker and painful to move even a smidgen. The muscles in his shoulders felt as if they were tied into proverbial knots. He became obsessed with the idea that his head might implode, squeezing his brains out of his ears. Even the *thought* of food sent waves of nausea crashing over him and he hadn't eaten in two days. "I wish they would hurry up and invent aspirin!" he said at one point, unaware that he had foreseen this medical marvel in his delirium.

He had tried valiantly to work, but thinking clearly on the solution to even a trivial differential equation was impossible when reality kept stretching and bending. One moment he felt as if he was ten feet tall and could barely see his feet, the next he felt as compressed as if he had his chin on his instep. Then the room would begin to swirl like a Dervish, or the walls would flex like India rubber. It was all most distressing. He opened his diary and recorded the single word 'migraine', followed by a small sketch of a black stone (incongruously done in purple ink).

He kissed the day good-bye and went to bed early, though he doubted that he could possibly go to sleep since that was problematic even under the best of conditions. He just wanted to be still; for the world to quit swimming; for the pain to subside, even a trifle.

He tried to think of some pleasant thought, like playing imaginary croquet games with Alice Liddel in the deanery garden (but the moving balls made his head spin). He thought about all of the wonderful qualities of the number forty-two. He thought of golden summer afternoons in his childhood, but the sun hurt his mind's eye and he didn't have sunglasses. He finally gave up and concentrated on imagining infinite fields of colour. But he found that images of things kept rudely intruding: a sheep popped out of a field of crimson; a walrus swam by in a field of blue. It went on like this for hours, until finally God had mercy on him and put him to sleep and he dreamt that he saw

*   *   *   *
*   *   *
*   *   *   *

Captain Imholtz supervising the lowering of the dinghy and personally seeing to it that everyone was safely aboard the small craft before they set out for the channel between Gloom and Doom Islands. The surf was low and they made good time. Those who weren't rowing took the opportunity for bird watching as they passed by the sheer cliffs of Gloom Island where innumerable sea birds nested and squabbled. Slowly but surely they rowed on and soon entered through the Gates of Hell into the Night Lagoon.

Back at the Temple, the High Priest bent forward and looked at the Jabberwok's head. His face broke out into the first smile it has displayed in the last thirty years. "What's this? Have you killed the Jabberwok?" Stobo didn't respond. "Ka-LOO-ka-lay!" the priest shouted, then danced a small jig. He opened wide his arms, and said, 'Come to my arms, my beamish boy!"

"No thanks," Stobo said.

The High Priests smile flew away like a frightened brillig bird. He re-folded his arms and stiffened his back.

"I'm lucky to be alive, and you know it! You dumped me out there on the edge of the wabe, knowing full well that the Jabberwok would come looking for me. Didn't you?"

"Of course not! Why would I do a thing like that?"

"Because you're afraid of it. I would imagine that you've had several close calls with it yourself. You were happy to see if I could deal with it, not caring in the least if I ended up dead in the process."

"That's not true!" the High Priest insisted.

Stobo didn't believe him. "Well, there it is anyway; dead as dead can be. Whether or not it's the only one of them is a fifty million-clamshell question, however. They do breed, you know, and as I understand it, that requires at least two. Its mate's probably not going to be any too happy."

"There may be hundreds of them. Who knows? One less is good riddance, however. But that wasn't the reason I sent you out to Massacre Marsh."

"Oh?"

"I needed to see if you had control over the snarks." He looked out at the pack standing in a protective semi-circle around Stobo. "You obviously do; more control than I have. They would have ripped me to bits had I gone out alone onto the wabe."

"Why did you need to know about my gift?"

"Darksnark has a plan to take back what is rightfully his."

"Which is?"

"The seven other Snark Islands. They've been under Quarksnark's control far too long."

"And this has something to do with me?"

"Everything. Darksnark has told me for ten years that a Snarkmaster would soon appear, having unsurpassed control over the snarks. We have been waiting for you with keen anticipation. But we had to be sure that you were really the promised one."

"What do the snarks have to do with all of this?"

"As you've seen, the snarks on Skarn are almost invincible."

"Almost," Stobo agreed. "But they are terrified of Jabberwoks."

"Really?" the High Priest asked. "How do you know?"

"When that Jabberwok attacked me last night the snarkangel of this pack who was with me ran for the jungle when he heard it coming. He didn't come back until after I had killed it."

"You mean you killed this thing all by yourself?"

"Yes."

"With what?"

"My grandfather's vorpal sword." He pointed to it hanging from his side.

"My word! You ARE *impressive!"*

"So what's your plan for the Skarn snarks?"

"We will build an invasion fleet of rafts and ferry them over to the main island of Snark. You will lead them into battle against the combined armies of the Quarksnarkaiser. I have no doubt that you will be able to defeat them."

"Why should I risk my life doing that? The snarks may be almost invincible, but I'm certainly not! A spear or an arrow can easily kill me."

"It would be worth the risk."

"Maybe to you."

"Think of it; you would become Minister of Defence to the Darksnarkaiser!"

"And you *would presumably be the Darksnarkaiser?"*

"Of course!"

"Let me see if I understand this; I *take the risk, but* YOU *reap the reward?"*

"I have been taking risks here on Skarn for decades. I am a marked man. There have been dozens of attempts by the Quarksnarkaiser's troops to kidnap or assassinate me. And this is MY *plan;* NOT *yours."*

"I thought you said it was Darksnark's plan."

"Yes, his, too; we speak with one voice."

Stobo was silent for a moment, considering the plan as outlined. Finally he said, "What's your name?"

"I told you that I don't reveal that to people."

"I remember. However, I won't do anything else unless you reveal it to me."

"Nonsense!"

"It's a condition; take it or leave it."

The High Priest was silent for a moment. "Very well. It's Grun-dee."

"You shouldn't have done that," Stobo told him. "You knew better."

"Why did you say that?"

"Well, Grun-dee, I don't have any desire at the moment to be a Darksnarkaiser or a defence minister. What's more, even if I did, I wouldn't want to have to kill half of the residents of Snark to be either one of them. In fact, I've taken a strong liking to this particular island, and I think I could be quite content with being the Darksnarkian High Priest."

"I would never allow that."

"What would you do about it?"

"I'd have your blue-scaled snark tear you limb from limb."

"Give it a shot, Grun-dee."

The High Priest glared at him. "You had your opportunity," he said. "And you've blown it. You're a dead man!"

"You seem to have forgotten that you've revealed your name to me, Grun-dee."

"That little bit of information will DIE *with you."*

Stobo didn't look too worried. He knew that the ears of all of the snarks except Blue were packed with watercress.

"Snarks!" the High Priest shouted. "Kill Stobo! Now!"

Bille stepped forward to obey, but stopped in his tracks when Twilight, who was much larger, made a VERY *threatening growl. None of the other snarks responded to Grun-dee.*

"Kill Stobo! Now!" the High Priest repeated, even louder. This time Blue stayed back.

"You seem to have a problem, Grun-dee," Stobo said with a smile. "If they won't obey me, they won't obey you either!"

"I wouldn't be so sure about that," Stobo said calmly. The High Priest suddenly looked very worried.

"I meant to ask you: did you talk to Darksnark about Boob, like I asked you to?"

"Of course not!"

"Now THAT *really makes me mad! In that case, this is for you, Grun-dee!" Stobo held up one finger, well above his head so that*

the snarks could all clearly see it. He then stepped back to get out of the way of the charge that he knew would follow.

Twilight led the attack, and they reduced the High Priest to bloody shreds within minutes, then consumed all of him except his inedible skull.

Stobo turned around to see if a second finger would be required, but none of the Darksnarkian priests, acolytes, temple servants, and slaves who had bolted for the jungle had returned. Blue was hiding under the veranda.

Stobo went over to the snarks and cleaned out their ears. "Good snark," he said to each one as soon as it could hear again, and patted it on its broad head.

"Here, Blue!" he called. Blue crawled out from under the veranda and came over to him, dragging his tail in the dirt. "Good boy!" he said, and patted his *head as well. "All is forgiven!"*

Blue leapt to his feet and went tearing around the temple yard as fast as his legs would carry him; then he jumped high in the air, happy again.

Fit VIII
The Landing

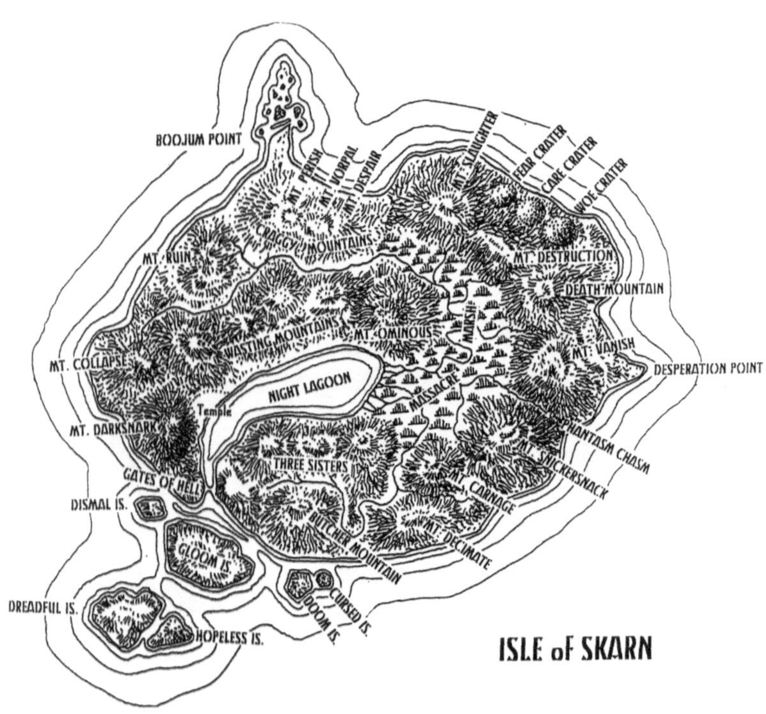
BOOJUM POINT
MT. PERISH
MT. VORPAL
MT. DESPAIR
MT. SLAUGHTER
FEAR CRATER
CARE CRATER
WOE CRATER
CRAGGY MOUNTAINS
MT. RUIN
MT. DESTRUCTION
DEATH MOUNTAIN
WASTING MOUNTAINS
MT. OMINOUS
MARSH
MT. VANISH
MT. COLLAPSE
DESPERATION POINT
NIGHT LAGOON
Temple
MASSACRE
MT. DARKSNARK
PHANTASM CHASM
THREE SISTERS
MT. SNICKERSNACK
GATES OF HELL
MT. CARNAGE
DISMAL IS.
BUTCHER MOUNTAIN
GLOOM IS.
MT. DECIMATE
DREADFUL IS.
CURSED IS.
DOOM IS.
HOPELESS IS.
ISLE of SKARN

FIT THE EIGHTH

The Landing

About this time the little dinghy carrying the crew of the *Forks and Hope* came paddling up the entrance to the Night Lagoon. Stobo saw their boat when it was still just a speck on the horizon, and as a precaution, told the snarks to retreat to the jungle and stay out of sight. He went with them and climbed up near the top of the Sacred Tumtum Tree that grew behind the temple, so that he would be able to see who they were and what they wanted without revealing himself.

The little boat made steady progress and Stobo was fascinated by its design, having never seen anything other than a canoe. They pulled up at the landing and a tall man with hair growing all over his face (something that Stobo had never seen in his life, as none of the islanders grew facial hair) got out first and waved something in his hand that made a marvelous ringing sound. Not having metal on any of the islands, he was the first Snarkian to have ever heard the sound of a bell. The tall man, who was wearing an odd limp hat, a striped shirt and tall boots, stood in the shallows and helped his crew ashore. The final creature to disembark looked to Stobo like some sort of large rodent, not unlike a mome rath except for its peculiar flat tail, though he couldn't imagine why anyone would want such a smelly beast on board a canoe.

The crew fanned out, exploring the Temple and its environs for several hours, as if they were looking for something, though Stobo couldn't imagine what. They gradually tired of their explorations and got back in the boat, with a great deal of confusion and bickering, and paddled off in the direction of Massacre Marsh. Stobo climbed down from the tree and called for Twilight.

"We need to go and see what these odd-looking bleached-out people are up to," he told Twilight. "They appear to be heading for the wabe. I can't make good time on foot and need a ride."

Twilight swung his head towards his back to indicate he should come aboard, which he did. With a shout, the pack took off around the northern shore to see if they could get there before the boat. But the boat had the advantage and they landed on the southern side of the lagoon well before the snark pack made it around the lagoon and across the delta that drains the wabe.

They finally spotted the crew climbing around on the lower slopes of the southern peak of The Three Sisters. While they were exploring Stobo and Twilight rode over to their dingy and had a look at the marvelous little boat. They had brought along a few boxes with food for their lunch and Stobo took the opportunity to open one and see what was inside, which just happened to be bride cake. It had the appearance of food, so he broke off a piece and tasted it, but found it disgusting and immediately spit it out. Having satisfied his curiosity he climbed back aboard Twilight and they went back into the jungle so as not to be seen by any of the crewmen climbing around on the rocks and crags high above them.

They got within a few hundred yards of some of the crewmen and watched and listened as they spoke in an incomprehensible, harsh-sounding language, often yelling back and forth at each other, arguing and screaming about one thing or another. The only word he heard which he understood was "snark", a word which they used quite frequently.

The crew slowly made their way around the base of the mountain and then around the southern edge of the wabe. After a lengthy discussion they all set out in single file up the slopes of Mount Snickersnack. "They had better be very careful," Stobo remarked to Twilight. "They may encounter a Boojum. I think we'll stay well back."

They watched from a distance as the crew made their way over to the edge of Phantasm Chasm and noticed that one of them split off from the rest and sprinted up the edge of the cliff, having evidently seen something of interest. A few minutes later there was hysterical laughter, followed by a burst of golden light, then silence.

"That would be the Boojum," Stobo told Twilight. "It's high time to go back, before we all join that one face-to-face with Zarksnark."

For THAT snark WAS a Boojum, as you well know.

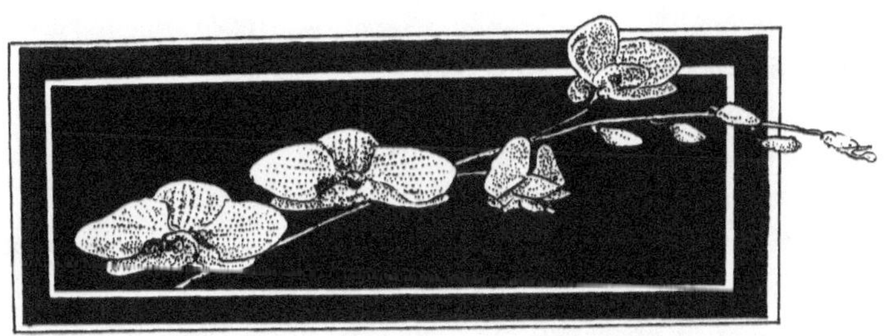

Skarnawakan-English Glossary

bandersnatch *n.* a large, arboreal mammal, with a long prehensile tail and distinctive black and white banded fur.

Boojum *n., pl.* **Booji.** 1: metaphysical snark. 2: species of tree, characterized by its tall, spindly, spiny appearance.

Darksnark *n* demonic Prince of Snark; regarded by the inhabitants of The Snark Islands as the god of evil; opponent of Quarksnark.

Darksnarkian[1] *n.* a member of the cult of Darksnark.

Darksnarkian[2] *adj.* pertaining to the worship of Darksnark.

grun-dee *v.i.* to initiate or transmit gossip; to snoop.

Jabberwok *n.* a large, winged creature.

jubjub *n.* large flightless bird, standing 3 metres (10 feet) tall and weighing up to 450 kilograms (1000 pounds).

kaboodle *n.* a pyramidal pile of skulls, thought to ward off evil.

ka-LOO-ka-lay *interj.* an exclamatory phrase used to express triumph.

mome rath *n.* large three-toed rodent.

Quarksnark *n.* demonic Prince of the Snark Islands, considered to be the god of both life and goodness; opponent of Darksnark.

Quarksnarkaiser *n.* the hereditary male ruler of the Snark Islands.

Quarksnarkian[1] *n.* a member of the orthodox religion dedicated to the worship of Quarksnark.

Quarksnarkian[2] *adj.* pertaining to the worship of Quarksnark.

Sharksnark *n.* God of the sea.

Skarnawakan *n.* 1: language spoken throughout the Snark Islands. 2: pictographic writing system for Skarnawakan.

slithy tove *n.* species of venomous snake, characterized by its thin bright emerald-green body and bulging red eyes.

snark *n.* any of the forty-two different species of legged or winged creatures comprising the family *Snarkius problematicus.*

snarkabana *n.* the common shelter or hut used by coastal residents of the Snark Island, usually with an open side facing the beach.

snarkabbage *n.* an edible leafy green plant used as a vegatable.

snarkabin *n.* the common shelter or hut used by inland residents of the Snark Islands.

snarkaboodle *n.* a collection of bleached snark skulls displayed at the entrance to a snarkabana or snarkabin as a magical protection against wild snarks.

snarkactus *n., pl.* **snarkacti** any of a family of plants that have succulent branches protected by thorns and lacking leaves, typically found in the Great Jabbersnatcher Desert on Snarkadia Island.

snarkaddy *n.* a small wooden box, usually covered in snarkskin, used for storing objects when not in use.

snarkaeopteryx *n.* an extinct, prehistoric winged snark known only from the fossil record.

snarkaic *adj.* of or relating to primitive snarks or prehistoric snark culture or worship.

snarkangel *n.* the alpha male of a snarkpack.

snarkattle *see* **snarkow.**

snarkave *n* underground chamber or series of chambers in which a wild snark lives or nests.

snarkaw *n.* the loud, raucous call of certain winged snarks.

snarkbark *n.* the characteristic alarm call of a snark.

snarked *v.adj.* 1: stymied. 2: enchanted, bewitched. 3: vanished.

snarker *n.* 1: a snark hunter. 2: one who handles or trains snarks.

snarkfarm *n.* a small private farm for raising snarkattle.

snarkful *adj.* characteristic of snarks.

Snarkian *n.* resident of any of the Snark Islands.

snarkilian *adj.* snark-like.

snarking *n.* the act of hunting or pursuing snarks.

snarkish *adv.* 1: pertaining to snarks. 2: extremely graceful or beautiful.

snarkiss *n.* the affectionate lick of a snark.

snarkist *n.* 1: a snark specialist. 2: someone knowledgeable in the care and husbandry of snarks.

snarkle[1] *n.* the high pitched scream or call of a wild snark.

snarkle[2] *v.* 1: to scream like a wild snark, with modulated groans and trills of varying pitch and intensity. 2: to fish with a spear.

snarkling *n.* an immature snark.

snarkmeal *n.* snark food.

snarkmew *n.* the sound made by a domesticated snark.

Snarkon *n.* a local tribal chief.

snarkophony *n.* the loud, dissonant calls characteristic of snarks when fighting for dominance or during mating.

snarkow *n.*, *pl.* **snarkattle** a domesticated snark, regardless of sex or age. *In pl.* domesticated snarks held as property or raised for use as meat or other purposes.

snarkpack *n.* a related group of snarks which forage in a group and defend a territory.

snarkpee *n.* snark urine.

snarkprey *n.* an animal taken by a snark as food.

snarkscat *n.* snark faecal droppings.

snarksign *n.* snarkscat; snark footprints; scratches left on trees by snarks; or other various signs indicating the presence of a snark.

snarkskin *n.* the essentially indestructible, long-wearing skin of a snark, similar to shark or eel skin in texture.

tammoo tree *n.* a large flowering tree, characterized by small aromatic purple blossoms in perpetual bloom, and broad dark green leaves with yellow spots which resemble splattered paint.

tumtum tree *n.* a sacred species of gigantic hardwood with a very broad trunk, often thirty of more feet in circumference, and an umbrella-shaped canopy well above its base.

vorpal sword *n.* a sword fashioned from a shaft of tumtum tree hardwood, set with two opposite rows of snark's teeth to form double serrated edges.

wabe *n.* a watercress marsh.

watercress *n.* staple food of omnivorous snarks.

Zarksnark *n.* demonic assistant to Darksnark; regarded by Snarkians as the God of the Dead.

The Millennium Snark Trilogy

Atchafalaya Boojum

Foreword to the 2014 edition of *In the Boojum Forest*

Byron Sewell has been writing or illustrating—or writing *and* illustrating—works inspired by Lewis Carroll's *The Hunting of the Snark*[1] for decades. Most of these were issued in very small limited distributions to his Carrollian friends and were never properly published. One early exception was his illustrated edition of *The Hunting of the Snark*, published by Catalpa Press of London in 1974. In 2012 I published some of Byron's more recent work along with some of his illustrations in *The Haunting of the Snarkasbord*,[2] together with a short piece entitled "Forks and Hope". I also published part of Byron's "Millennium Trilogy", which was written in 2000. This was *Snarkmaster*,[3] which Byron also illustrated.

This present volume publishes another part of "Millennium Trilogy", namely "In the Boojum Forest", a novella written in 2006, along with a shorter novella "Atchafalaya Boojum"

1 The publisher quite naturally recommends the Evertype edition, published in 2010 (ISBN 978-1-904808-36-7)

2 *The Haunting of the Snarkasboard* (ISBN 978-1-904808-98-5)

3 *Snarkmaster: A Destiny in Eight Fits* (ISBN 978-1-78201-002-9)

and its even shorter sequel, "Blue Boojum" (2005), as well as a charming piece callled "Southern Fried Snark" (2005).

Many of Byron's works, both Snarkian and Alician, are set in locations where he has either lived or visited. A year living in Australia—where he illustrated *Alitji in the Dreamtime* (1975)—explains his interest in the South Seas and is part of the inspiration for *Snarkmaster*. Byron was born and reared in the Southwest, which explains his inspiration and interest in the themes of "In the Boojum Forest". He lived for a year in Kenner, Louisiana, near to the Atchafalaya Swamp, which gave rise, in part, to "Atchafalaya Boojum".

Some comments on Byron's illustration for the cover of this present volume may interest the reader. The Bellman and his crew have been searching for snarks in the midst of the famous Boojum forest in the desert climes of Baja California. Byron's attire for the Bellman is appropriate desert gear (in the style of Roy Rogers' sidekick, Gabby Hayes). He carries a pitchfork and is ringing his bell as a warning to his crew that he has encountered a rattlesnake. On the left-hand side of the back cover can be seen in the distance a small mesa that in reality is located a few miles south of Tucumcari, New Mexico, where Byron was born in 1942. In case you've missed it, there is a rather obvious visual puzzle in the illustration.

I am pleased to tell fans of Byron Sewell's sometimes violent, amusing, and eclectic Carroll-inspired tales that Evertype plans to publish many of his Alician fantasies and parodies in due course. Some of these were co-authored or inspired by Byron's own famously humorous sidekick, August A. Imhlotz, Jr.

The third part of the "Millennium Trilogy", the tale of a serial killer who murders some of the crewmen in a secret Snark Club in California, has also been published in 2014 as *Murder by Boojum*.[4]

Michael Everson
June 2014

4 *Murder by Boojum* (ISBN 978-1-78201-079-1)

Contents

"How doth the little crocodile,
Improve his shining tail,
And pour the waters of the Nile,
On every golden scale!

How cheerfully he seems to grin,
How neatly spreads his claws.
And welcomes little fishes in
With gently smiling jaws!"

—Alice's Adventures in Wonderland

"The fifth is ambition. It will be right
To describe each particular batch:
Distinguishing those that have feathers, and bite,
From those that have whiskers, and scratch."

—The Hunting of the Snark

CHAPTER I

Cocodrie

Georges LeBlanc poled his flat-bottomed boat slowly up the bayou as quietly as he could manage. His neighbour and fishing buddy, Mathieu Gaudet, sat up at the front, aiming the beam from a handheld spotlight that they had hooked up to a 12-volt car battery. They were searching for the tell-tale bright eyes of *cocodrie,* as they called alligators, which might be lurking in the water hyacinth. There was a thin slice of moon just above the horizon, but its faint light didn't penetrate into the dark backwaters and branches off of the big bayous. The particular backwater they were on at the moment was some ten feet wide and was relatively deep. Its low banks were overgrown with thick brush and trees, some of which bent so far over that their tops dipped into the water, their washed-out roots unable to hold their trunks upright. Every once in a while a snake would drop from a branch with a soft splash and swim silently away into the darkness ahead of them. The swamp was surprisingly noisy from the calls of frogs hiding in the trees or perched on the thick water hyacinth and lily pads. The high intensity beam of the spotlight made it obvious that the heavy, musty air was aswarm with mosquitoes and other insects. Georges and Mathieu had put on so much repellent that the *cocodrie* could probably smell them coming. Still, it didn't do them all that much good; the hungry bugs bit them anyway.

So far, it hadn't been a good night for hunting *cocodrie.* They had seen a few small ones, not worth the trouble of shooting with the .22 rifle they carried in the boat. You could get a dollar for a small alligator skull, which sold well to tourists in the curio shops in New Orleans, especially to little boys, but it was messy work cleaning and bleaching them and there was a limit to what a person would do for a buck. However, there was real money to be made from the bigger alligators that were four to six feet long, and both Georges and Mathieu considered them to be good eating as well, especially deep fried in a fiery mustard and Tabasco batter. Catching one that big would make their night's efforts well worthwhile.

A sudden, very loud splash a short distance ahead startled them both, and Georges instinctively jammed the long pole into the thick mud to slow their boat.

"*¿Que diablo?*" Georges exclaimed.

Mathieu aimed the bright light in the direction where the noise had come from, but the beam hit the overhanging branches and only penetrated a short distance. "I'm not sure," he said, the tone of his voice revealing that he had been badly startled. "Something *really* big hit the water up ahead of us."

"What could be that big?"

"I dunno; maybe a panther fell out of a tree."

"Not likely. I been in these swamps all my life and I ain't never seen a panther."

"Oh, they're in here all right. I've heard other people say they've seen em. I heard one scream once."

"Well, if it's a panther, I sure don't want it leapin in the boat with us! Let's pull back to more open water."

“Now wait just a minute,” Mathieu said. “If we leave, we’ll wonder for the rest of our lives what it was; might be a big *cocodrie*,” he suggested.

“How big?”

“I dunno; maybe ten or twelve feet. That could really be worth something!”

“How we goin to get anything that big back, even if we *could* kill it? We couldn’t even get it in the boat; it’d probably sink it!”

“We could tie it up to a tree and go back for my power boat, then come back and fetch it. We could even tow it alongside if need be. We wouldn’t have to get it into the boat with us.”

“How much you think we could get for one that big?”

“It might fetch $500; maybe even more.”

Just then the entire surface of the water around the boat vibrated intensely from a spooky low frequency noise that caused the bottom of their aluminium boat to hum, as if it had been touched by a tuning fork.

“*Mon Dieu!* You ever hear or feel anything like that before?” Mathieu asked, suddenly very afraid again.

The vibrations suddenly stopped, as if someone had tripped off a power switch.

“No, but I seen something like it once on a nature show on TV. A big bull *cocodrie* makes a noise like that when it wants to mate. That sound can travel for miles underwater and attracts females. It makes the water dance all around him when he does it.”

“And probably attracts his rivals, too.”

“Yeah; them too. If another bull responds there’s usually a terrible fight for mating rights.”

“You think that might happen here?”

“Maybe. Worse yet he might think our boat is another big bull.”

“Oh, great! That’s all we need.”

"Don't get too upset. I got my pistol." Georges patted the handle of the .44 magnum he carried in a holster on his hip. "I don't care if that *cocodrie* is fifteen feet long; this pistol's able to crack an engine block at fifty feet. Any *cocodrie* sticks his head up where I can see it is goin to have a splittin headache for his last memory." He took the pistol out of its holster.

Suddenly the water all across the width of the bayou vibrated again, this time with more energy. They could clearly see beads of water lift into the air and dance across the vibrating surface like water hitting a frying pan full of hot grease.

"That SOB must be right under us!" Mathieu said, his voice revealing genuine terror at the possibility.

"Shine your light down here into the water," Georges said, pointing at the water beside their boat with the barrel of his pistol. "Let's see if we can see anything."

Mathieu aimed the spotlight at the water, but the beam could only penetrate a few feet into the murky pea green water. It didn't reveal so much as a perch. "Nothing!" Mathieu said. Georges moved the beam around, scanning the water across the width of the bayou. Suddenly a dark shadow in the water, as big as a pickup, rushed by, less than five feet away from the boat, travelling fast in the direction they had come from, as if trying to cut off their escape.

"You see dat?" they both asked each other in nearly perfect unison.

"Looked like a killer whale!" Georges said, in utter disbelief. "I saw something like that at Sea World in San Antone once. You'd see this dark shadow moving fast through the water, then the killer whale would come clean up out of the water, then belly flop. Looked just like that!"

Mathieu urinated in his pants.

"We've got to get out of this boat! Right now!" Georges said as he shoved his pistol back in its holster and frantically poled the boat over to the bank.

"*Vite! Vite!*" Mathieu was yelling, urging him on.

They were out of the boat in a few moments, grabbing at low limbs to keep from going deep into the water, and searching with their feet for underwater logs or cypress knees to stand on.

They were only a few feet back into the trees when they felt a rush of air, as if something huge had breached, followed momentarily by a loud, crunching splash as it landed square on top of their boat. A sheet of water cascaded over them through the surrounding trees. They both screamed instinctively, unable to control their own voices in this moment of panic.

Everything in the surrounding swamp went silent, except for the sound of water dripping from the trees. Even the frogs had momentarily stopped croaking. Then the ankle-deep water they were standing in vibrated again, and this time they could feel it on their boots and legs.

"Let's get back into them taller trees!" Georges said. "It likely can't follow us back in there."

"There's snakes in there!" Mathieu said, hesitating.

"To hell with the snakes! We've got a lot better chance against them than against whatever that thing is!"

They frantically fought their way through the tangle of brush and vines until they reached a small island of mud and moss, with a cypress rising up out of the middle. "Let's get up in this tree!" Georges said. "Here; I'll give you a boost up to that first limb and you pull me up after you. *Vite!*"

In a minute they were heading up the tree like black bear cubs, climbing as high as they dared, and both nearly out of breath, gulping the heavy, humid air, their hearts pounding.

Then they heard it come up out of the bayou and make its way towards them. Its steps made a sucking sound as its feet lifted out of the thick mud. Then it roared, or rather screamed; it was hard to describe. It sounded like it was directly below them, at the base of the tree. Georges and Mathieu both took death grips on the tree trunk, not sure what to expect.

"*Mauvais!*" Mathieu said through clenched teeth.

That's when it hit the tree. It felt as if a car had rammed it, and it was all they could do to hold on and not be knocked from their precarious perches. Georges decided that it was time to do something and pulled out his pistol. He fired three random shots towards the base of the tree, not able to see what he was shooting at it in the pitch-blackness.

This caused another terrible roar, this time from directly below and then they heard it retreat back into the bayou. A few minutes later the swamp reverted to its normal background noise of croaking frogs and buzzing insects. The smell of gunpowder was heavy in the thick, motionless air.

They stayed in the tree all night and until well into midmorning, afraid to descend, even though they could clearly see the ground now and that there was nothing waiting for them. "Well, we can't stay up here for days," Georges said. "I don't want to spend another night up here. And anyway, we'll eventually starve if we don't get back. We're going to have to try to work our way over to the main channel and see if we can flag down a fishin boat."

Mathieu knew he was right, but dreaded going back down, still terrified at what might be lurking below. Georges led the way and dropped down into the muck. Mathieu was soon down beside him. "Let's see what's left of our boat," Georges suggested. "I'd like to get a life vest if I can find one. I don't like the thought of drownin out here."

"What if it's still there? Just waitin for us to return?"

"Come on! It's a night creature. It's not going to expose itself like that. We're safe enough. And anyway, I can see to shoot now, and I've got three rounds left."

They made their way back to where they had come from, looking ahead for any sign of the creature's footprints, but the water had swallowed up any such evidence hours ago. They found what was left of their boat, smashed almost beyond recognition, half out of the water and half up against a tree. It looked like it had been through a hurricane. "Look at this! Can you believe it?" Georges asked.

"It's a damn good thing we weren't in it!"

"I reckon. We'd have been dead in an instant!"

They looked around for debris from the boat. Their ice chests were shattered and pieces were floating along the bank. However, their life vests were intact, having survived the impact better than anything else. They retrieved them and put them on, even though they were wet.

"Come on, let's get the hell out of here, just in case that thing hears us," Mathieu pleaded.

"Okay," Georges agreed. "We'll go back into the swamp a ways and try to follow along the edge of the backwater till we hit the main bayou." He thought for a minute, then said, "Look; we can't never tell nobody about this. We'll become the laughin stock of the parish. Probably lose our jobs and have to move away. Folks'll say we was attacked by the Boojum. We'll never hear the end of it."

Mathieu nodded. "I reckon you're right. No point anyway. Iffen I heard about it, I wouldn't believe it neither, so I don't figure anybody else would. What we goin to say happened to us?"

"We'll just say we rammed our boat on a snag and it sank. No one's ever goin to find what's left of our boat back in there. Who's goin to know or care?"

Mathieu nodded. "It'll be our secret. But I'll tell you this; I ain't never comin back out here into these deep swamps at night again. No way!"

"Me either. I'm goin to switch to bass fishin out on wide-open lakes in the daylight."

Mathieu nodded. "Georges, you know something?"

"What's that?"

"I don't believe that was any big *cocodrie*."

"No, me neither. I've heard big bulls bellow, and they don't sound nothin like that scream we heard last night."

"No, that weren't no *cocodrie* gruntin!" he agreed. "That sounded more like something straight out of Hell."

"Or the movies. Reminded me of *Jurassic Park*."

"Yeah; more like that."

"That's something else I ain't never goin to do again."

"What's that?"

"Watch them damn *Jurassic Park* movies."

"Yeah; me neither; too realistic!"

"Yeah!"

It took them several hours of struggling through the swamp to finally reach the main channel. Three hours later a boat finally approached and they started yelling their heads off to attract attention.

Dave Thibodeau pulled his bass boat up alongside the trees where they were perched like egrets.

"Thank God you heard us!" Georges said. "We wrecked our boat. We need a ride back into Morgan City."

"You want *me* to take you?"

"Yeah. We've been out here all night."

"I look like a taxi to you?"

"Well, no. But we really need help."

"I been out on a rig for two weeks. I just finally got here to do a little fishin. If you think I'm going to spend the next two hours takin you two idiots back to Morgan City you're crazy."

"We'll pay you."

"How much?"

Georges thought for a moment. "Fifty dollars."

Dave laughed. "Hell, I make that much in thirty minutes out there on that rig."

"Okay, then. How much you want to do it?"

Dave thought for a moment. "Five thousand dollars," he told him with a straight face.

"Five thousand dollars?"

"That's what it would take for me to throw away my day runnin you two up and down the bayou."

George turned to Mathieu. "How much money you got?"

"On me?"

"No, in the bank."

"Last I checked I think maybe I had $300."

"I only got $1,500." He turned back to Dave. "We only got $1,800 between us."

"Then you're up the bayou without a boat *or* a paddle," Dave said. "Looks like you two are goin to have to wait for the next bus."

"You don't mean that you're goin to just leave us out here, do you?" Georges asked is disbelief.

Dave didn't even bother to answer him, but revved up his boat and pulled away.

"Can you believe that son of a bitch?" Georges said. "You should have shot him."

"Yeah, I probably should have. But I'd rather save the bullet for that thing that tried to eat us, just in case it's been trackin us."

It was two hours before another guy in a boat finally saw them and picked them up. He didn't demand a fare.

Chapter II

Gray's Bayou

Dallas "Tizzy" Tizzard and his three companions approached the funky Boojum billboard as they drove west from Gibson towards Morgan City, heading for the boat launch, where they would put their bass boat into the Atchafalaya. "ST. MARY'S PARISH / HOME OF THE BOOJUM!" the sign announced. The faded sign needed a new coat of paint. The rain, sunlight and salt air had taken a heavy toll. Whoever had painted the sign had imagined the parish's legendary monster as having the head of a T. Rex, the feathered body and wings of an enormous rooster, and the scaly legs of a giant iguana. It was really something to behold. Bigfoot and Nessie seemed a lot more plausible.

Tizzy laughed out loud as they drove past the sign. "That damn Boojum always gets me right in my funny bone!" he said, pointing at the sign through the open window. "It looks like it came right out of one of ole Colonel Sanders' nightmares!"

Tom Guppy, Alan Twardy, and Leon Rocheleau, his old high school buddies at Central Catholic High in Morgan City, laughed with him. It *was* an undeniably funny sight.

"Yeah," Alan added. "They could serve it at Kentucky Fried Boojum."

"KFB!" Guppy added.

"Original or extra crispy?" Leon asked, pretending to be the one serving at the counter. This made them all laugh again. Not that it was all that funny; they just liked being with each other.

"What would you do if you was to meet something like that thing out in the swamp?" Guppy asked Alan. They all liked Tom's last name so much that they had never called him by his given name.

"Get the hell out a there as fast as I could!" Alan responded without hesitation. "What'd you do, Guppy?"

"I'd take its picture and sell it to CNN for a hundred thousand big ones," said Guppy.

"Take a picture with what? You bring a camera?"

"Of course not," Guppy said. "I'm goin fishin, not takin wildlife pitchures."

"There you go; you might miss the chance of a lifetime cause ye're too lazy to bring along a camera!"

"I don't reckon the chance of us actually seein that creature's any too high," said Tizzy.

"No; bout as high as seein Godzilla squash the Huey P. Long bridge!" Alan said.

"I reckon," Leon agreed and laughed at the thought of Godzilla rising up out of the muddy Mississippi to terrorize the Baton Rouge rush-hour traffic.

"I don't know. Tonight might be just the night to see it. You read in the paper about them two missin fishermen?" asked Tizzy.

"No. What about em?"

"Their families reported them missin when they didn't come back from huntin gators last night. They still ain't found any sign of em. The Coast Guard and game wardens have been searchin for them back in the Bayou Cocodrie."

"Hell, they probably just changed their minds and went into the French Quarter and found themselves some girls. Lot more fun than shootin gators!"

"No, the paper said they was good Christian boys; don't drink or nothing."

"I don't understand how anyone could not want a beer now and then!" Guppy said. "What're you sayin? You think the Boojum ate em?"

Everyone laughed at this preposterous idea.

Tizzy grinned big and went along with the joke. "Maybe. You know the legend. That hungry Boojum comes up outa the swamp every couple a years and eats a few folks, then goes back to wherever it lives for another two years. Them boys might'a been dinner."

"Yeah, right!" said Guppy, not buying it.

"I can tell you ain't a believer in our famous legendary monster," observed Tizzy.

"Are *you*?" Guppy asked, a big funny grin on his face.

"No; but something happens out there in the swamp every couple of years, almost like clockwork; about Labor Day. That's just a little over a week from now, you know."

"People just get out there in the swamp and lose their bearins and get lost," said Guppy. "Or they have boat trouble, or run out of gas, or drown water skiin with the snakes. Lots of things can happen out there. Some people probably even get themselves murdered."

"I figure that's why the phone company invented cell phones," said Alan. "Some big ole swamp Boojum jumps out at you, you call in the Coast Guard; or a squadron of F-4s to drop napalm."

"Call them from where? Inside the Boojum's belly?" Tizzy asked.

"Well, no. I reckon, that'd be a mite late to go makin any 9-1-1 calls."

"Yeah. A mite." Tizzy laughed as he pulled into the narrow parking lot at the ramp and then backed the boat trailer into the murky water. His companions jumped out and quickly released the boat, then climbed aboard. Tizzy pulled the empty trailer out of the water and parked the SUV. There were about thirty SUVs and pickup trucks already there, most with empty boat trailers. Sometimes it seemed like there were more SUVs and pickups than cars in South Louisiana. He locked up and waded out to the boat and clambered in. His friends already had the outboard engine idling.

It was early morning, and the sun hadn't quite come up over the cypress swamps between there and New Orleans, off to the east. It was late summer and the morning was already hot. They set out south from Morgan City at full throttle, into the main channel that led to Sweet Bay Lake, passing the shrimp boats just coming in from a night out in the Gulf. They hadn't been on the water more than fifteen minutes when the sun came up, and the dark water briefly lit up like golden neon from the reflected sunlight. All four of them put on their sunglasses at the same time, as if saluting a superior officer. They kept to the western side of Sweet Bay Lake and turned up the Big Wax Bayou for a short distance until they came to the main fork that put them into Gray's Bayou.

The water in the bayou was so still that it looked like polished marble. Every few hundred yards they would scare up egrets, or sometimes even a scarlet ibis, from out of the dead top of a tall cypress or from a perch on an old log. The birds would fly ahead of them, often just above the water, a mirrored brilliance of white or red on the dark water. Turtles would sometimes slip off of fallen trees or almost submerged cypress knees along the banks as they approached.

It took them another fifteen minutes to spot the plastic jug they had hung from a low branch to mark the location of their trotline. Tizzy cut the throttle back and they glided quietly into a backwater branch overhung with tree branches. He slowed the motor to a crawl as they approached their first float, an empty plastic milk container on which they had spray painted a big red “X” to identify it as theirs. “Okay, boys; let’s see what we got,” Tizzy said.

Guppy leaned out and tugged on the line to test its weight. “Something big on this one!” he said. He quickly pulled it up, hoping that it wasn’t a big snapping turtle or a gar. In a moment there was a nice four-pound channel cat swinging in the air, struggling hard against the hook. The blackish-green skin on its back was as shiny as if it had been dipped in cooking oil.

“All right!” Leon said. “*Numero uno!* That’s a keeper.” Guppy plopped it down inside the boat and Leon stepped on its bony, flat head to keep it from hooking him with its erect dorsal fin while he deftly removed the hook with a practiced hand. He tossed the fish into an ice-filled cooler. “I can taste catfish and hush puppies already,” he said. The only thing he liked better than catfish was shrimp, any way you could fix them. Leon reached into an old Styrofoam cooler and produced a chunk of rotten chicken that they’d left out in the sun for two days to ripen, and re-baited the hook. Then Guppy lowered it back into the dark water. Leon rinsed the slime off of his fingers in the bayou.

They worked their way along the line, pulling up three more catfish of a similar size and one three-foot long gar, which they hit in the head with a hatchet to kill before throwing it back in the water for the *cocodrie* and turtles.

"What's that?" Guppy said as they approached the next float, pointing to something white snagged on the float just below the surface.

Everyone looked in the direction he was pointing. "Net it," Tizzy suggested. "Maybe we can use it for bait."

"Oh, shit!" Guppy exclaimed when he lifted the net up out of the water. "It's somebody's hand! It's still got a weddin ring on!"

Alan turned to the other side of the boat and vomited his grits over the side; a little breakfast for the perch.

"Now what?" Guppy said, holding the net at arm's length, as if he thought the severed hand might make a sudden grab for him like Thing from *The Addams Family*.

"I reckon we'll have to take it in to Sheriff Paquette," said Tizzy. "Might belong to one of them missin guys they're searchin for."

"I wonder where the rest of him is?" Leon said, looking around the boat and over to where the black water filled in around the base of the trees. Alan was still throwing up.

"I vote we don't stay around and try to find him," Tizzy said. "Toss them catfish in with the beer and we'll put the hand in there on the ice."

Leon quickly transferred the fish and Guppy dumped the hand into the box, then covered it with ice. You could see the white of the broken wrist bones. Tizzy swung the boat around and headed back towards Morgan City as fast as the boat would take them.

"I figure the Boojum ate him, and that's all that's left," Guppy said, with a Cheshire Cat grin spread across his face. He had recovered his sense of humour once they had gotten back out into Sweet Bay Lake, well away from where they had found the hand.

"Yeah, right!" Tizzy responded, but half-believed him. It was spooky out in the swamp when something had scared you like that, and he was anxious to get back to civilization. Alan had finally quit throwing up and was sitting up in the bow, as far away from the cooler as he could get, breathing the rush of humid air, and trying to resist the black nausea that kept trying to overwhelm him.

They went straight into town and over to the Parish offices. They had decided to leave the hand in the cooler. Tizzy held one handle and Leon the other; not that it was all that heavy. It was just that neither one of them wanted to carry it up close.

Sheriff's Deputy Maurice LeClaire was seated at the front desk. He looked up when they came in. "You boys bringin me a mess of shrimp?" He'd known the four of them all their lives, all the way through high school.

"We wish," Tizzy said. "You got a strong stomach, Maurice?"

Maurice considered that to be an ominous question. "You pull people out of car wrecks and you soon get a strong stomach, or else you go find a different line of work. What you got in there? You better not be bringin some dead animal or a snake in here. You do, and you'll all spend the night back there in one of them cells."

"Well, I reckon it's dead alright, but worse that any snake," Tizzy said, setting the cooler on the floor in front of his desk and lifting the lid up. Maurice put his hand on his pistol grip just in case something mean came flying out of the cooler. Some of these kids had a weird sense of humour.

He peered in. "All I see is ice," he said.

"You got a pencil I could use for a prod?" Tizzy asked.

Maurice handed him a ballpoint pen, and Tizzy used it to scrape the ice away to reveal the hand.

"Where'd you get that?" Maurice asked, quite taken aback by what he now saw in the cooler.

"Back in Gray's Bayou. We was workin our trotline and this thing was snagged on one of our floats. We figured it might belong to one of them boys you guys are lookin for."

"Could be. Don't touch it."

"No problem!" Tizzy assured him. "You can have the damn cooler, too. I ain't never puttin that back in my boat."

"Where's Gray's Bayou?" Maurice asked. There were so many bayous in the lacework of waterways that cut through the delta that it was hard to remember all of them, even when you'd lived your whole life in the area.

"West of Sweet Bay Lake. It joins the Big Wax Bayou."

Maurice nodded, remembering it now. "You boys excuse me a minute while I go radio the Sheriff." He got up and went back into a small inner office. He quickly related what had happened to Sheriff Paquette, then went back out to where the four boys were standing, well back from the cooler. "The Sheriff says he wants us to meet him down at the Coast Guard Station. They'll have a boat down there waitin to pick us up. You boys are goin to have to take me back out there and show us exactly where you found that." He pointed at the hand in the open cooler. He went over and covered it back up with ice and closed the lid, then phoned the State Police to make arrangements for them to pick it up to send to the lab. "Should be easy enough to identify who that belonged to; what with a complete set of fingerprints and a weddin band."

"How will we get back?" Tizzy asked, not at all excited about the possibility of spending all day out there with the police and divers poking around for a body, or what remained of it.

"You show us the spot and we'll get you right on back; probably by airboat or helicopter."

"All right!" Guppy said. "Ain't never got to ride in one of them choppers before."

"It's not a promise," Deputy Maurice told him, "just a possibility; don't get your hopes up."

They went back outside to the parking lot. "You boys follow me on down to the Coast Guard Station; there ain't enough room in my squad car for all of you."

They followed Maurice and parked their rig, taking up three spots. The sun was well up now and it was already in the lower nineties. The filthy water had a strong smell of dead fish and diesel as they made their way down to the dock. A large airboat was waiting for them, with a Coast Guardsman holding a map. They climbed aboard and introduced themselves to Captain David Hunka, who opened the map. "Can you show me about where you found the remains?" he asked.

The map was mostly solid green indicating a vast swamp and marsh, but crisscrossed with narrow blue waterways. Tizzy pointed at a spot on Gray's Bayou. "Okay. I'll get us as close as I can to that location, then you can lead us to the exact spot. You guys have a seat." He pulled out a two-way radio and repeated their destination. "There'll be several boats with police and divers that'll meet us out there," he said. "Cast us off, will you?" Leon untied the boat and pushed them a few feet away from the dock. The big engine revved up and they glided out onto the channel, where they were soon roaring through the waterway at breath-taking speed.

They were met by several other boats on Sweet Bay Lake near the entrance of Big Wax Bayou. It took their small flotilla only about fifteen minutes to reach the entrance to the backwater where Tizzy and his friends had their trotline. Tizzy signalled to slow down the boat and they eased up to about the spot where they had found the hand. "It was caught on our sixth float," Guppy said. "But it could've just floated in here, so no tellin where it came from."

"There's not much current back in here and the natural flow is back out to the bayou, so there's a good chance the body might be close by," Maurice said. He signalled for another boat to come alongside. "They found the hand in this area," he told them. "Try draggin through here first. We might get lucky and snag the body. If that doesn't work then we'll need a couple of your divers to go down here and take a look-see. We'll pull on back out of here and give you guys some room to work. Pull that trotline up so none of you get hooked."

They made their way back out to the channel and tied off to wait for the search effort to get on.

"I don't see no chopper," Guppy said, obviously very disappointed.

"It's probably workin over towards the swamps south of Amelia," Deputy Maurice said. "We had a report of some clothes in the water over there and they're checkin it out. That's where Sheriff Paquette is. We'll probably have to take you guys back in one of these boats. We'll wait awhile and see if they come up with anything."

"I should've brought a fishin pole," Tizzy said as he sat down and tried to get comfortable. "I'll be amazed if they're able to find anything in that water. You wouldn't be able to see more'n a foot in front of your nose down there."

"What if they come up on a gator in there? They's some right big ones back in these bayous. My Dad and I was out here when I was a kid and we saw a big one, that was maybe twelve feet long; a real monster."

"People don't see many that big these days," Maurice said. "Still, there could be one. They'll post a couple of guys on the boats with high-powered rifles to keep an eye out for them. I reckon they'll be safe enough from the gators. I'd be more worried about steppin on a big snapper, if it was me in there."

"Who are these guys that are missin?" Alan asked.

"Couple of boys from over towards Gibson. They got big families over there. Their wives have been callin me about every hour wantin to know if we've found their husbands yet."

"What do you think might of took off that hand?" Tizzy asked Maurice.

"Hard to say; but it ain't easy to cut off a hand like that, except with an axe or a chainsaw."

"Or maybe he got a little too close to a big gator," Guppy suggested.

"I doubt it," Maurice replied. "A gator doesn't bite things off like that. They'll just latch on to an animal and drag it under to drown it; must have been something else."

"Like what?" asked Leon.

"Oh, people try to dispose of bodies sometimes," said Maurice. "Cut em up in little pieces and dump them out here in the swamp, hopin the gators will eat them and get rid of the evidence."

"That's supposed to be what happened to Jimmy Hoffa," Alan said. "I heard the Mafia cut him up in little pieces and fed him to the gators down in the Everglades."

"I heard that, too, but I don't believe it. Most likely they put his body in the trunk of a car and had it smashed in one of them wreckin yards. The Mafia controls most of those in New Jersey and New York. That mushed up mess would have then gone into a blast furnace, and they'd have never found a trace. A lot more efficient that feedin the wildlife."

"You guys catch any fish on your trotline?" Maurice asked, trying to change the subject.

"Yeah, we pulled up three nice channel cats, and one fair-sized gar," said Leon. "We killt the gar and tossed it in for the turtles, so's they'd have something to eat besides our bait. Those divers in there will likely be findin that gar afore long."

"You don't eat gar?" Maurice asked, smiling.

"Well, I eat most things; but not gar. The dang things are all bones and taste too strong. I don't like my fish to taste *that* fishy; I like white meat if I can get it; sand trout or Jew fish."

"I caught a freshwater gar one time in a river in Texas," said Tizzy. "This Mexican feller I was with kept it; he said it made good soup; wouldn't let me throw it back. He scaled it and took it home for supper."

"I'd have to be damn hungry to eat gar soup!" Leon allowed. "Even with lots of Tabasco. I hope I ain't never that hungry!"

"It might not be too bad in gumbo," Guppy allowed. "You can put almost anything in that and it'll taste real good."

"I was over to the Shark Rodeo at Texas City once, several years back," said Tizzy. "I saw a saltwater gar big enough to eat a kid or a big dog."

"No way!"

"I'm tellin the truth. They were catchin all sorts of big fish out in Galveston Bay and bringin em in to be weighed. They'd string em up on telephone poles using electric hoists. They had half a dozen eight to ten foot sharks strung up. While we was lookin at em, a pickup drove up to the weigh station with this gar about eight feet long and at least two feet across his gut. It was about one third teeth. And it wasn't dead, even though it must have been out of the water for half an hour. They climbed in and hooked it with a steel cable and winched it up a pole. That dang monster kept floppin and twistin around, trying to take a bite out of anybody that got within reach. It was still floppin around when we left about thirty minutes later."

"I'd of liked to have seen that!" Guppy said.

"This guy who was there and lived over in Galveston said that the canals around some of them fancy resort homes down by the water's edge on the backside of the island have those big saltwater gar in them. People's dogs jump in there to fetch a stick or something and the gars hit them. He said they lose lots of dogs that way."

"You'd think they'd lose a few kids that way too," observed Alan.

"You'd think; but I've never heard of that. I guess you have to teach them to be careful and not to fall in."

"I know one thing, after seein the sharks they drug out of Galveston bay, I never want to go fishin out there," said Tizzy. "You fall overboard and there's some real monsters swimmin around with you."

"Big as Jaws?" asked Leon.

"Well, no; not *that* big. But for sure big enough to take off a leg with one bite."

"I don't recall hearin about any shark attacks down at Galveston," Maurice said.

"Maybe not; but if you'd seen the size and nature of them sharks and gars you'd think twice about going too far out in the surf fishin for bone fish or sand trout."

They went on talking about big fish to kill the time while they waited for the divers to finish their search. About an hour later a deputy pulled up beside them in a small boat to talk with Maurice. "All they come up with down there on the bottom was a baseball cap and two toes."

"Two toes?" Maurice asked, a bit shocked by the news.

"Yeah, a big toe and a middle one; they aren't sure which one exactly, or even if they're even from the same foot."

"You callin it quits then?" he asked.

"Yeah; they say they've searched everywhere. I think they swam about a hundred yards up and down the bayou. They've even searched back in the swamps on both sides for about fifty feet, in case something drug a body out of the water back in there to eat on. Nothing back there though."

"All right, let's head on back," said Maurice. "They got those toes in plastic bags and in ice?"

"Yeah, they're packed up nice in zip-lock bags."

Maurice told Captain Hunka that they were ready to leave and they were soon speeding back to Morgan City.

When they were back in the parking lot Maurice came over to the four of them as they were getting ready to get in Tizzy's SUV. "I'm goin to need to ask you boys to keep quiet about this for a while. Don't talk to anyone about what you've seen, okay? Let the Sheriff make any sort of necessary announcements."

"Why?" asked Tizzy.

"We don't want to panic everybody around here, especially seein as how the Shrimp-PetroFest is startin next week," Maurice explained. "We wouldn't want folks to think there's someone or something out there in the swamps killin people and cuttin em up in little pieces to feed the gators; wouldn't be good for attendance."

"I suspect you're wrong about that," Tizzy said. "If you made an announcement that the Boojum got hungry and ate a few more people you'd have so many sightseers in here lookin for it that you wouldn't be able to handle the crowds."

"Yeah," Guppy agreed. "Folks like that kind of stuff. You wouldn't be able to rent a boat around here for weeks, people out looking for the monster."

"Either way, it likely wouldn't be good for the festival. We'll let the Sheriff and the folks in charge of the festival make that decision. Can I count on you boys to keep quiet about this?"

They all reluctantly nodded. "I expect you won't be able to keep a lid on it for long, though," Tizzy said. "There's too many folks will have heard about it. There's your deputies and the Coast Guard guys. There's the divers. Then there'll be the State Police or whoever does the lab work on the bits and pieces. And then, of course, there'll be the family of the victim once you identify him. They're sure to raise hell, wantin you guys to find the killer; whoever or whatever it is."

"You're probably right," admitted Maurice. "Still, I'd appreciate it if you don't say nothin till there's an official announcement. It'll make my life a lot easier. As soon as news of this gets out there'll be everybody from CNN to reporters from the Baton Rouge *Advocate,* the Lafayette *Daily Advertiser,* and even the New Orleans *Times-Picayune* in here wantin to know about what happened, and whether or not anyone's seen a Boojum. It's goin to be a damn circus!"

"Okay," Tizzy said. "We'll keep it quiet." The other three nodded.

"What if someone does see a Boojum?" asked Guppy. "You'll have reporters in here from as far away as Beijing, Moscow and Rio de Janeiro. You'll even have National Geographic film teams, and the Sierra Club in here trying to protect it as an endangered species. You sure won't get any sleep for weeks; maybe months!"

"There ain't no such thing as a Boojum, and you know it!" Maurice said. "That's just something somebody on the town council dreamed up to pull in a few tourists."

"I don't know," Tizzy said. "About every two years people start disappearin out in the swamps around here. I think this fits the cycle pretty good."

Maurice just shook his head. "You boys just keep a lid on it for now," he said as he walked off and got into his squad car.

Sheriff Justin Paquette was waiting for him when Maurice got back. "What'd you all find back in there in Gray's Bayou?" he asked.

"More body parts. Two toes. And a baseball cap. It probably belonged to the same victim."

"That it?"

"That's it. They searched hard underwater for about a hundred yards up and down the bayou, and back into the swamps on both sides for about fifty feet."

"You think they might have overlooked anything?"

"Well, the backwaters got lots of water weed in it, so they might have missed something small, I suppose; maybe another little toe or an ear or something. They wouldn't have missed anything big, though; like an arm or a leg. Did the State Police lab techs show up and collect the hand?" he asked, looking around for the cooler.

"Yeah they came and got it about an hour ago. They're goin to drop by the missin men's houses and try to get some prints from their dirty dishes and their tooth brushes; that sort of stuff, so they'll have something to compare the prints against."

"Too bad they didn't find the whole body. I just hope that there aren't bits and pieces strewn all over the swamp and people keep findin them here and there."

"If they *are* strewn all over the swamp then the turtles and gators will soon take care of em."

"You find anything over in Bayou Cocodrie?"

"No; it was a waste of time. The families can't identify the clothes that were found, so it's likely they didn't belong them."

"How we goin to handle the press when it gets out that the hand and toes of one of these guys has been recovered?"

"We likely won't know if those bits belonged to them for another few days. We don't have to say nothing until the lab reports come back. If they don't belong to one of the missin then we can just keep it low-key and say they're still missin. and we're workin on some recently discovered evidence. We don't have to say what. I sure hope those pieces don't belong to them. The timin couldn't be worse, what with the festival openin next week."

"I swore Tizzy and his three buddies that found the hand to silence, at least until the papers get wind of it. You might want to talk with the Captain Hunka and see if he can get his men to keep quiet as well."

"I called him already, but it may be too late for that. Hard to keep something like this quiet for very long. It's pretty sensational."

He had no sooner said this than Claude Généroux of *The Atchafalaya Advocate* came in. "*Allo,* Sheriff," he said. "Maurice."

"*Allo,* Claude. What can we do for you?"

"I hear someone found a severed hand out in the swamp this mornin."

"Now who told you that, Claude?" Justin asked.

"An anonymous source; he didn't give me his name, and I didn't ask for it. Any truth in it?"

"We're not ready to say anything about any on-goin investigation. We're waitin for some lab results."

"So there *was* a hand brought in!"

"I didn't say that."

"But you don't deny it."

"Look, Claude. The Shrimp-PetroFest's this next week. You don't want to go spreadin panic about something you don't know anything about. Wouldn't be good for business. Lots of folks depend on that festival for a good chunk of their annual income. You wouldn't want all these folks mad at you for spreadin rumors and hurtin them would you? I mean, you might have to go lookin for somewhere else to live if you did something real dumb like that."

"I ain't goin to spread any rumors. That's why I'm here askin for confirmation."

"Like I said, I can't confirm anything just yet. We don't know exactly what happened."

"Well, just suppose, for argument's sake, that there *was* this hand brought in. What might be a reasonable theory to explain somethin like that?"

"I'm sure you've got a bigger and better imagination than I do."

"Well, I guess it could be a murder," he suggested.

"Yeah; or—just for argument's sake—maybe an industrial accident," Justin suggested.

"An industrial accident? Out in the swamp?"

"Sure. There's lots of oil and gas drillin goes on out there. You know that. Roughnecks get their fingers chopped off with some regularity."

"Yeah, but I've never heard of one gettin his whole hand chopped off."

"Now, Claude; I haven't said anything about a whole hand, now have I?"

"No; but you haven't denied it either; and that's what my source said it was. I tend to believe him."

Sheriff Paquette was silent.

"Okay," Claude said. "I don't want to cause no trouble for anyone; you or the Festival. Will you let me know when you plan on makin any public announcements? You do that and I'll wait."

"I'll let you know first."

"Okay. Deal." He turned to leave and then turned back. "You find anything over at Bayou Cocodrie? I believe you were out there lookin for two missin fishermen. "

"No, there was just some T-shirts; that's it. The family didn't recognize them. We're still searchin."

The next day Deputy LeClaire received the lab report from the State Police by FAX, and quickly read it over before taking it in to show Sheriff Paquette. It wasn't good news. He walked into his office without knocking, since he knew that there was no one with him. "The State Police report just arrived. That hand didn't belong to either Ledoux or Poirier." He handed the FAX sheet to the Sheriff over his desk.

"Whose is it then?"

"They don't know. It says they don't have any matchin prints on record."

"They're comparin DNA from the hand and toes to see if they're from the same person. No point in contactin the Ledoux and Poirier families till we know that. We'll likely be gettin a request for blood samples from their wives and kids pretty soon."

"*Allo,* LeClaire," came a shout from the front counter.

"Lemme go see who dat is," the Deputy said in his best Cajun accent. It was Claude Généroux. "*Allo,* yourself. What you need, *mon ami?*"

"You seen today's edition of the Lafayette *Daily Advertiser?*"

"No; I don't subscribe."

"There's an item here on the front page about that severed hand I asked you about; the one you didn't want to admit to havin."

"Lemme see dat." he said, reaching out for him to hand it to him. "There, on the lower right."

"Yeah, I see it."

BODY PARTS RECOVERED FROM GRAY'S BAYOU

LAFAYETTE (UPI)— An anonymous source close to a Morgan City Sheriff Department investigation has revealed that a severed hand was discovered Monday by fishermen in a backwater off Gray's Bayou, west of Sweet Bay Lake.

The remains have been sent to the State Police crime lab for identification. Speculation is that it might belong to one of two Amelia men reported missing Sunday: Émile Ledoux and Eugène Poirier.

The Coast Guard, Louisiana Game and Fish wardens, St. Mary's Parish police, and the Morgan City Sheriff's Department have been searching for the missing men for several days, without success, concentrating on the alligator infested swamps around Bayou Cocodrie.

These recent disappearances, along with the new grisly discovery, have renewed speculation that the St. Mary's Parish "Boojum", a legendary monster said to inhabit the swamps around Morgan City, has re-emerged to feed on hapless human victims after a two-year fast.

The disappearances of Benoit Girard and Eugène Giroux two years ago in the same swamps have never been solved. Local legend is that these two men were the last victims of the Boojum, up until these recent disappearances.

"Did they get it right?"

"Just a minute, Maurice. I need to consult with Justin."

He took the paper with him into the Sheriff's office and closed the door behind him. "Well, the severed hand's hit the front page over in Lafayette." He handed the newspaper to him. "Down on the right."

"Well, all hell's goin to start breakin loose around here now," he said after he had read the article. "I thought you swore them boys to secrecy."

"I did. I doubt it was one of them. More likely someone at the Coast Guard Station, I figure. Anyway, what's done is done. Claude Généroux wants confirmation about the story. He's not too happy about bein scooped by an out of town paper."

"There's no point in tryin to hide it any longer. I'll go out and talk with him."

"*Allo,* Claude. Maurice tells me you're lookin for confirmation of this story."

"Yeah. I feel like you didn't do me right on this one. I held back waitin for you to make a public release and you didn't do it. Now it looks like I don't even know what's goin on in my own backyard."

"I'm sorry. We aren't sure who leaked it. I reckon it'll all start comin out now. You can go ahead and confirm part of the story."

"Which part?"

"About findin the hand. But the lab report says that it didn't belong to either Ledoux or Poirier. The prints don't match."

"Whose is it then?"

"We don't know."

"You don't know, or you're not sayin?"

"We don't know. Prints from the fingers didn't match up with any prints on record."

"You owe me something more on this. What else can you tell me?"

"Well, you can report that the search around Bayou Cocodrie came up negative; all we found was just a couple of unidentifiable T-shirts."

"That it?"

Sheriff Paquette hesitated. "No. I guess you might as well know that police divers also recovered a couple of toes where the hand was found."

"What?"

"Two toes; one a big toe. The crime lab is tryin to determine if they belong to the same body the hand came from. They'll have to use DNA analysis to do that, so it'll be awhile before they know for sure."

"Anything else?"

"Only that we'd like for you to downplay the 'Boojum' thing."

"Was there any evidence of a monster?"

"Like what?"

"I don't know; big tracks or claw marks on the tree trunks; that sort of thing. Anything that might indicate that there was a big animal in the area."

"No, there wasn't anything like that."

"You sure? Or are you stonewallin me again because of the Shrimp-PetroFest?"

"No; I'm bein straight."

"Well, I'll report that you don't have any evidence for the 'Boojum', but the connection with it'll make good copy, and I'm not goin to downplay it any more than that."

"Well, there's freedom of the press, and I can't stop you. Just be careful you don't incite something. People start racin off out into the swamps day and night lookin for monsters and there'll likely be more dead and missin. If there is, there'll be blood on your hands; morally anyway."

"Yeah, I understand your concern. I'll keep the hype low and caution the readers about goin out into the swamps ill-prepared. I appreciate your tellin me what you have. I might be able to keep my job now."

"*Au revoir*," Sheriff Paquette said, then turned and went back to his office.

"*Au revoir*," he replied as he walked out the front door.

Deputy LeClaire picked up a copy of *The Atchafalaya Advocate* the next day to see what Claude had written. It was worse than he had dreaded. The front page had a headline story about the discovery of the body parts out on Gray's Bayou. There was an interview with the Ledoux and Poirier families, who were understandably still hysterical about their missing menfolk. But worst of all, they had included a big special center insert, titled "The St. Mary's Parish Legendary Boojum". This special section recounted the local legend of the Boojum that was said to live out in the swamps south of the city, and how it fed on hapless humans on a two-year cycle around Labor Day. This included a list of all eight of the missing persons that were thought to be the Boojum's possible victims over the last decade, along with what personal information was known about them, and a map of the swamps showing where they were last seen. There was also a reprinting of a large portion of Lewis Carroll's nonsense poem, *The Hunting of the Snark,* along with some reproductions of two of Henry Holiday's original illustrations. They had even included a large photo of the goofy sign east of the city that depicted what the St. Mary's Parish Boojum was supposed to look like. And, keeping his word, there was a small, boxed inset that cautioned people about the dangers of going out into the swamps looking for the monster without being fully prepared, with the headline: "DON'T BECOME THE BOOJUM'S NEXT VICTIM".

Deputy LeClaire went on into the office and took the newspaper into Sheriff Paquette. "You seen this yet, Justin?"

"No." He took the paper and started to read it. "Check out the center section."

Just then the phone rang and Maurice went to answer it at his desk.

"St. Mary's Sheriff's Department," he said in a neutral voice. "May I help you?"

"This is Rhonda Ledoux, over in Amelia. I'm Émile Ledoux's wife. I just read the paper and they say that my Émile has gotten hisself eat up by that Boojum monster!" She practically screamed the last sentence.

"Now, Mrs. Ledoux, you just calm yourself. I've read that newspaper and it doesn't say that at all. It just speculates about it. People like to read sensational stuff like that. There's not one lick of evidence that such a monster even exists, and even less that he attacked your husband. You cain't believe things you read in the papers. Don't you know that? You just put that paper to good use by lining your birdcage with it. There's a whole lot of folks still out there, night and day, lookin for your husband and his friend. I believe that they'll find them. You just got to keep your faith up and say your prayers. If we find out anything, we'll call you, first thing."

"Do you promise?" she asked, then sobbed.

"I promise. You'll be the first to know. Now you just keep prayin and ask the Blessed Virgin to protect them till we find them."

"I will. That's all I've been doin for three days and nights."

"*Bon.* You try to get some sleep, now, you hear?"

"Okay."

"*Adieu.*"

"*Adieu.*"

He went back into the Sheriff's office. “That was Rhonda Ledoux. She was real upset by the paper this mornin. I'd like to punch Claude Généroux in the nose for scarin her like that. She was convinced that the Boojum had eaten her husband!”

Sheriff Paquette shook his head. “I'd like to find the person that started this Boojum rumor and put him in jail for a few years.”

The phone rang again, and Deputy LeClaire went to answer it. “St. Mary's Sheriff's Department,” he said. “May I help you?”

“Hey, Maurice. This is Marcel.”

“Marcel! What you up to?”

“Five foot four and hatin it,” he said, then laughed. Maurice joined him. “What you got?”

“I'm callin from New Orleans. I thought you might be interested in what's in the *Times-Picayune* this mornin.”

“I'm afraid to ask.”

“Well, it's about that Boojum you all got stompin around the swamps down there. There's a local radio station here that's offering a $50,000 reward for verifiable evidence the monster exists.”

“Oh, no!”

“That's what it says. It's got a pretty good-sized article, too; all about the legend and the supposed victims. You all might want to start makin preparations for a lot of craziness down there in them bayous. This ought to be the most exciting Shrimp-PetroFest yet!”

“We likely won't survive it,” Maurice said. “We might have to call in the National Guard.”

“Yeah; I reckon you might. Well, I got to go. I just wanted to tell you about that big ree-ward.”

“Thanks, Marcel. You take care.”

Marcel rang off, and Maurice went right back into talk to Justin, who was on the phone. He stood patiently and waited till he was through.

"Good news!" Justin said when he hung up. "That was Captain Hunka over at the Coast Guard Station. They just found those two missin boys out in the swamp. They'd run out of gas and got lost. Had to get under some trees so they wouldn't burn up. They spotted the empty boat from the air and sent in a rescue team. Just in time, too. They were badly dehydrated and ate up by mosquitoes. But they're expected to survive."

"Well, that's good news for sure!" Maurice said. "We could use some good news around here for a change. But you know how it goes."

"How what goes?"

"I'm afraid I got some bad news right behind it." Sheriff Paquette stared at him, afraid to ask what.

"My friend Marcel Gautreau just called me from New Orleans. He tole me there's a local radio station offerin a $50,000 reward for verifiable evidence of the Boojum."

The Sheriff let his head droop until it bumped against his desk. "Oh, no!" was all he could manage to say.

"My very words," Maurice said. "We're about to get invaded by Boojum hunters."

Chapter III

Cover Up

Game Warden Jacques Menard had spent most of the last two days scouring the interlacing waterways and bayous west of Sweet Bay Lake looking for any evidence of an accident that might be related to the severed hand that had been turned into the Sheriff in Morgan City. He had grown up in Morgan City and knew the wetlands as well as anyone in the area.

Towards late afternoon he headed up a dead-end branch off of Big Wax Bayou and came across the crushed *bateau* abandoned by Georges LeBlanc and Mathieu Gaudet. It was just as they had left it, except that their Styrofoam coolers had finally floated out into the main bayou and off towards the Gulf. He got in close and examined the boat and was able to determine the boat's registration number. He put on hip waders and went into the trees and looked around for any evidence of foul play, but found nothing at first. It was just when he had turned to leave that he spotted a shattered tree root that looked like it had a slug in it.

He decided that it was time to call in investigators, and went back to his boat where he radioed the Louisiana State Police. “This is Warden Jacques Menard. I’m out in the swamps west of Sweet Bay Lake, on Big Wax Bayou, where I’ve just found a crushed boat and evidence of what looks like a large calibre slug buried in a tree. I’d like to request a forensics team to come in here and check this out. I’ll wait out in the main channel for you.” He then looked at his global positioning satellite readout and gave them his precise location.

It took the first of the State Police about 45 minutes to arrive on an airboat. A powerboat showed up about thirty minutes later. Warden Menard showed them the tree root, and the investigating team set about to saw out the section of the root containing the slug from the tree to take back to the lab. They scoured the area for other evidence, but found nothing obvious that might be of benefit in an investigation. They then phoned in the boat’s registration number and quickly determined that the owner was Georges LeBlanc. It took them only a few minutes to hook up ropes to the remains of the boat and drag it out into the main channel, where they lashed it to the side and covered it with plastic sheeting to take it back into Morgan City for examination.

A pair of detectives was sent out that evening to interview Georges LeBlanc at his home. Detectives Eugène Giroux and Alain Maisonneuve knocked on his front door.

Georges answered the door, his dog beside him, barking wildly.

“Georges LeBlanc?”

“Yes.”

“I’m Detective Eugène Giroux and this is Detective Alain Maisonneuve of the Morgan City Police Department. We’d like to ask you a few questions.”

“Just a minute,” Georges said. “Lemme put the dog in the bedroom. He might try to take a piece out of your leg.”

He reappeared momentarily, the dog's barking now muffled behind a closed door. Georges invited them into the living room and turned off the TV, which was tuned to a fishing show. His wife appeared in the door to the kitchen with a questioning expression.

"It's okay, Angela." Georges reassured her. "These men are from the police; they just want to ask me a few questions."

"About what?" she demanded.

"I don't know, *ma chère.* They haven't told me yet."

Angela frowned, but didn't say anything more, and went back into the kitchen. The delicious smell of red beans and rice filled the house. Georges and the detectives sat down on the couch beneath a framed picture of the Blessed Virgin holding a baby Jesus.

"Do you own a boat?" Giroux asked.

"Yes, sir."

"Where is it?"

"I wrecked it out in the swamp."

"When was that?"

"Last Sunday night. I was out hunting *cocodrie.*"

"Do you have a licence to hunt alligators?"

"Yes, sir."

"May I see it, please?"

Georges went over to a table and got his wallet, from which he produced the licence. He handed it to him. "It's current," he said. Giroux looked at it then gave it back to him.

"How did you get back into town after you wrecked your boat?"

"Two fishermen picked me up and brought me back to Morgan City."

"What were their names?"

"François and Louis. I don't know their full names."

"Where do they live?"

"I didn't ask."

"What exactly happened to your boat?"

Georges was silent for a minute.

"Do you have something to hide?"

"No."

"Then what happened to your boat?"

"It sank."

"No, it didn't; your boat was found and is now at the State Police lab in Lafayette."

Georges was silent again.

"Were you alone when this happened?"

"No."

"Who was with you?"

"My friend Mathieu Gaudet."

"What is his address?"

"Why?"

"We'd like to talk with him to verify your story."

"He lives just across the street at 407."

"We'll talk with him later. Now, I need to know what happened to your boat. It's evident looking at what's left of it that it was crushed with great force. How could this have happened out in the bayou where it was found?"

Georges was silent again.

"You really need to tell us. If you have done nothing wrong there will be no repercussions. Do you own a gun?"

"Yes. Several."

"Did you have one with you when you had this accident in which your boat was destroyed?"

"Yes."

"What kind of gun?"

"A Smith & Wesson .44 magnum pistol. We also had a .22 rifle."

"Why would you need such a powerful handgun?"

"In case I encounter a really big *cocodrie*. Or something else that might want to harm me. You never know out there."

"Did you discharge this handgun at the site where you abandoned your boat?"

"Yes. How did you know?"

"You left a bullet in a cypress tree root. Did you fire this weapon at someone?"

"No."

"What then? You get real mad at that tree and try to kill it?" Alain tried to suppress a laugh.

"No. It's just that if I told you what happened then you wouldn't believe me,"

Georges finally said. "Try me."

"It's a real strange story. I know you won't believe it."

"I've heard some mighty strange stories since being a detective, I can assure you."

"Okay. Well, my friend Mathieu and I was out huntin *cocodrie*. We went up this bayou. Mathieu was holdin the spot, shinin it across the water to look for their bright eyes. Suddenly we heard a terrible noise up ahead of us. Mathieu shined the spot in its direction, but we couldn't see nothing because of the limbs hangin down in the water. Then the water starts to vibrate wildly. Little drops of water were bouncing all over, and the bottom of the boat started buzzin."

"That was probably just a large bull alligator," Eugène said. "Males make that noise when it's mating season."

"I know. But this was very powerful! Mathieu shined the spot into the water, lookin for some big *cocodrie*, but we couldn't see nothing. Then suddenly this shadow as big as a pickup passed by underwater, goin real fast. A minute later the water started vibratin again, but this time even stronger. Drops of water was dancin all over the width of the bayou. We got real scared and poled over to the bank and got out as quick as we could, heading back into the swamp. Then we heard this terrible noise as something crashed on top of our boat. We climbed up a cypress as fast and as far as we could. This thing that had crushed our boat came ashore, stalkin us. It rammed the tree so hard that we felt that we might fall out. I shot three times into the darkness at the base of the tree to try to scare it away. I must have hit it, cause it screamed and went back into the bayou. We stayed in the tree until morning, then came down and worked our way through the swamp to the edge of the channel. The fishermen finally rescued us several hours later."

"So, you think it was a gigantic alligator?"

"No way! I been huntin *cocodrie* all my life. I've heard stories from the old timers. This don't match. Its screams didn't sound nothing like a *cocodrie.* I've heard them. That's more like a deep gruntin, bellowin sound."

"What you think it was then?"

Georges was silent again.

"Well? I'm just askin your opinion. I'm not goin to arrest you or anything."

"I figure it was a Boojum."

"A Boojum?" Giroux asked.

"Yeah. That *zombi* that lives out there in the swamp and eats people once in awhile when it gits real hungry."

The detectives were silent, staring at him. "See, I told you that you wouldn't believe me."

"Well, you're right; it *is* just a bit hard to believe," Giroux said. "Tell you what. We're goin over to your friend Mathieu's house and see if he tells us the same story. We'll be back in bit." They got up and walked across the street to Gaudet's house. Mathieu grudgingly told them the same story, with just enough added detail to make it believable.

"Mathieu, I wonder if you'd mind comin with us back over to Georges' house for a few minutes?"

"I reckon I don't mind."

"Good."

They walked back across the street and knocked. Georges let them in and they went back into the living room and sat down.

"Now, we're goin to have to write something in our report," Giroux said. "I don't think we can write down that you boys were attacked by a Boojum. The papers would have a field day with that. You'd probably have to move to Godawful, Texas, to start a new life."

"What's your plan then?" Alain asked.

"Well, we can't deny the damage to the boat."

"No, that's true."

"I think what we should do is just say you boys told us that you were attacked by a very large alligator. How big a gator you figure it would take to flatten your boat like that?"

Georges thought for a moment. "Twenty, maybe even twenty-five feet, I reckon."

"What do you think, Mathieu? You agree that it would have to be that big?"

"Yeah; at least."

"Do they even get that big?" Giroux asked.

"None that I ever heard of," said Georges. "The biggest one I ever saw was when I was a kid was maybe fifteen feet long."

"How bout you, Mathieu. You ever heard of one gettin that big?"

"No. But there's lots of strange things out there in them swamps. It might be possible."

"All right, so in theory, one might get that big, if it lived to be 75 or 100 years old. I seem to remember that Australian saltwater crocodiles can get that big."

"At least the one in *Crocodile Dundee* got that big," Mathieu said, as if he believed it to be a true-life documentary.

"There you go!" said Eugène. "Lots of folks have seen that crazy movie. So, they'll probably agree that it's at least a possibility."

They all nodded.

"Okay. We're goin to put in our report that you were attacked by a very large alligator; perhaps twenty-five feet long. It smashed your boat and you had to run for your lives into the swamp and up into a cypress."

They all nodded. "If any of you ever change that story I will personally blow your head off. I won't take kindly to anyone sayin that I faked a report. My pension might be dependin on this." He said this with real menace and none of them doubted him for a minute. "If some damn reporters show up at your houses wantin to know what happened you tell them this story. I don't want to read anywhere that you think you was attacked by a damn Boojum. Clear?"

"Clear," said Georges.

"Clear," said Mathieu.

Giroux and Maisonneuve got up and left.

"You hungry, Mathieu?" Georges asked.

"Yeah; I'm always hungry."

"How's about some red beans and rice? Angela's cooked up a nice mess with some real good *andouille.* And I think she's been makin *beignet,* too! Go on home and get Dora and the kids. I'm sure we got plenty."

Chapter IV

Alan in Zombiland

Tizzy, Alan, Guppy, and Leon sat in the shade of a big oak tree in Lawrence Park eating mudbugs, drinking beer and listening to "Michael Douchet and The Cajun Swamp Snarks" playing their own version of Nathan Abshire's *The Good Times Are Killing Me.* A ten-foot high cutout of a shrimp wearing a hardhat and playing an accordion was mounted above the stage. Its tail had been mounted on a pivot and motorized with an electric motor and a V-belt so that it continuously moved back and forth, as if keeping time to the lively music. It was a fine, hot day, and there was a huge crowd of perhaps 10,000 people, most of them trying to squeeze in under the shade of the trees to get out of the direct sun. Rows of food stall awnings lined the edges, selling everything from Crawfish *Étouffée* to *Jumbalaya.*

"I've been thinkin about that $50,000 reward," said Tizzy as he peeled another crawdad. "We ought to go back where we found that hand and have a better look around to see if there's any evidence of some sort of monster. That's a lot of money."

"Speaking of that, did you guys see that picture of a crushed boat in *The Atchafalaya Advocate?*" Guppy asked.

"Yeah; two guys claim a big gator smashed it," Alan replied.

"Said it was twenty or twenty-five feet long! Silliest damn thing I ever read. They don't get that big."

"They probably did before white men showed up and started shootin everything in sight," Alan suggested. "I'd sure like to see one that big."

"A gator would have to live a very long time to get that big," Guppy observed.

"I was thinkin that maybe that big gator's responsible for bitin off that hand we found; and them toes. Maybe those bits and pieces were sort of like the crumbs after its meal."

They were quiet for a moment as they each visualized this.

"Well, if that's what it was then it might be real dangerous to go in there lookin for it," Guppy said.

"We could each take a deer rifle," Tizzy said. "And pistols as backup," said Alan.

"What would we do if we found it?"

"Take some videos, I guess."

"What if the Radio station says that a big gator doesn't qualify as finding a Boojum?"

"We should call em and ask first," Tizzy said. "I'll do that."

"When you want to go?" Guppy asked.

"Let's go in the mornin."

They all agreed to meet at Tizzy's house. He got up and went to look for a pay phone while the others sat back and listened to The Cajun Swamp Snarks and watched the couples dance the Zydeco Two-step on the small temporary dance floor that had been laid out in front of the stage.

Tizzy returned fifteen minutes later, wearing a new T-shirt. It had "BOOJUM BLUES" across the top, with what looked like a dancing cartoon T. Rex playing an accordion below it.

"Where'd you get the T-shirt?" Guppy asked.

"They're sellin em in a booth over there."

"How much?"

"Fifteen dollars. I talked to the radio station. They said that if we can document a gator bigger than 20 feet in length in the swamps south of Morgan City that this would qualify. But they have to have hard evidence, preferably a dead alligator. I called the Department of Game & Fish. They said that as long as we have a valid licence we can shoot one as big as they come. But they laughed at the idea. They said they hadn't heard of one bigger than 16 feet since the early 1900s. They told me that if we did find one that big it'd be worth more alive than dead, but didn't think it would be too smart for us to try to catch anything that big and powerful. They strongly advised us to leave it alone if we found one."

"I vote we go for a dead alligator," said Guppy. "I like my hands and other extremities still attached to my body."

A loud round of applause went up from the crowd as The Cajun Swamp Snarks wrapped up their set. "Those guys were real good! Who's up next?" Alan asked. "It's supposed to be Wayne Toups," Leon said.

"When's Doug Kershaw playing?"

"Not till about four o'clock, I think."

"I need another beer," Tizzy said. "You guys need one, too."

They all allowed as how they did, and Tizzy made another beer run.

The following morning the boys were out on the water by seven o'clock, heading for their old trotline. They were armed to the teeth, looking like a small band of mercenaries setting off to topple some tiny fourth-world government. Tizzy pulled their boat up the backwater, recognizing their old marker, and tied off about a hundred yards back from where they had found the severed hand. He landed his crew with care, then handed each of them their rifle once they were safely on the muddy bank. He passed his own rifle ashore, then the camcorder and finally climbed out himself, managing to get pretty soaked in the process.

They spread out a bit, trying to find small clumps of grass and logs to walk on, and looking hard for snakes. They went perpendicular to the bank until they finally reached a small area of what passed for solid ground, though it was really just decades of grass that had packed down. It was eerily quiet, the frogs having all retreated to their daytime hiding places, and it was stifling hot. There was absolutely no movement of air in the grove of cypress and brush.

"I don't see any tracks," Guppy said.

"I doubt we'll find any," Tizzy said. "The ground's too waterlogged. Let's just look around for any areas where the brush and grass are pressed down, where something huge might have passed by. Let's head over that way," he said, pointing.

They were all eager enough and set out in that general direction. They slowly made their way for several hundred yards until they arrived at what appeared to be a cut through the brush that led down to the bayou.

"This could be something," Guppy said, quite excited at what they were looking at. "It would be big enough for a large alligator to pass through."

"Something's obviously been through here," Tizzy agreed. "The grass and weeds are all flattened and broken." Tizzy turned on the camcorder and started to film the run. Guppy posed in the middle, acting like a great white hunter, posturing with his rifle.

Suddenly a loud guttural bellow came from somewhere back in the swamp directly behind them, and they all wheeled around.

"Run!" Guppy screamed, already moving back in the direction they had come from.

"*Vite! Vite!*" Leone yelled right behind him.

In a moment all four were rushing as fast as they could over the stumps and snags. Tizzy whirled around to see if they were being chased just in time to see a large bull alligator heading down the cut towards the bayou. He filmed it for a moment, then jerked up his rifle. "Shoot!" he yelled and then put two bullets into the alligator behind its front shoulder.

Alan was the only other one with enough presence of mind to turn and get off another shot. It struck the alligator harmlessly near the base of its enormous tail. The alligator collapsed and came to a rest.

They stood still, looking at the huge alligator for a minute, afraid to approach it. Finally Tizzy started to walk back, stopping every few steps to film it with his camcorder. Within a few minutes they were all four standing near the head, about ten feet back, studying the monster.

"Now what?" Guppy finally said. "What if it isn't dead?" Leon asked.

"It looks dead," Alan said.

The alligator took this as a cue and suddenly lurched forward a few feet, obviously not quite dead yet. They all four screamed and jumped back, then started laughing at themselves. Tizzy finally walked up and put two more shots into the alligator's head, right between its eyes.

"This is the biggest damn gator I've ever seen in my life!" Guppy said. "I just hope it's at least a twenty-footer." He reached into his pants pocket and pulled out a small tape measure. "Here, help me measure," he said to Tizzy.

They taped it off, from the tip of its snout to the end of its tail. "Eighteen feet, three inches," Guppy said, his voice heavy with disappointment.

"Damn!" Tizzy said. "There goes our fifty thousand."

"It might still be worth a lot," Alan said, "if we could get it back, but there's no way we're ever going to drag that thing out of here. We'd have to have winches."

"It probably weighs a thousand pounds."

"At least," Guppy said, who got down on his knees and put his shoulder up against it, fruitlessly tried to budge it.

"Let's go back into town and get help," Tizzy said. "I know this old guy named Gaston Arseneault who's hunted gators for forty years. I can probably get him to come out here and help us skin this thing. We could cut off its head and take it back. The skull and belly skin have got to be worth a bundle." Tizzy went up to the alligator's head and pulled open the enormous jaws to reveal an amazing set of eighty yellowed teeth, several of which had been broken in fights with other males. "First though, let's take some pictures. You guys all get up on its back with your rifles and I'll film you."

This seemed like a very good idea and they all clambered up, posing with their rifles. At which point the alligator lurched again, and all three jumped off and ran a short distance. Tizzy captured it all with the camcorder.

"Shit!" Guppy said. "I thought it was dead!"

"I'm going to start calling you guys Larry, Curly, and Moe," Tizzy said, laughing so hard that he had to hold his stomach.

The Three Stooges joined him in laughing at themselves. Tizzy sat the camcorder down on a log then went up and put another shot through the animal's head. "I wish I knew where this thing's tiny little walnut of a brain is," he said. "Don't keep pumpin shells into it. You'll destroy the skull and we won't be able to sell it for as much."

"I just don't want it to get up and slide into the bayou!" Tizzy said.

"It ain't goin anywhere," Alan assured him.

"All right. Let's head back and get help. One of you guys needs to stay here and guard it."

"No way!" Leon said with finality.

"Me neither," said Guppy. "You guys might not come back. That boat leaves, I leave."

"I'll stay," Alan said. "Leave me the bottled water, a life jacket, and a knife."

"Okay. It shouldn't take us more than three hours. Even if we can't get Gaston to help us skin it we'll come on back out and get you before dark."

"You'd better! I'm not going to be too happy if I have to spend the night out here with things like this monster roamin around lookin for supper." He kicked the alligator in the ribs.

Tizzy went back for the water, life jacket and knife, and picked up the axe for good measure.

When they were ready to go, Guppy went up to Alan and said, with melodramatic feeling, "Well, Alan, ole buddy, it's really been great knowin you!"

Alan didn't think this was all that funny, but Tizzy and Guppy thought it was hysterical.

"Don't worry," Tizzy told Alan. "We'll come back and get you; at least what's left."

"Ha ha!" Alan said, but wasn't smiling.

Tizzy, Guppy and Leon made their way back to the boat and set off for Morgan City to look for Gaston. Alan went over and sat on a log where he could look at the enormous alligator and take a drink of water. It hadn't moved now for about fifteen minutes, and Alan assumed that it had finally died, but he was still leery.

A wood duck suddenly winged through the trees with a rainbow flash of colour, startling him a bit. It was unbearably hot and there was no movement of air. But worst of all, the mosquitoes had found him. He got out the repellent and put on a thick layer and idled away the time by smacking the mosquitoes that landed on his jeans to try to bite him through the thick denim.

He didn't really hear the Boojum coming up behind him until it was less than twenty feet away. When he finally heard the wet sucking sound as it raised a hind foot Alan jumped up and whirled around, then froze, momentarily too terrified to scream or run. Recovering, he grabbed for the rifle propped against the log on which he'd been sitting, but the Boojum closed the gap between them before Alan could get the rifle up to his shoulder. The gun discharged harmlessly into the top of a cypress, knocking down a six-foot strand of Spanish moss.

The Boojum bit Alan's head off as easily as you'd pull the head off of a crawdad, and spit it out. It then ripped him apart and ate most of him. While this was happening the alligator recovered enough to get back up on its short legs and slide down the run into the bayou. In less than an hour there was essentially nothing left of Alan except his head. The Boojum retreated back into the swamp.

Two hours later Tizzy, Leon, and Guppy, accompanied by Gaston Arseneault, returned to find Alan's bloody clothes and his head, which seemed to be staring back into the swamp where the Boojum had gone. The grass around the log where he had been attacked was covered in blood and the swamp water itself had turned from pea green to blood red. Tizzy, Guppy and Leon ran into the bushes in three different directions and threw up. When he had recovered slightly, Leon went back to the boat, refusing to look anymore. Gaston, inured to the sight of blood from years of skinning alligators, walked carefully around the gore and over to where the huge alligator had been.

"Dis where dat *cocodrie* was at?" he asked.

Tizzy came over to him. "Yes. We shot it least six times. I even shot in three times in the head at close range; right between the eyes. I don't understand how it could have gotten up to attack Alan."

"Dem *cocodrie* is mighty tough, dat for sure. Strange though."

"What?"

"It bitin off his head like dat. I never seen dat before. *Mauvais, mauvais.*"

"Do you think it drug Alan into the bayou?" Tizzy asked, looking down the cut.

"No. Whatever killed your friend ate him right dere." He pointed to the spot.

"What do you mean? Are you saying that the alligator didn't eat him? That something else did?"

"Maybe." Gaston went back over to where Alan had been killed and walked a ways back into the swamp, studying the ground, with Tizzy and Guppy right behind him. Guppy was carrying his rifle at the ready, just in case something rushed them, though it was unlikely that he would have had the courage to stand and shoot if it charged. "Look here!" Gaston said, pointing to what resembled a very large footprint in the soft muck.

Tizzy and Guppy bent down to examine what he was pointing at.

"That's the biggest alligator print I've ever seen!" Tizzy said. "How big would the gator have been?"

"*If* dat *was* a *cocodrie,* maybe twenty-five feet."

"What do you mean 'if'?" Tizzy asked.

"Might not be a *cocodrie.*"

"Then what was it?"

Gaston shrugged his shoulders. "Maybe dat was a *zombi.*"

"A *zombi?*" Guppy asked. "You mean the living dead?"

"No, not dat voodoo stuff you see in movies. A *zombi* is a bad swamp spirit; a Boojum."

Tizzy and Guppy both straightened up and scanned the swamp, as if they might see it lurking there, hiding behind one of the big cypresses.

"Well, I think we had better go back and tell the Sheriff what's happened here."

"*C'est bon,*" said Gaston, quite happy to get away from this evil place.

"Should we take Alan's head with us?"

"No, do'n do dat," Gaston said. "De Sheriff will consider dis to be a crime scene; you do'n want to go touchin nothing. Leave dat rifle, too!"

Gaston led the way back to the boat. They all climbed in and sped back to Morgan City.

Chapter V

Tizzy's Tale

Sheriff Justin Paquette and his Deputy Maurice LeClaire sat in the sheriff's office watching Tizzy's home video for about the tenth time. "That's sure one hell of a *cocodrie!*" Justin said as he looked at the scene where Guppy, Alan and Leon were standing on the alligator's back with their rifles, clowning around and acting like great white hunters. If it wasn't for Alan's tragic death, the scene where the alligator moved and they all fell off would be worth sending into *America's Funniest Home Videos.* It would be sure to win the $10,000 prize."

"It must have been real bad to be attacked by that monster," Maurice said. "Makes you want to stay the hell out of the swamp!"

"No chance of that for us."

"I don't understand how they could have shot that thing five or six times with high powered rifles and it still be able to attack and eat Alan, then escape into the bayou."

"I figure it'll die eventually," Justin said. "From internal bleeding or infections."

"I hope."

Someone rang the bell on the counter out front and Maurice went to see who it was.

"*Allo,* Maurice."

"Claude! What's up?" Claude was also wearing a "BOOJUM BLUES" T-shirt. They were evidently selling well.

"I understand that there's a video of the big alligator that ate Alan Twardy."

"Yeah. Justin's back there lookin at it."

"Any chance I can watch it?"

"I doubt it."

"Would you mind askin?"

"Okay; I'll ask." Maurice went back to make Claude's request.

Justin came out to talk with him. "Claude," he said when he came up to the counter.

"Mornin, Sheriff. I was wondering if you might let me watch Tizzy's home video. That be possible?"

"I can't let you. Tizzy might though; it's his property. I'll be givin it back to him later today."

"You think that big alligator's dead?"

"I ain't got any way a knowin," Justin said. "But I hope it is. I'm gettin real tired of cleanin up after it."

"You think that gator was what folks call the Boojum?"

"Likely. I hope so anyway. I'd like for that legend to die."

"You goin to Alan Twardy's funeral this afternoon?"

"Yeah. Maurice'll be lookin after the store while I'm gone."

"What are they going to *bury?"*

"I believe they have cremated the remains."

Claude nodded. "Makes sense."

"You sure I can't take a quick look at that video?"

"You got to go see the Tizzards."

"Okay," Claude said, deciding it was best not to press the matter. "*Adieu.*"

"Take care," Justin said. "You stay out of dem swamps, hear?"

"No problem," Claude said.

The next day Claude went over to Tizzy's home and knocked on the door. His mother answered. "Yes?"

"My name is Claude Généroux from *The Atchafalaya Advocate.* I wonder if I might speak with your son, Dallas?"

"Just a moment," she said, but didn't invite him inside.

In a minute Tizzy appeared at the door. "You want to see me?"

"Hi, my name is Claude Généroux from *The Atchafalaya Advocate.* I wonder if I could talk with you for a minute."

"I reckon." Tizzy came out onto the porch. "Have a seat," he said, pointing to one of two plastic lawn chairs. Claude sat down in one chair and Tizzy sat in the other. "What is it?"

"I was wonderin if you could tell me about what happened out in the swamp that resulted in your friend Alan's death?"

"This for the paper?"

"Yes. I want to do an article. People are very interested."

"Well, we went out to see if we could locate the big gator that bit off the hand that we had found earlier in the week workin our trotline. We were thinkin about the $50,000 reward offered by the New Orleans radio station for evidence of the Boojum."

"But that was for a legendary creature, not an alligator."

"I called and asked them how big an alligator would have to be to qualify. They said if we found one over twenty feet long they'd give us the money."

"How big was the one you shot?"

"We measured it with a tape. Eighteen feet and three inches."

"So it didn't qualify for the reward."

"No."

"Why was Alan alone when it attacked?"

"We went back to Morgan City to get help from a gator hunter I know; to skin it. We figured the head and hide might be worth some real money. We left Alan to guard it."

"By himself?"

"Yeah. We thought it was dead anyway. That was a mistake. If there'd'a been two of us there he likely wouldn't a been killt. I blame myself. I feel real bad about that. Guppy and Leon feel bad, too."

"Guppy and Leon?"

"They were the other friends that were with us. Tom Guppy and Leon Rocheleau."

"Sheriff Paquette tells me that you took a video of the alligator, before you went back into Morgan City."

"Yeah. He brought it back yesterday. He'd borrowed it."

"I wonder if I might watch it?"

Tizzy thought for a moment. "I guess there's no harm. Come on in. I'll put it in the VCR in the den."

They got up and went into the den, where Claude watched it. It took less than five minutes."

"I wonder if I might have a still photograph of the alligator, with your friends standin on its back for use in the next issue of *The Atchafalaya Advocate*?"

"I'll ask Alan's folks if they think that's all right. If they say yes then I'll have one made and drop it by your paper's offices, if you'll pay for the cost."

"That would be fine. Do you think that this alligator was the legendary St Mary's Parish Boojum?"

"No, Sir."

His answer surprised Claude. "Really? Why not?"

"My friend, Gaston, who went back out there with us to skin the gator, found a big footprint back from where Alan was killed. He said it was too big to belong to a mere eighteen footer."

"A *mere* eighteen-footer? How big did he think it was?"

"He guessed maybe twenty-five feet."

"Twenty-five feet?"

"Yeah."

"There's never been one that big. I checked on the Internet. They don't get any bigger than six meters; that's about 20 feet. And they haven't seen one that big since the early 1900s."

"I know."

"Even the biggest crocodiles in Africa don't get bigger than seven meters. That's just twenty-three feet."

"I know. Scary thought, ain't it. Those African monsters can bring down a zebra or a wildebeest. I've seen it on TV. You goin to report that?"

Claude thought for a moment. "No, I don't think so. It's just speculation. Even if it's right, it would just result in hunters going back in there to find it. Someone else might get killed."

"Likely."

"Do you plan to go looking for it?"

"I don't know. I've thought about it."

"Wouldn't you be afraid?"

"Of course."

"How would you protect yourself?"

"I was thinkin about getting me one of them new .50 calibre rifles I've seen on the news. They can crack an engine block from a mile away. Fires a single .50 calibre machine gun shell. I reckon that ought to do the trick."

"They're very expensive."

"Yeah. About two grand, I think. It'd be worth it to kill that damn thing. And I can resell the gun after I'm through with it."

Claude looked at him for a moment. "I think if I was you I'd just let it be."

"Well, he wasn't your friend."

"No, he wasn't. Still, you might end up the next victim if you go messin with it."

"I don't think so. I know what I'm lookin for now; and I know about where to find it."

Claude thanked him and got back in his car. He drove over to interview Georges LeBlanc. Georges was out in the front yard mowing his lawn when Claude drove up. He parked his car in the driveway behind Georges' pickup and got out. Georges killed the mower when he saw him get out of his car.

"Good morning," Claude said as he walked over to him.

"Morning," Georges responded. "You sellin something?"

"No, no; nothin like that. Are you Georges LeBlanc?"

"Yeah. That's me. Who are you?"

"Claude Généroux," he said, extending his hand. "From *The Atchafalaya Advocate.*"

Georges shook his hand. "What can I do for you?"

"I read in a police report that you were attacked out in the swamp by a large alligator. I'd like to talk to you for a minute. I'm sure our readers would be very interested in hearin about it."

"I told the police all about it. I imagine it's all in their report, which you said you've read."

"Well, actually the report's a bit sketchy. All it said was that you and a friend," he looked at his notes, "a Mathieu Gaudet, were out in the swamp when you were attacked by an alligator estimated to be between twenty and twenty-five feet long. It destroyed your boat. You managed to escape and were picked up by fishermen, who brought you back to Morgan City."

"Yeah, that sounds about right."

"I went over to the police yard and saw your boat," Claude said. "It was quite a sight. Looked like it had been through Hurricane Katrina."

"We managed to jump clear of the boat before it was hit."

"I've never heard of an alligator as big as twenty feet long, and certainly not twenty-five feet. Did you actually see it?"

"No, it was at night and very dark. We were shinin a spotlight into the water but all we saw was its shadow as it moved through the water beneath the boat. It was a *very* long shadow. That's how we guessed at the size."

"Where were you exactly?"

"South."

"But where, exactly? Southwest or southeast?"

"I don't want to say."

"Would it happen to be somewhere near Gray's Bayou?"

"I don't want to say."

"Why not?"

"I might want to go catch that damn thing. I tell folks where it is and they might go try to do that their self."

"I suppose it might be worth a lot of money; an alligator that big."

"Could be."

"Even photographs."

"Could be."

"How old do you think such an alligator would be? To get that big, I mean."

"I don't know."

"Maybe a hundred years old?"

"Maybe."

"Well, thanks for your time, Mr. LeBlanc."

"No problem."

"You might want to pick up a copy of our next issue. There will be a short article about your experience; and a picture of what's left of your boat."

Claude walked across the street to go see if Mathieu would tell him anything else, but it proved to be a waste of time.

CHAPTER VI

The Hunting

Tizzy bought a single shot .50 calibre rifle in New Orleans two weeks after Labor Day. It took a week to get it after he'd paid his money, since they didn't have them in stock. He didn't bother with a scope. He figured if he ever got to use the rifle that it would be at close quarters in the middle of a swamp, and a scope would actually get in the way. He also bought a .44 magnum pistol for use if the monster got close enough that he felt threatened and he couldn't reload the rifle, and a set of starlight night vision glasses.

He decided that the best and safest way to find the monster was to bait it. He'd read somewhere about a missionary in New Guinea who remarked at a feast about how wonderful the ham he was served tasted, only to find out that it was roasted human flesh. Evidently we taste a lot like pork when we're roasted. So he went to a slaughterhouse and bought a whole fifty-pound pig, cleaned and dressed. If this monster had a taste for human flesh then this was the best he could manage. He put his camping gear in his truck, hitched up his boat and drove to the boat ramp. In another two hours he was back at the site where Alan had met his death.

Tizzy went ashore, armed with his cannon, and searched carefully to be sure that nothing was lurking close by while he put out the bait. He had brought a length of steel cable and he attached a loop to the pig's neck using clamps. He tossed the end over a cypress tree limb and pulled the pig up a few feet off of the ground so that a normal sized gator couldn't reach it. He then anchored the end of the cable to the tree. The monster might eat it off of the cable, but that was the only way this pig was going anywhere. He figured that the carcass might have to hang in the hot sun for a day or two to ripen so that the monster could smell it, and he was prepared to wait.

He went over to the nearest tall cypress with a clear view of the pig and spent the next two hours installing the portable tree stand he used for hunting deer, twenty feet up. He attached a rope and tackle and spent the rest of the afternoon getting his rifle, food, water, high intensity beam flashlight, and mosquito netting up to the stand, and securing them in the branches. It was almost dusk by the time he was finally ready.

Nothing happened that night, the next day or the following night. By the second day he was able to smell the rotting pig and the first turkey vulture appeared. He hadn't planned on that, and since it was a Federal crime to shoot them, he couldn't just start popping them off. He wished that he'd had the good sense to bring a slingshot and a bag of marbles, or even a BB gun; but there was nothing to do about it now.

He watched in frustration as the birds began to slowly but steadily consume the pig, fighting and sparring with each other for a perch on the pig's shoulder. By evening there was little left of the bait, but what there was still had a terrible smell, so he waited, unwilling to leave his perch and go all the way back into Morgan City to buy another pig.

Just after dark he heard the unmistakable sound of something *very* large walking slowly through the muck and water. His heartbeat jumped as adrenaline raced through his body. He put on his night vision glasses and scanned the swamp in the direction of the noise, but couldn't see anything because of the undergrowth, long strands of Spanish moss and tree branches. He decided to focus on the bait.

Whatever was out there was apparently wary. The footsteps had stopped, but after an hour it had not come out from its cover to investigate the ripe bait. "Perhaps it isn't yet hungry," Tizzy thought; "it's only been a few weeks since it ate Alan." He knew that large reptiles like anacondas and crocodilians could go for months between meals.

After another hour Tizzy decided that the creature must have slipped away, and turned off his glasses to get a drink from a plastic bottle. As he was unscrewing the lid he was startled by a loud scream. He dropped the plastic bottle and clicked his night vision glasses back on just in time to see what looked for all the world like an animal straight out of *Jurassic Park* rush out from the brush and snatch away the remains of the pig. It was over in no more than two seconds, and all that was left was the steel cable swinging back and forth. It had been such a fleeting glimpse that Tizzy couldn't even properly describe what he'd seen. All that he could say was that it was reptilian, with a long tail, huge legs and a large head. It obviously had a lot of teeth.

"That goofy billboard with the St. Mary's Parish Boojum isn't that far off," he thought; "though I'm not sure where they got the idea it had feathers. Someone else has seen this thing before, but won't admit to it!"

The monster failed to reappear, and about midday Tizzy descended from his cypress perch with his rifle to go back into town for more bait. He was hopeful that the thing hadn't destroyed his boat, and was relieved to see it intact when he reached it. In another two hours he was back home. His parents had found his note and had begun to get worried. He said hello to his parents and told he was just having fun in the swamp. To their dismay, he informed them that he was going back out. He decided that he wouldn't mention the Boojum. They probably wouldn't believe him anyway, and might well put up a fuss about his return if they did.

He went by the Morgan City mayor's offices and inquired about who had designed the billboard depicting the Boojum west of the city. They referred him to Claude Généroux over at *The Atchafalaya Advocate.*

He went to the newspaper office and found Claude working at his desk, typing away on a PC. He looked up when he walked in.

"*Allo*, Tizzy," he said. "What can I do for you?"

"I'm trying to find out who designed that billboard of the St. Mary's Parish Boojum that's out at the parish line. I was told you might know."

"I do. The sign was based on a description given by an old-timer who said that he'd seen it. He's dead now. The guy who painted it used that as a basis, but embellished it a bit, by puttin feathers on it."

"Why'd he do that?"

"In Lewis Carroll's poem *The Hunting of the Snark* it says that some snarks have feathers and bite. He was just goin along with the poem. Why do you ask?"

"Well, I saw it last night out in the swamp; and it didn't have feathers." Claude's jaw dropped. "You saw it?"

"For only a few seconds, through night vision glasses."

"But how? Where?"

"I baited it with a three day old rotten pig, and climbed into a deer stand I'd mounted in a tree. I was up there for three nights. I meant to shoot it, but it was too fast. I never even managed to get to my rifle up to my shoulder."

"You serious?"

"Yeah; dead serious. It looks just like that picture on that billboard, except without the feathers and wings."

"You were up in a tree with a rifle waiting for it?"

"Yeah; I got me one of them 0.5 calibre rifles, like I told you I was thinkin about doing."

"I don't know whether to believe you or not."

"Don't matter. I saw what I saw. But don't go writin an article about it. You do and I'll come back here some night and burn this place down."

"Are you threatenin me?"

"No; just makin a promise. I don't want anyone out there disturbin that thing until I can get a shot at it."

Claude was silent for a moment. "Let's just say that you actually manage to shoot this thing; will you let me be the first to publish the story?"

"Yeah; no problem."

"Okay. Deal." Tizzy turned to leave. "You be real careful."

"I'm bein so careful you wouldn't believe it. I've seen that thing and I'm not takin any chances." He left and went down to the hardware store and bought a BB gun before going back to the slaughterhouse for another pig.

It took him the rest of the day to string up the new pig and get back into his tree house perch. This time he'd attached the cable to the carcass by wrapping it around it five times so that it wouldn't be so easy to snatch away.

Two days later the first vultures reappeared, but this time he was ready for them. Every time one would land on the bait he would bounce a BB off of its butt. But they were persistent and didn't fly away from nearby trees, too mesmerized by the smell of the rotting pig. Before nightfall there were twenty of them perched in the tops of the trees.

On the third night Tizzy once again heard the monster approach, drawn by the now familiar smell of the bait. Tizzy was ready and focussed his glasses on the pig. This time the Boojum didn't wait so long, and came charging out of the brush after only twenty minutes. When it struck the bait it found it impossible to snatch it away, and whirled to roar in frustration. Tizzy got off one round from his rifle, but it missed, and the Boojum turned to face him, uncannily aware now of where he was.

Before Tizzy could reload the Boojum had crashed through the brush and into the bayou, with an enormous splash. Then all was quiet again. Tizzy scanned the brush along the bank of the bayou, but saw nothing. Then he heard, or rather felt, a strange low frequency noise; it vibrated the tree. A minute later he heard an incredible crash as the Boojum destroyed his boat. At first Tizzy couldn't figure out what had happened, but it slowly dawned on him.

Over the next several nights the Boojum would make fleeting appearances, too quick for Tizzy to get off a shot with the huge rifle which was designed for sniping at long distance, not for a shootout. He was too terrified to descend from the tree, knowing that the Boojum was waiting for just that. He had calculated that his limited provisions would last for only another five days, even if he rationed them carefully. He could manage to get water by coming down the tree just long enough to fill a bottle with the greenish swamp water that surrounded the tree, but he knew that if he was stuck in the tree for weeks he would likely starve.

On three occasions he tried to bait the Boojum with himself, to get off a shot, but the huge rifle was much too unwieldy for an animal as quick as this one. By the time he would get it up to his shoulder it would have disappeared once again. He finally gave up on the rifle, even though he realized that it was probably the only thing he had with enough force to kill it. He tried the same tactics with his pistol. But that wasn't much better. He got several opportunities to shoot, but found that his aim was too bad with the pistol. Finally down to one remaining bullet he decided to save it for himself, if worse came to worst.

A game warden found him two weeks later during a huge manhunt that was organized after the pleading of Claude Généroux and Tizzy's family. He had put a bullet through his chest, still perched up in the tree. Heavy rain had long since obliterated the Boojum's tracks, and it was a matter of wide debate and discussion about why Tizzy had killed himself up in a tree. Claude didn't tell them that he knew why he was up there. He didn't want to be responsible for anyone else trying to hunt down the Boojum. Somehow he felt responsible for what had happened, since he hadn't tried harder to stop him, or advised the Sheriff what he was up to. Perhaps they could have rescued him had they known his approximate location.

The biggest mistake Tizzy made was not taking along a cell phone. He could have used some F-4s for close ground support.

Chapter VII

The Boots

Dave Thibodeau took his bass boat out on Big Wax Bayou for some night fishing. He had lived in the Morgan City area all of his life and worked offshore on drilling platforms and on salt marsh oil rigs. He needed fresh air and wide-open spaces to recover from the stifling close living quarters and the sulphur-laden air on the platform. He loved the outdoors and went hunting and fishing whenever he could.

He had been divorced for eight years and didn't really miss anything about Terra except her fine Cajun cooking, which, unfortunately, had clogged his arteries. His two girls were grown and married, one of them living over in the New Orleans suburb of Kenner, where she and her husband owned a little hole-in-the-wall Cajun restaurant, and the other over in Lake Charles, where she worked as a cocktail waitress in a casino. So he had nothing to keep him at home. He spent most of his money on gambling, drinking, cold-hearted women, boats, guns, and fishing trips.

He had just caught a little three-pound bass and was taking the hook out of its mouth when the Boojum came straight up out of the water right behind the fish, so fast that Dave didn't even have time to jump back out of the way. All he saw was a huge gaping mouth lined with rows of six-inch long serrated teeth. He tried to scream, but the Boojum ate the sound when its jaws closed over his head. When the Boojum sank back into the bayou Dave went with it. He had vanished suddenly enough, though not quietly, and certainly without any glee. The bass escaped to tell the tale to his fishy buddies.

About fifteen minutes later Dave's right foot, still in his boot and bitten off at the ankle, floated up from the bottom of the bayou and washed up against the bank. It would eventually float down the bayou, out into Sweet Bay Lake, and then on out into the Gulf, where it would finally be netted by a shrimper, ten days after a game warden found his expensive boat tied up along the bank of Big Wax Bayou.

DNA analysis of the foot would later confirm that it had belonged to Dave Thibodeau. Out of fear of getting AIDS from tainted blood, he had donated some of his own blood for an upcoming coronary bypass; so the police were able to say with certainty that the foot had indeed once belonged to him. Because of the circumstances of his terrible demise the paper referred to him as "The Boots", a name that would stick in the chronicles of the local Boojum legend.

There wasn't really enough left of him to justify a coffin, but his daughters wanted a proper funeral, with something to bury. So the undertaker put Dave's foot and boot in a child's coffin, along with some fishing lures that the girls dropped by the mortuary before they sealed the coffin. They wanted him to have something to catch flying fish with on the other side of the rainbow.

Terra came to the funeral, dressed in black from her hat to her shoes, but really wasn't at all sad to see Dave go. The priest tried to assure her and the girls that, being a Catholic, he'd gone to heaven to be with Jesus, the Blessed Virgin, and the angels. Terra knew better; if there was room in Heaven for someone as mean as Dave Thibodeau had been in life, then Hell would surely prove to be an almost empty place.

Murder by Boojum

A Mystery in Eight Fits inspired by Lewis Carroll's *The Hunting of the Snark*

Byron W. Sewell

Illustrated by the author

The Millennium Snark Trilogy

Murder by Boojum

Foreword to the 2014 edition of *Murder by Boojum*

Snark Clubs

There are at least two genuine snark clubs. Perhaps the oldest, and certainly the most famous, is The Snark Club, founded in 1934 at the University of Cambridge. However, that society is not (at least now, anyway) a secret society and has become quite public in their activities, inviting the public to apply to attend one of their annual meetings, though how often such an invitation is extended is unknown to me. They even have a website (www.snark.com) in case you might like to apply. They recently posted a group photograph of those in attendance at the 2013 annual meeting. One person of note in the photograph is Dr Selwyn H. Goodacre (first row on the left-hand corner), the world's foremost textual authority on the *Alice* books and author or editor of many articles and books about Charles Dodgson and his works, including *The Hunting of the Snark*.[1]

The other functioning English snark club (The Universal Snark Club; TUSC) attempts to remain more-or-less secret,

1 The publisher quite naturally recommends the Evertype edition, published in 2010 (ISBN 978-1-904808-36-7)

but in spite of their vows of secrecy some of their activities have become known (or at least rumored). The TUSC meets annually at Christ Church in Oxford.

Both of these English clubs have only ten members at any given time; each assigned a name of one of the crewmen from the poem. Their chairman (Captain, in this sense) is designated "The Bellman". At each meeting someone (or perhaps more than one) typically makes (or procures) in a very limited number something related to snarks (usually of an original or creative nature) to be distributed to those in attendance as a keepsake or memento. These are understandably rare, since they were produced in very limited editions and usually enter the private Carroll collections of most of those in attendance. They are prized collector's items, only rarely (if ever) appearing on the market. For example, I have never seen one of these keepsakes offered on eBay, though this doesn't necessarily mean that they have never appeared. One particularly clever and funny item by the late Alan White, *Report of an Investigation / into Bellman Enterprises' Snark Safari*, written for the TUSC's 1996 meeting, was published in 2011 for members of The Lewis Carroll Society and The Lewis Carroll Society of North America.

Unlike the Cambridge Snark Club, the Oxford club is not open to the public and those in attendance are by invitation only, though some members are known to be accompanied by their spouses, so there will typically be more than ten people in attendance.

At one time there was a West Coast Chapter of The Lewis Carroll Society of North America (LCSNA), founded by Dr Sandor G. Burstein, a prominent Carroll collector. However, as far as I know, there was never an organized snark club associated with the West Coast Chapter. The snark society described in this book is fictitious. Further, there is no actual American Lewis Carroll Society.

Unlike the infamous Victorian-era "Cannibal Club" founded by Sir Richard Burton (see Wikipedia for a brief description), there has never been so much as a hint of anything outrageous, deviant or criminal happening during a meeting of a snark club. That may be disappointing to some of you. Hopefully, this present violent tale will make up for that unfortunate fact

For those of you who are interested in such things, an earlier unillustrated version of this tale was originally published privately in a very limited edition for private distribution in 2000 as one of three stories in what I refer to as my "Millennium Snark Trilogy", under the title "SNARK! A Murderous Agony in Eight Fits". This present publication is the third in the trilogy, the other two ("Snarkmaster"[2] and "Atchafalaya Boojum"[3]) having already been published by Evertype.

Byron Sewell
Hurricane, 2014

2 *Snarkmaster: A Destiny in Eight Fits* (ISBN 978-1-78201-002-9)

3 *In the Boojum Forest* (ISBN 978-1-78201-078-4)

Contents

Fit I

Forks

Fit the First

Forks

The heavy padded mailer looked innocent enough to Fred Poole. It had a picture of a trout on the lower left-hand corner and the return label was for the California Department of Fish and Game. Even though he hadn't ordered anything from them, he assumed that it contained a book and went ahead and opened it without phoning them to verify that they had actually sent him one. It was the biggest mistake of his life. The full force of the bomb struck him in the chest, tore off two fingers, blinded an eye, and ruptured an eardrum.

The explosion was loud enough for the receptionist in the insurance agency next door to his own office to place a 911 call. Sirens screamed, shrill and high, rending the shuddering sky as the police, rescue squad and a fire truck arrived. He was still alive when the EMTs found him. Since it was apparent that there had been a bomb explosion they got him out of the building as quickly as possible and set to work, trying to keep him alive until they could get him to a hospital. Firemen did a quick search of his office and found his missing fingers, which they rushed down to the ambulance, where they were packed in ice in hopes that it might be possible to reattach them.

Police quickly organized an evacuation of the building in case there was a second bomb, herding the occupants leaving the building a block down the street as a precaution. Since it was almost lunchtime, most of the evacuees went into the Three Oceans Chinese restaurant, which was close to the staging point, and enjoyed their blistering Szechwan buffet while awaiting the all-clear signal. Bomb specialists donned full body armour and used sniffing dogs to thoroughly search the building. Having assured themselves that there were no additional explosive devices in the building, they allowed its occupants to return to their offices several hours later. Six ATF and FBI agents in dark suits soon arrived from Los Angeles.

Bombings were rare in Fresno and the FPD, who had local jurisdiction, didn't have investigators who specialized in them. So the case was assigned to Homicide Detectives Brad Pinkman and Jesse Jinks. They had been partners for eight years and neither one of them had ever had occasion to personally witness the aftereffects of a bombing. But even if they had seen them on a regular basis they would have found this one unique. Whoever had built the bomb had packed it with pieces of silverware to create shrapnel; forks to be exact. The hospital report, a copy of which the ATF Agency had condescended to send them the next morning, indicated that surgeons had removed three tines from Mr. Poole's chest. This shrapnel had punctured both lungs, miraculously missing his heart, and he had almost bled to death before they could repair the damage, which had involved the removal of one lobe. He was listed in stable but critical condition, and was expected to survive.

It was another two days before the ATF and FBI shared a copy of the crime lab report with the FPD. A number of fork fragments had been dug out of the walls and ceiling of the office, along with the pieces that had even been extracted from Poole's chest and from a stuffed bull elk head that hung over his desk. Photos of the fork fragments were attached to the report, clearly showing where the fork handles had been sawn off and discarded. They had been identified as being from patterns sold at Sears, Penny's and Montgomery Wards in the 1940s.

"There's no way they're ever going to trace those," Jinks remarked.

"I expect you're right," agreed Pinkman. "The bomber could have bought them at any of thousands of flea markets or antique shops."

The ATF report also identified the explosive as Semtex, the explosive of choice for many of the world's terrorists, primarily because they could manufacture it themselves, using the instructions in a little red booklet that had been readily available at gun shows until it had been outlawed. However, the most interesting thing in the report was that there had been a message placed in the bomb, carefully engraved onto a small strip of stainless steel designed to survive the blast. It read: "They pursued it with forks and hope". The ATF had identified this as a quote from *The Hunting of the Snark*, a rather obscure Lewis Carroll nonsense poem. Pinkman remembered it from an English course he had taken in junior college. "What I tell you three times is true," he thought; it was the only other line from the poem that he could recall.

The bomb had been mailed from Chowchilla, north of Fresno, and the FBI had already interviewed the post office there, finding that no one could remember it. That was all that was in the report. Other than the quote from the poem, there wasn't much to go on.

"I wonder if there's a Lewis Carroll society." Pinkman asked.

"I wouldn't be surprised," said Jinks. "These days there's a society for just about everything, from beer cans to license plates. We could check the internet," he suggested.

Pinkman quickly found the home page for the American Lewis Carroll Society, an elaborate site with over a hundred pages, filled with sophisticated graphics, Dodgson photographs, texts, and chitchat about Carroll in the popular culture. When he e-mailed the Society's secretary, Alicia Wunderlich, he found that the FBI had already contacted her as well, something that they had failed to mention in their report. Mrs. Wunderlich e-mailed him a copy of the same membership list that she had given to the FBI. He printed it out, then emailed the English Society, requesting a copy of their membership list as well. The English Society's secretary responded that she had no intention of releasing their membership list to someone she didn't know without instruction from the Foreign Office, and told him to make any such requests through the British Consulate. He decided to drop that idea for the time being. "Can you believe this?" he said. "There are Carroll societies in Canada, Brazil, The Netherlands, Italy, Germany, Japan, Australia, Iceland, Nigeria, and even Papua New Guinea!"

"Papua New Guinea?"

"That's what's listed. There are 2,500 names on this list for the American Lewis Carroll Society! Thankfully two dozen of them are listed as deceased, so that helps a little, I suppose." He did a quick count. "There are forty members who are universities and other such institutions. If we eliminate all of those it still leaves about twenty-four hundred. I wouldn't have thought that Carroll was *that* popular."

"Who'd a thought? Tracking down that lot should keep the FBI busy for a while! Talk about dog work!"

"Half of them are probably school kids and little old ladies."

"That'd be my guess," replied Jinks. "Let me see the list." He studied it for a few minutes then said, "I vote we concentrate on members with California addresses, especially members of their California Chapter. Look! Here's our victim." Jinks held up the list, pointing to a name. "Fred Poole's a member of both the American Lewis Carroll Society and their California Chapter."

"You have to wonder why a taxidermist like Poole would be interested in Lewis Carroll."

"You have to wonder why any adult is," responded the Jinks. "If you ask me, these people are all stuck in their childhood."

"Like you and basketball?" Pinkman responded.

"Low blow! That's different," Jinks protested.

"Yeah, right! Let's give the California Chapter's president a call and see what he can tell us." Pinkman dialled his listed work phone number, and Jinks got on an extension.

A woman with an Australian accent answered. "Doctor Kerr's office. May I help you?"

Pinkman identified himself, then asked to speak with Dr. Kerr. "I'm sorry, but he's with a patient. Can he call you back in about ten minutes?"

"That'll be fine." He gave her the number.

About fifteen minutes later Dr. Kerr was on the line. Pinkman introduced himself. "We're investigating a bombing that happened here in Fresno. You may have heard or read about it."

"Indeed. It's been big news in the L. A. papers and on local TV."

"Were you aware that the victim, Mr. Fred Poole, is a member of your California Chapter of the American Lewis Carroll Society?"

"Yes. I recognized his name. The Chapter sent flowers. I've met him on several occasions, at various Chapter meetings. I don't know him well, though."

"Can you think of any reason why anyone would want to harm him?"

"As I told the FBI, I haven't any idea whatsoever. You have to understand that we are a literary society. With rare exception, we don't get to know each other on a very intimate basis. We correspond occasionally and sometimes see each other at meetings; that's usually about it. No one would ever talk about his or her enemies."

"Are you aware that the bomb included a quote from a Lewis Carroll poem?"

"Yes, I read that in the papers; a line from *The Hunting of the Snark.*"

"Is there anyone in the Society who has a special interest in this particular poem?"

"Of course. Many of us do. Almost any Carroll collector would have copies of the book. However, there is a much greater interest in *Alice*, of course."

"Do any of your members have an exceptionally large collection of Snark editions?"

"Well, I have about three hundred copies."

"Really?" Pinkman asked, amazed at what he had heard.

"Yes." He paused. "I hope that doesn't mean I'm a suspect!"

"I didn't mean to imply that. I'm curious; why do you have so many?"

"My wife has asked me the same thing on numerous occasions. I don't know, really; I just like them. Can't get enough of a good thing, I suppose."

"Are there other collectors who would have that many editions?"

"I doubt it. But I can think of at least a dozen collectors who would have twenty or thirty copies: there are several in New

York, one in Maryland, two in Massachusetts, one in Illinois, half a dozen or more here in California ... "

"Can you give me the names of the California ones?" Pinkman interrupted him.

"Well, there's me, as I said earlier. Then there's Cooksley, Schwartz, Barnett, Clapham, Imhoff, Cleaver, and, oh yes, Fred Poole; your victim."

"Fred Poole?"

"Yes, I think so. I've never had the opportunity to see his entire collection, but I know that he has some rare things associated with *The Snark*, so I would definitely say he had a more than casual interest in it."

"What kind of special things does he have?" Pinkman asked.

"Well, he has a couple of presentation copies from Dodgson to some child-friends, one of which is a rare purple binding variant. And he has some original art from Mahendra Singh's edition of *The Snark*. Things of that nature. "

"Did Poole have any enemies in the Society?"

"Not that I know of. In fact, I don't know of anyone in the Society that has enemies. Our members are pretty nice people: academicians, housewives, school children, artists, and collectors; that sort of thing. Our meetings are all very genial and fun. If anyone has enemies they don't talk about them at our functions."

Pinkman thanked him and rang off.

"That group sounds about as boring as watching a curling match," Jinks said.

"You don't like curling?"

"Well, to tell the truth I've never seen a match; just a few clips on TV. It's always some squatting woman with her mouth wide open, yelling like someone just dropped her stone on her big toe. So now what?"

"Let's go pay Fred Poole's wife a visit; see if she has any ideas."

"The FBI would have been there already."

"I know; they seem to be omnipresent. But they aren't going to share much with us; and perhaps they haven't yet followed the *Snark* trail."

"Before we go let's check with ATF and find out if there are any open cases with Lewis Carroll associations," Jinks suggested.

"That's a good idea. Our bomber may be interested in *Alice* as well as *Snarks*."

Jinks placed the call and took a few notes. "They had already checked this angle. There isn't much to go on here. There was a theft of a first edition of *Alice* from a rare book room at the University of Illinois at Urbana-Champaign back in 1953; it's never been recovered. In 1956 there was an armed robbery in Sistersville, West Virginia in which some guy in a ski mask stole a can of film for a 1933 *Alice in Wonderland* movie at gunpoint. In 1967 some guy was shot dead in his Memphis living room while reading *Through the Looking-Glass*. That's all they came up with. There haven't been any previous bombings associated with anything Carrollian."

"Perhaps this bombing has more to do with Poole being a taxidermist than with Carroll," Pinkman suggested.

"How's that?"

"Oh, 1 don't know. Perhaps some environmental nut doesn't like him because he's associated with hunting elk. He has that big one on the wall behind his desk."

"I kind of doubt it; the bomber didn't include a quote from some famous tree-hugger."

"True." Pinkman turned and checked his e-mail again. "Listen to this! Ms. Wunderlich sent me another e-mail. She says that one of their former members wrote a parody of *Alice in Wonderland* back in 1974, entitled *R. A. V. E. N., or The Dormouse Who Came in from the Cold*. It's about a republican plot to overthrow the Queen of Hearts, by assassinating her with a homemade bomb made out of an explosive mixture of pepper and treacle. She thought we ought to check this guy out, since he seemed to be fascinated with bombs."

Jesse groaned. "This case is going to be really weird."

"And you said their Society was boring!"

Just as they got up to walk out to their car Detective Cox handed Pinkman a copy of the local newspaper. "Thought you guys might enjoy today's edition," he said. "The headline blared POLICE HUNTING FOR SNARKS. You guys watch out now," Cox told them with a big grin. "You bump into a BOOOO-jum Snark and you just might vanish!"

Everyone in the squad room had been listening and they all laughed. Then Cox suddenly yelled, "BOO!" at the top of his voice, which caused Pinkman to instinctively jerk his hand up to his pistol grip. This made everyone laugh even louder. "You better go take a Valium, Brad," Cox said.

"Very funny," Pinkman responded. He and Jinks walked on out to get in their car. Pinkman kept the newspaper.

"Let's drop by and visit Ms. Cookesly before we go over to Poole's place. Her house is on the way."

They drove there and got out. Pinkman knocked on the front door and an attractive, conservatively dressed woman opened it. He showed her his ID badge, then introduced himself and his partner. She invited them in.

"We're investigating the Fred Poole bombing," Pinkman told her. "Did you know him?"

"Quite well," she said. "It's so tragic. I do hope he will recover."

"I believe that's the prognosis. How did you know him?"

"Through a Carroll society we both belong to."

"The American Lewis Carroll Society?"

"Yes. How did you know?"

"If you've read today's newspaper, you know there was a quote from *The Hunting of the Snark* in the bomb."

"Yes, I read that. Very strange! I kept the paper actually; for my collection."

"You have a collection about bombings?"

"No, no! I kept it for my Lewis Carroll collection."

"Oh; I misunderstood you." He chuckled.

"Actually, I keep everything I find that has anything to do with him. Most Carroll collectors I know find it impossible to throw anything away that has even the slightest reference to Lewis Carroll."

"That reminds me of the bumper sticker about toys," Pinkman said. "I can imagine one that says: THE ONE WITH THE MOST CARROLL STUFF WHEN HE DIES WINS THE GAME."

She laughed. "Yes. That's a good idea. I think I'll see if I can get the California Chapter to have some printed up."

"Well, because of the reference to *The Snark* that was found in the bomb debris we obtained a list of members of the various Carroll societies here in America and your name came up."

"Why would my name come up?" suddenly alarmed that she might be a suspect.

"Dr. Kerr said that you shared a special interest in *The Hunting of the Snark* with Fred Poole."

"Oh, I see. Yes, that's correct; as I said, I'm a rather omnivorous collector. I have a relatively large number of editions of *The Snark*, as does Fred."

"Can you think of anyone who would have wanted to kill him?"

"No one; he's a very nice person."

"I wonder if we could ask you a favour? Would you mind showing us a few *Snarks* from your collection; just to educate us a bit? It's not something you find on the shelf of your local Barnes & Noble."

"No, it isn't. I'd be delighted to show you what I have. I keep my Carroll collection in my bedroom." She stood up and led them through the house. Her collection was prominently displayed in bookcases on a wall next to a large Victorian brass bed, covered by a frilly lace spread. The walls were lined with framed posters from various Disney productions of *Alice in Wonderland*, some in foreign languages. Pinkman could recognize Japanese, Hangul, Hindi, and Russian.

"How many books do you have?" Pinkman asked, looking at the full shelves.

"I'm not sure. I've never counted them. There's probably something like a few thousand items in my collection, though they're not all books. There might be a thousand books I suppose."

"I assume these would be quite valuable," he said.

"Well, yes. I have the collection insured for two-hundred-thousand dollars. But, the way prices keep going up on this material that likely wouldn't replace it if something happened to it, God forbid! I can only rarely afford to buy anything to add to my collection these days. Books I used to buy for $20 or $30 now fetch $250 to $500."

Pinkman whistled. "So this is an investment?"

"Sort of, I suppose; though I wouldn't sell it for anything." She went over to a shelf and pulled down a couple of books. She handed a tan book to Pinkman and a large black one to Jinks. "This is the standard 1876 first edition," she said to Pinkman. "The one I gave you, Detective Jinks, is a strange 1974 production, published by the Catalpa Press in London. Here let me show you." She took the book back and walked across the large bedroom, and laid the book on the floor. She then proceeded to pull the folded pages out to a length of about fifteen feet. "This is called concertina style," she explained.

"The Victorians used to make books that way. This crazy long boat in the illustration is the first chapter, or 'Fit' as Carroll called it, and depicts all of the ten crewmen who went hunting for Snarks. The illustrations are rather naively adapted after the original ones by Henry Holiday. Here, you can see the originals in the first edition you are holding, Detective Pinkman." They looked at a few.

"Have there been lots of different editions?" Jinks asked.

"Not lots; nothing like the *Alice* books, which probably runs into the thousands. A new edition of *The Snark* comes out every five years or so. There's just not a mass market for it, though it is well known. My favourite modem edition is from the 1940s, by an English illustrator named Mervyn Peake." She went to a shelf and pulled down a slim yellow volume and handed it to Pinkman.

He thumbed through it. "Strange illustrations," he said.

"Yes, sort of surrealistic Gothic horror," she said. "Peake also did a magnificent *Alice*. I've never been able to find a copy of the first edition of it for sale, and probably even if did I wouldn't be able to afford it!"

"Didn't he write The *Gormenghast* trilogy?" Jinks asked.

"Yes; that's him."

Pinkman looked at him in amazement.

"Hey! I read too!" he protested, silently proud of himself for having recognized the author.

They handed the books back to her. "Thanks very much for taking the time to show them to us," Pinkman said. "They're quite interesting."

"Not at all. It's been my pleasure." Julia left the Catalpa edition lying across the blue carpet and escorted them back to the front door.

"Here's my phone number," Pinkman said, handing her a card. "Give us a call if you see or hear anything suspicious."

"I will."

"Don't open any packages, unless you're certain who sent them," Jinks advised her.

"Why?"

"You never know; it could contain a bomb. I'd say that you're a bit of a high risk target, because of your association with Poole and Snarks."

"I see," she said. "Yes, I'll certainly be careful with the mail from now on," she assured him.

They went back to their car. "Could you believe that? How many copies of *Alice in Wonderland* does a person need, for Pete's sake?" Pinkman said.

"She's obviously a bibliomaniac," Jinks said.

"A what?"

"She's got a neurosis; an obsession with collecting books."

"You just make that up?"

"No, it's a real condition. I read about it once."

"Where? In the *Gormenghast* trilogy?"

"No. I don't remember; *Psychology Today*, maybe."

"You a subscriber?"

"No, I ain't a subscriber! I read them once in a while—while I'm waiting in my dentist's office."

"Are they dangerous?" Pinkman asked.

"Yeah; dentists are real dangerous." He grinned.

"Not dentists, idiot! Bibliomaniacs."

"Not usually. Of course, every once in a while one of them gets into the bomb making business," he said, still grinning.

"In that case, we should have checked her kitchen," Pinkman said.

"For what?"

"Pepper and treacle." They both laughed as they eased out into the traffic.

They made their way across town to Fred Poole's home, a modem brick house with a manicured yard. There were gum trees growing behind it in the backyard and the air was heavy with the fragrance of eucalyptus. There was an old white Volkswagen Rabbit in the driveway, with a vanity plate that read 'I'M LATE.' Mrs. Poole answered the door and invited them in, once they had identified themselves.

"I was just on my way over to the hospital to see my husband," she said as they sat down in the living room.

"What's left of him!" Jinks thought.

"We won't keep you long," Pinkman assured her. "We just wanted to ask you a few questions about your husband."

"I've already told the FBI everything I know about all of this, which is next to nothing. I can't imagine why anyone would want to harm Fred. He's such a dear!"

"Unfortunately, the FBI doesn't always feel obligated to keep us informed of everything they learn. Quite frankly, they regard us at about the same competence level as Barney Fife. But sometimes they miss things."

"I understand. I don't mind talking to you."

"I appreciate that. We understand that your husband is a Lewis Carroll collector."

"Yes. He inherited a collection that his mother started when she was a girl, and he's added to it over the years. He's always been interested in it. He has a number of good friends in the various Carroll societies."

"We talked to Dr. Kerr of the California Chapter and he said that your husband has a large collection of things associated with *The Hunting of the Snark*."

"That's right. It's his favourite book. He quotes from it all the time. 'What I tell you three times is true!' he'll tell me when he really means something. He's always looking for something new to do with it, to add to his collection."

"Would you mind showing us his collection?" Pinkman asked.

"Not at all. He keeps it in his study. I haven't been in there since he was injured, so it might not be too tidy."

"That's not a problem," he assured her.

She led the way and they entered a bedroom that had been converted into a study. The mini-blinds on the windows were closed to block out the sunlight, which could fade the spines of his books. She flipped on the light.

"Oh, my God!" she said.

"What's wrong?" Jinks asked, half expecting to see a body on the floor. "Someone's stolen the paintings!" She pointed at an empty wall and rushed over to it, as if looking closer at the wall might tell her where they had gone. "There were three framed illustrations from an edition of *The Hunting of the Snark* hanging on this wall the last time I was in here! Someone's stolen them! Oh, dear, this will be very upsetting to Fred." Her eyes had filled with tears.

"Were they valuable?"

"Well, yes, to a Carroll collector." She took a Kleenex out of her pocket and dabbed at her eyes. "They were from an edition published recently. Original art, especially anything associated with *The Snark*, is very hard to come by."

"Please look around and see if you can tell if anything else is missing," Pinkman told her.

She scanned the shelves for a few minutes. "Not that I can tell, but Fred knows his collection much better than I do. We probably won't know until he comes home and does an inventory."

"Were the paintings insured?"

"I doubt it. You have to pay a fortune for someone to appraise them in order to get the insurance. He probably thought it was so unlikely that anyone would take them that he didn't bother."

"I'm sorry," Pinkman offered. "Please phone the FPD when you get back from the hospital and report this. They'll send someone out to take the information on the theft and open a case."

"Do you think this might have anything to do with the attempt on Fred's life?" she asked.

"Quite possibly," he said. "But it's hard to say. It is an odd coincidence, though."

"Should I call the FBI and tell them too?"

"That's up to you." He hoped she wouldn't.

"Can you describe the paintings?"

"They were rather garish watercolours, by an artist named Gruszecki; very bright and colourful in the Slavic, surrealistic style one often sees in Czech and Russian children's books. One was a picture of the Bellman standing in the surf. Another was a picture of the Banker being pursued by a dragon-like beast. The last one was of the Baker vanishing away like a Cheshire Cat."

"Actually, I'm having trouble imagining them. Do you happen to have a copy of the edition they were made for?"

"We did. I hope the thief didn't take that, too." She scanned the shelves. "Oh, good! Here it is!" She took it off of the shelf. "This book was hard for Fred to obtain. A friend of his picked it up in Prague when he went through on a business trip a few years ago. He also tracked down the artist through the publisher and got Fred in touch with him to buy the paintings." She leafed through the book to find the pages that were the same as the missing paintings and showed them to the detectives.

"Could you possibly take this by an express copy shop and get colour copies of the missing paintings for us? It might help us find them."

"Of course. I'll do that tomorrow and then drop them by the station for you. Do you really think you can find them?"

"I honestly doubt it. Stolen art can take a long time to resurface. In fact, most of it never does. I wouldn't want to get your hopes up too high; but you never know." They thanked her for talking with them and left.

After weeks of searching the only one of the California *Snark* enthusiasts that they hadn't been able to locate was George Clapham. They had an old address in Canyon Muerta, east of L. A., so they drove out there to look around. They had a hard time locating it. The house was closed up and the yard overgrown with waist-high weeds and brush. "The first time there's a fire through here this place will be gone," Jinks observed as they walked up the dirt drive to the front door. They poked around outside for a while, scaring the lizards, and peered through the dirty windows. They hadn't brought a search warrant, which was just as well.

There was nothing exceptional to see; no sign of anyone having lived in the house for years.

They got in their car and drove back to their motel. Pinkman checked with LAPD, but they had no records on Clapham. They went down to the Denny's next to the motel restaurant to get some lunch. The seated themselves in a booth. It was noon and the place still smelled like breakfast.

"So far all we have is 'a perfect and absolute blank,' Pinkman said, quoting from *The Snark*.

"Pretty much," Jinks agreed. "Where do we go from here? You got any ideas?"

"Oh, you know me; I've always got ideas. They're not always good ideas, however."

"What have you got at the moment; good, bad or ugly?"

"I was thinking that we might go into Hollywood and visit a few antiquarian book stores to see if anyone's ever dealt with our guy Clapham."

"That might be worthwhile," Jinks agreed. "What else?"

"I've been trying to imagine the bomber, what he might do with himself in his spare time."

"You mean besides torture small animals?"

"Who knows; he might do that, too. I was thinking that he might like to think of himself as a member of the crew of the boat in the poem. You know; he might be a sailor; own a yacht or something. We could check with the Coast Guard and see if there's a boat named 'The Snark' or a boat registered under his name."

"You think he might be that careless, to leave an obvious trail like that?"

"Who knows?"

"Okay, we can do that easy enough. What else?"

"That's it. How about you; you got any ideas yourself?"

"I was wondering if maybe we could set a trap for him by convincing the California Chapter to hold a symposium on *Snarks*. That might well bring him out of cover. I don't see how he could stay away. We could be waiting in the wings and nab him."

"I don't know; we might get some innocent people killed doing that."

Jinks considered this for a moment. "Yeah, I suppose you're right. He might be crazy enough to set off a car bomb and take out the whole Chapter."

"We could ask Dr. Kerr to give us a description of Clapham, since he's met him a few times; we need to put a face on this guy."

The waitress finally showed up. "What can I get you?" she asked Pinkman. "I'll have a piece of bride cake," he said, grinning.

"Yeah, right. Real funny!" she said, though not smiling. "This look like a wedding chapel to you?"

"I don't suppose you have any mutton boiled in sawdust either?" Pinkman asked.

"No," she said, obviously irritated. "The last person who ordered it choked on it and died. The management took it off of the menu. "

"In that case I guess I'll just have to settle for a Caesar salad and a Diet Coke."

"Watching your figure?" she asked. "Good idea!" she added, looking disapprovingly at his paunchy stomach pressed up against the table. "And you, sir?" she said, turning to Jinks.

"I'd really like a nice thick Jub-jub steak," Jinks said, grinning at her.

"You guys are a real riot! Sorry, we're fresh out of Jub-jub. Real popular today."

"Shucks!" said Jinks. "In that case, I guess I'll settle for a double-cheeseburger and fries, with a side of onion rings."

"Everyone's a comedian," she said as she walked away.

"Touchy!" Pinkman said.

After lunch they went into the Coast Guard offices. He identified himself to a clerk, then said, "We're trying to find out if there are any boats named Snark." The clerk laughed hysterically. "You're kidding, right?"

"I'm quite serious. Why's that so funny?"

"SNARK is the world's largest manufacturer of sailboats. There are thousands of them out there. One popular model is the Super Snark."

Pinkman groaned. "Oh. I see what you mean. Well, can you check the registry for anyone named George Clapham?"

"Just a moment. I'll search our database." A few moments later he responded. "Yes. He's got a sailboat that he's named *Snark III*. It's registered in Long Beach."

"Do you have a home address in your database?"

"Yeah; 206 Sea Cliff in San Francisco. I don't know if it's still current, however."

"You want the registration number for the boat?"

"Yes," Pinkman said, and the clerk wrote it down on a piece of paper for him.

They went back to the parking lot.

"Let's go down to Long Beach and see if we can find his boat."

"I just wish I'd brought my trunks" Jinks said grinning broadly.

"Yeah, right; dream on, Alice!"

"You're starting to talk like these people," Jinks said.

Pinkman shrugged. "You're right; this stuff is contagious!"

They drove down to Long Beach and toured around the harbour, which was full of boats. "Just the place for a Snark!" Pinkman said as he parked their car with care.

"Aw, nuts!" Jinks said, stopping and looking up at the sky.

"What is it?"

"We forgot to bring the bathing machine!" They laughed as they set off down the wharf to a cluster of moored sailboats. Gulls screamed overhead, angry that they hadn't brought bread.

They spent the entire morning going up and down the harbour, checking the names on sailboats and asking people if they knew George Clapham. They couldn't find the *Snark III*, and they didn't find anyone who would admit to knowing George Clapham.

"You look a bit uffish," Pinkman said. "How about some lunch?"

They walked over to The Walrus and The Carpenter Oyster Bar and ate raw oysters and had a beer, even though they were on duty. Feeling refreshed, they went back to their car then drove north to Hollywood to check out the bookstores.

Their first destination was the Hollywood Hills Bookstore, a small shop that had been designed to look like a bookstore one might see in London, with dark custom made bookcases with locked glass doors. They went in and Pinkman identified himself, asking for the manager.

She came over from where she was sitting at an old roll-top desk at the back of the store. "I'm the manager. May I help you?"

"Perhaps," said Pinkman. He showed her his badge and identified himself, then introduced her to Jinks. "We're looking for a gentleman who might be one of your customers. His name is George Clapham. Do you happen to know him?"

"Yes. He's a regular customer."

"What sort of books is he interested in?" Pinkman asked.

"He always inquires about editions of *The Hunting of the Snark*. That's a nonsense poem by Lewis Carroll, who wrote *Alice's Adventures in Wonderland*."

"I know," Pinkman said.

"I'm sorry; I didn't mean to talk down to you. Not everyone is familiar the poem. *The Hunting of the Snark* seems to be his only interest."

"He had just one idea - and that being 'Snark'," Pinkman said.

"Oh, 1 see that you know the poem very well!"

"Just a few lines. Yes, that would be him. When was the last time he was in your shop?"

"I don't recall an exact date. It was probably within the last month."

"I wonder if you could describe him for me?"

"I'm afraid that I'm not very good at this sort of thing, but I'll try. Let's see; he's middle-aged, thin, with wavy grey hair. He wears wire-rimmed glasses and dresses rather oddly, usually on some nautical theme; a captain's hat, with an anchor crest; that sort of thing. My staff refers to him as Toasted Cheese."

"Why would they do that? I thought Toasted Cheese referred to the Baker."

"My goodness! You're right, of course. You obviously know more than a few lines of the poem. For a policeman, you must be as rare as a Jub-jub's tooth!"

Pinkman grinned. "You wouldn't happen to have his address by any chance?"

"No, I'm sorry; not even a phone number. He's very private, and always pays with cash."

Pinkman was disappointed, but not surprised. "I'd like to send a police sketch artist around and see if you and your staff can help him come up with a likeness. Would that be all right?"

"Of course. Why are you looking for him, if I might ask?"

"We just want to talk with him. He's very difficult to find. You've been a big help today already."

"If he comes in again shall we tell him that you're looking for him?"

"No, that would be a very bad idea. You may find this hard to believe, but he might be quite dangerous. Just give us a call the next time he comes in to your shop." He gave her his card. "If you could manage to get a license plate number when he leaves that would be wonderful, but don't put yourself or your staff at risk."

"Oh, dear," she said.

Then Pinkman added, "You don't happen to have a surveillance camera in the shop do you?" He looked around at the ceiling.

"No, I'm sorry; just a burglar alarm."

"Too bad. I was hoping that you might have caught him on video. The sketch artist should be here tomorrow morning. It shouldn't take him more than an hour. One other thing."

"Yes?"

"Do you have any *Snarks* in stock?"

"Only a few. They sell very quickly. We have a standard first edition in reasonably nice condition. "

"Could I see it?"

"Of course. Just a moment." She went over to a case and unlocked it, then pulled out a book. "Here it is. The spine is a bit sunned and the comers are bumped. But it's a tight, bright copy."

"How much is it?"

She took it back from him and looked at a code penciled on the back endpaper. "Four-hundred dollars."

Pinkman tried not to gasp. "Do you have anything a little less expensive? I was thinking of buying a copy, but I can't afford a week's pay for it."

"Well, we do have a problem copy of the first edition, which is much cheaper."

"What's a problem book?"

"This one is lacking a page, and the condition is generally poor."

"Could I see that one?"

"Of course." She went to an open shelf and came back with a well-worn copy. She opened it and showed him where an illustration had been torn out by someone. "People do this sort of thing, usually to frame an illustration."

"How much is this one?"

"I would be pleased to let you have it for ten dollars," she said.

"Now that's more like it," he said and pulled out his wallet, then paid her.

"Thank you."

"Not at all. I hope that you will enjoy the book."

They said good-bye and left.

"You thinking of becoming a book collector?" Jinks asked once they were outside.

"Yeah. Who knows? I might just join the Lewis Carroll Society."

"Thinking of doing a little undercover snooping?"

"Maybe."

"They'll see right through you, like a biker at a Sunday School picnic."

Two days later Pinkman received the sketch artist's rendering by e-mail. It showed a very nondescript man who could likely blend in almost anywhere if he gave up his nautical garb and tried. The artist had dressed him in a striped sailor's tee shirt; he looked like he'd jumped ship from a Russian destroyer.

George Clapham came into The Hollywood Hills Bookstore two weeks later, wearing his captain's attire, including a dark blue blazer and white turtleneck.

The bookstore's all-female staff went suddenly quiet and as nervous as the Beaver sitting next to the Butcher. George Clapham sensed their tension immediately, making him nearly as nervous as they were.

The Manager was the only one brave enough to come forward to wait on him. "Mr. Clapham; how nice to see you again," she lied in a tremulous tone. "How can we help you today?" She accidentally dropped her glasses and had to stoop to pick them back up, then bumped her knee when she straightened back up.

"Oh, you know me; I'm always searching for *Snarks*;" he said, and then giggled nervously, trying to figure out why she was acting so strange.

"No, no; nothing unusual, I'm afraid. We know your interest, of course, and we always set them aside for your first refusal." Then it occurred to her that she might be able to get his address. "We would be happy to phone you or drop you a note whenever a *Snark* comes in if you will only give us your number or address. It would save you unnecessary trips in to check with us." She smiled as innocently as she could, though she was just about ready to jump out of her skin.

George couldn't get out quickly enough. "That won't be necessary," he said. "I don't mind the trip. Thank you anyway." He bolted for the door, and once outside literally ran, in the opposite direction of where he had parked his car. He ducked into a shop and waited to see if anyone was following him.

The manager phoned Pinkman immediately. "George Clapham was here just a few minutes ago," she told him. "We tried to act normal, but I'm afraid we frightened him. He literally ran out of the bookstore when I asked him for his phone number. I'm sorry."

"It's okay," he assured her. "Thanks for trying." Pinkman knew that George Clapham would never again visit the bookshop, even if a live Snark decided to nest there.

Fit II
Soap

Fit the Second

Soap

Alison Cooksley, one of Fresno's most successful real estate agents, came home from showing a house late in the afternoon. When she reached the front door she found a plain white plastic bag hanging from the doorknob. She peeked inside without touching it, now paranoid about bombs, but only saw a free sample of Radiance shampoo in its familiar maroon plastic bottle. She liked the brand. "Good timing!" she thought, as she was nearly out of shampoo. She took it with her into the shower later that evening just before going to bed. She washed off and got the free shampoo bottle. When she twisted the lid the force of the explosion slammed her into the wall of the stall, killing her instantly.

The blast set off her smoke detector and automatically dialled the fire department. Firemen burst through her front door a few minutes later and rushed in to find her crumpled body in the shower, the water still running. They turned off the shower and drug her out onto the bedroom carpet. She had no vital signs, but they spent ten minutes vainly trying to bring her back before giving up and calling for homicide. Since there had obviously been a bomb they left the house just in case there might be another.

Pinkman and Jinks arrived about fifteen minutes later and made their way through the familiar house to the master bedroom. A patrolman was standing guard at the door to be sure that evidence wouldn't be disturbed. "What can you tell us?" Pinkman asked him.

"There was evidently a bomb. There's a corpse over there on the carpet." He pointed at a body covered by a bedspread. "She died taking a shower. Seems like no where's safe these days!"

"Oh, lots of people die in their bathtubs," Jinks said.

"Not in explosions," he observed.

Pinkman nodded. They went on into the bedroom and the patrolman followed. Pinkman pulled up the comer of the bedspread so they could see her face. It was barely recognizable as a face. Both Pinkman and Jinks winced; the bomb had obviously gone off right in her face. He dropped the corner of the bedspread, having seen more than enough. "I'm pretty certain that this is Alison Cooksley," he said to the patrolman. "She lived here."

The patrolman nodded. "That's what we assumed. You seem to know her."

"Yeah. We interviewed her here a few months back after the Fred Poole bombing. She was a nice lady; too bad!"

Pinkman turned to go into the bathroom and noticed that several of the framed Disney posters nearest to the bathroom had been knocked off of the wall by the force of the explosion.

"Watch your step," the patrolman cautioned. "There's soap all over everything and the tiles are slicker than snot."

"Thanks," Pinkman said and proceeded with a bit more caution. The glass in the vanity mirror and the windows had been shattered. There were shards everywhere.

"Any forks laying around?" Pinkman asked.

The patrolman was surprised by his question. “No; but then most people don’t eat in the bathroom.”

“Most of the civilized ones don’t,” Pinkman agreed, as he continued to look around.

“Here’s something,” he said, squatting down and pointing at a small stainless steel strip

“You think it’s important?”

“I’m sure of it.”

Another man stuck his head into the bathroom. “ATF Agent Zabrodski,” he announced. Pinkman and Jinks stood up and looked at him.

“FPD Detective Pinkman; this is my partner Detective Jinks.” They nodded at each other, but didn’t shake hands.

“Hi, Jinks,” he said and then laughed.

“Kids in Junior High used to say that,” Jinks responded. “I used to knock their teeth out.”

“That a threat?”

“Take it however you want,” Jinks said coolly.

Pinkman interrupted them, pointing out the metal strip to Zabrodski, who produced latex gloves from a coat pocket. He put them on and picked up the metal strip by its edges to examine it.

“What’s it say,” Pinkman asked.

“They charmed it with smiles and soap.”

“That wold be a quote from *The Hunting of the Snark*,” Pinkman said.

“Not my idea of charming,” Zabrodski replied. “This clearly links this murder to Fred Poole’s attempted murder earlier this year.”

“Thanks, Sherlock,” Jinks said.

“Elementary, my Dear Watson,” Zabrodski told him with a sneer. “We’ll have a metallurgist compare the two strips.”

Evidence technicians soon arrived and began picking through the debris. They scraped up samples of the shampoo, which covered practically everything. They also collected every piece of the plastic bottle they could find, along with any bits of wire and metal.

"Can you please send me a copy of your report?" Pinkman asked Zabrodski.

The agent nodded. "No problem." He paused. "I understand that you two have been investigating the Poole bombing. You come up with anything we should know about?"

"Nothing concrete. We've been concentrating on Poole's associations with the California Chapter of the American Lewis Carroll Society."

"Anything interesting?" he repeated.

"There's one odd guy that we've been looking for who is very hard to find. He acts like he's hiding from the police. Don't know why. He doesn't have a record or any outstanding warrants."

"What's his name?"

"George Clapham."

"You have a photo of him?"

"No, just a police identi-sketch based on descriptions from some of his acquaintances. "

"Send me a copy," Zabrodski said, more like an order than a request.

Pinkman nodded. He'd have to cooperate if he expected him to share things with him.

"What can you tell me about him?"

"He has a keen interest in *The Hunting of the Snark*. So does Fred Poole; and Alison Cooksley, the lady on the carpet in there, did too."

"Why haven't you reported this to the FBI or to us?"

"It's just suspicion on our part; and, up until now, there hadn't been a murder."

"I"d like to come by and talk with you at length about this. You available later this afternoon? Say 3:00?"

Pinkman nodded.

"I'll be there at 3:00, sharp."

Pinkman and Jinks stepped out of the bathroom and left Zabrodski poking around in the broken glass looking for clues. They went over to the bookcases that held Julia's Lewis Carroll collection, tracking shampoo and little bits of glass across the blue carpet. Pinkman looked for Alison's *Snarks*. "They're gone," he said to Jinks. "Not a snark in sight!"

"You think Poole and Julia were killed for their books?" Jinks asked; the thought seemed ridiculous.

"Well, the books are worth a lot of money, and in this town you can get stabbed for less than five bucks. But, honestly, I doubt it. If someone wanted the books he could have simply burgled the house; no need to set off a bomb and bring the Feds in on top of you. Let's go back to the station and do some brainstorming; see if we can guess who might be the next victim."

"You obviously think there will be another one."

"Likely, I'd say. Don't you think so?"

"Yeah."

When they got back to the station Pinkman and Jinks went into a small conference room with a white board. Pinkman had brought along the problem copy *Snark* that he had bought at the Hollywood Hills Bookstore. He wrote the names of the ten crewmen on the board in a vertical column: Bellman, Boots, Bonnets, Barrister, Broker, Billiard-marker, Banker, Beaver, Baker, and Butcher.

"B seems to have been Carroll's favourite letter," observed Jinks.

"Yeah; just like a kid, he had lots of favourites: the letter B, the number 42, and purple ink. Okay, let's start with Clapham. He's probably the Bellman, based on the way he dresses the part; and he has a sailboat." He wrote his name on the board next to Clapham's.

"Poole could be the Billiard-marker," suggested Jinks. "Pool is an American derivative of billiards."

"A bit obtuse, but possible, I suppose." Pinkman wrote Poole next to Billiard-marker. "Now, Alison Cooksley."

"There weren't any women crewmembers," Jinks pointed out.

"Well, it could have been the Beaver. I imagine that it might be difficult to tell the difference between a male and a female beaver."

"Yeah. After all the Beaver was making lace, which sounds pretty feminine."

"However, Dodgson was a bachelor and didn't seem to care for mature women. A woman was probably the last thing he would want on his imaginary boat destined for a desert isle."

"The logical association would be Baker," said Jinks. "You know: Cook - Baker."

"Of course!" Pinkman penned in her name next to Baker.

"I take it you think that the bomber may be killing off a figurative crew?"

"The thought has occurred to me. What are the names of the other Snark enthusiasts that Dr. Kerr provided?"

Jinks pulled a small notebook out of his shirt pocket and read them off. "Blanche Schwartz, Charlie Barnett, and Julius Imhoff."

"Barnett sounds like 'Bonnets', spoken with a thick accent, so that could be him."

"What about Schwartz? Where's she fit in?"

"Here's a possibility. A boots was someone in Victorian times who blackened and shined a hotel guest's boots while he was sleeping. In German *swarz* means 'black.' So, I'm guessing that's her."

"Yeah, but her first name is Blanche, and *blanc* means 'white' in French," said Jinks.

"It is a strange name; sort of a mixed message."

"Anyway, what about Julius Imhoff? He's an accountant, right?"

"That's right. Perhaps he's either the Broker or Banker."

"Could be." Pinkman wrote Imhoff's name beside both. "That leaves the Barrister. "

"That doesn't seem to fit anyone we've heard of."

"There is someone on the list named Jurist. Let's get back to Dr. Kerr and see if she has any particular interest in *Snarks*."

Agent Zabrodski barged in without knocking. "It's 3:00," he said, which seemed to be his idea of a greeting.

"Take a chair," Pinkman suggested.

"Hi, Jinks," he said, then laughed.

Jinks had a difficult time controlling his anger. "Agent Broad-asski," Jinks replied as an acknowledgement. Zabrodski glared at him, but let it go. "What have you got for me?" he asked, as if Pinkman and Jinks worked for him.

"We were just summarizing it here on the board." Pinkman explained their theory.

"Based on this, you think Clapham is the bomber?"

"Could be; he's our prime suspect."

"I think you guys are in danger of losing your jobs, if not your minds. This is the biggest load of crap I've ever seen."

Pinkman and Jinks didn't respond at first, put off by his reaction to their theory. "I realize that it does seem a bit far-fetched," Pinkman admitted.

"A bit? What's the motive?"

"We aren't sure. Could be he's just a psycho. I guess we won't know if there's anything to any of this unless someone else on this list gets hit."

"What do you propose to do now?" Zabrodski asked, the tone of his voice still incredulous.

"We need to find George Clapham. The FBI could assist in that. Everyone on this list needs to be warned that his or her lives might be in danger."

"On the strength of that?" asked Zabrodski, pointing at the board. "Not a chance." He got up and left; didn't even say good-bye.

They were silent for a minute. "Perhaps he's right," Pinkman finally said. "I wish now that we had never explained our theory. He seems to think everything we do on this case is a big joke."

"Let's don't let him get us down. The ATF and FBI aren't making any noticeable progress, so they aren't nearly as smart as they act. Let's just do what we know to do and if someone gets hurt then it won't be because of any negligence on our part."

"You're right."

The crime lab report on Alison Cooksley came in a few days later. Once again the explosive in the device had been Semtex, the Czechoslovakian equivalent to C-4. The shampoo was ordinary stuff, available in half of the drugstores and supermarkets in the country. The bomber had taken great care to carefully scratch away the identifying codes on the plastic bottle.

Jinks had been on the phone. "Dr. Kerr says Rachel Jurist does have quite a number of *Snarks* in her collection. He gave me her phone number."

"Why don't you give her a call and just ask her to be especially careful, but try not to panic her."

Fit III
Spadework

Fit the Third

Spadework

George Clapham was a very paranoid individual. He had just learned a few weeks ago, from the owner of the Long Beach Marina, that two policemen were trying to locate him. Then, when the manager at the Hollywood Hills Bookstore had tried to get him to give her his address and phone number he panicked. He put his Lewis Carroll collection in vaulted, environmentally controlled storage, packed his bags and went to his country home in the hills west of Los Angeles to lay low. He imagined all sorts of people looking for him besides the police: his former wife, Mafia hit men, secret agents, and even aliens. He really believed it was probably the latter. Ever since his painful abduction experience three years ago he imagined these terrifyingly cruel little grey creatures behind practically every bush. Who knew? Perhaps they had even infiltrated the police departments. He wasn't about to let them find him again and perform any more excruciatingly painful experiments on his brain and sexual organs.

He was glad now that he had sold his sailboat. He would miss it, but knew that if someone tried hard enough they could probably trace him through it. When he arrived in L.A. he went straight to a Goodwill store and donated all of his nautical garb, including his collection of captain's hats. He didn't have any use for them any more without the boat, and he felt they made him look too conspicuous.

The house in the canyon was a mess since no one had lived in it in years. It would take him weeks to get it cleaned up to liveable standards. All of the stuffed furniture would have to be thrown out since mice had taken them over. And he would need a new bed and refrigerator. He decided to wait until tomorrow to go into town and buy new ones. He would spend the night in the RV he had driven. He was too exhausted to start cleaning, and went to bed early.

He awoke in the middle of the night to the sound of someone banging on the side door. He fumbled for the overhead light and checked the time. It was 2:30 a.m. The banging continued, but he was too terrified to see who it was or to find out what they wanted. The banging stopped momentarily, then he heard the terrible metallic sounds of the door being pried open with a crowbar. In a few moments the door flew open and a figure dressed entirely in black and wearing a ski mask entered the van carrying a spade.

The Snark said nothing and went straight to Clapham, who was sitting upright in bed, frozen in terror, like Scrooge awaiting the arrival of the next ghost. It took his attacker three hard blows to the head to kill him with the shovel, and by the time the attack was over the bed was awash with blood, which was also splattered across the walls and ceiling. Once back in L.A., the Snark stopped off at a pay phone and placed a call to LAPD, telling them where to find the body.

Pinkman first heard about the murder while watching the evening news. He called Jinks and they met at the station.

They began making inquiries to get the details, requesting a copy of the case and autopsy reports. The police report arrived within a few minutes on the fax, and they studied it together. There was no indication that LAPD had yet related the murder to the two Fresno bombings. The cause of death was a fractured skull and loss of blood. The murder weapon, a WW II foxhole shovel, available in hundreds of Army surplus stores, had been dropped outside Clapham's RV in plain view. The murderer had honed the shovel's edge to paring knife sharpness.

"The Boots and the Broker were sharpening a spade," Pinkman told Jinks, quoting from *The Hunting of the Snark*.

"So much for our theory that Clapham was the bomber," Jinks replied.

"Yeah; bummer. Well, we had tentatively identified Schwartz as the Boots," Pinkman said. "The poem might imply that she's our most likely suspect, since the Boots was the one who helped sharpen the spade. Schwartz is a stockbroker, isn't she?"

Jinks pulled out his notes. "She's a broker, she's a broker, she's a broker!" Jinks declared.

"Very funny."

"One thing that bothers me though is that the killer didn't leave his signature metal strip with a Snarkian quote. "

"Perhaps the killer thought it would be obvious from the cause of death. After all, the murder weapon was left in plain view. The killer obviously wanted it to be found."

"Maybe." Pinkman heard the fax, and got up to see if it was for them. "Here's the autopsy report on Clapham. Here we go! There was a plate! The pathologist found it in Clapham's mouth when he opened it to examine his teeth to confirm his identity against dental records. Guess what's inscribed on it?"

"Oh, I'm sure it's your quote about sharpening a spade."

"Right on!" Pinkman was proud of himself, and grinned broadly.

Detective Cox came over to their desks, carrying a newspaper. "You guys seen today's paper?" he asked. He handed it to Pinkman; Jinks looked over his shoulder.

SECOND GRISLY "SNARK" MURDER
Victim Encounters a Boojum

Los Angeles (UPI) - Local area resident George Clapham was found brutally murdered at his vacation home in Canyon Muerta in west L.A. yesterday.

LAPD reports that the cause of death was multiple blows to the head. The murder weapon, a foxhole shovel, has been recovered.

The autopsy revealed that his assailant inserted an engraved metal plate in his victim's mouth, with a quote from an obscure nonsense poem, *The Hunting of the Snark*, by Lewis Carroll, author of *Alice's Adventures in Wonderland*. The FBI says that this quote links his murder to two unsolved bombings in Fresno earlier this year, one of which was fatal. According to Dr. Grant Kerr, President of the California Chapter of the American Lewis Carroll Society (ALCS), the poem, first published in 1876, is a surrealistic tale of a crew of nine men and a beaver who set sail to an uncharted island in search of mystical creatures called Snarks.

According to Dr. Kerr, there are several different varieties of Snark, including one called a Boojum, which is invariably fatal when encountered. "You simply vanish away" he said.

Dr. Kerr confirmed that George Clapham, along with the two Fresno bombing victims, Fred Poole and Alison Cooksley , was a member of the California Chapter of the ALCS, and that all three were *Snark* enthusiasts and collectors.

Boojum is the name of a grotesque desert plant found in the Sonoran Desert, apparently named by its discoverer after this particularly lethal species of Snark, which for some reason he thought it resembled.

They were still reading the newspaper when Zabrodski stormed in. "Let's talk," he said to Pinkman and Jinks. "You got a private office we can go to?"

"We can use one of the interrogation rooms," Pinkman said as he got up. They all went down the hall to the room. "What can we do for you?" Pinkman asked when they had seated themselves.

"You've heard about George Clapham, I suppose."

"Yes."

"The last time I was here you two had a screwball theory about the Fresno bombings. Frankly, I thought you were nuts. But there obviously was a link between them, though, as I recall, you had postulated that Clapham might be the bomber. He evidently wasn't. I'd like to see the chart you had drawn on the board the last time I was here."

"My notes are back at my desk. It'll just take me a moment to get them." Pinkman left to retrieve them, grinning all the way. When he got back he wrote it all out on the white board again, and this time Agent Zabrodski took notes.

"So, as I understand this, you two believe that the killer might be Blanche Schwartz?"

"It's possible," said Jinks.

"Who else might be the killer?"

"It could logically be anyone in the ALCS, not necessarily someone from their California Chapter. So far, we've been working on the obvious assumption that it's someone who has a specific interest in *The Hunting of the Snark*."

"Have you guys interviewed Schwartz?"

"We talked to her some months ago by phone. The conversation was normal. She didn't give us any reason to believe she might be a bomber. We thought at the time that it was more likely that she was a potential victim and were just cautioning her to be careful. You might want to talk to her yourself," Pinkman said. "The FBI interviewed her as well."

"I'll look into that."

"Anything else?" Pinkman asked.

"No. Just let me know if you find any more links or associations will you? You have my number, right?"

"We've got it," Pinkman assured him

Agent Zabrodski got up and stormed out.

"Well," Jinks said. "We don't seem to be regarded as quite so full of crap as the last time."

They went back to their desks, and Pinkman found that he had a message to phone Dr. Kerr. He placed the call and the doctor came to the phone.

"Dr. Kerr," Pinkman said. "You called?"

"Yes. I wonder if we might talk the next time you're in the Los Angeles area? It's nothing urgent. I'd just like to see where the case is going. It's having a rather negative impact on our Society."

"Of course. Actually, as it happens, my partner and I are driving down to L.A. this afternoon anyway."

"In that case, perhaps you might drop by my home later this evening, about 7:00?"

"That will be fine."

"I'll see you then. I may not be punctual, since the traffic is hard to predict. You have the address, I believe. "

"That's not a problem. Yes, we have your address. Thank you. Good-bye."

Pinkman hung up. "Dr. Kerr wants to talk to me this evening at 7:00 at his home. I told him we were going down to L.A. this afternoon."

"We are?"

"I just told him that; I've been wanting to interview him anyway, and this is a good excuse. You want to join me? Could be interesting."

"Of course."

"If we leave now we can get there by 6:00, and we can grab a bite to eat somewhere."

Fit IV
Special Collections

Fit the Fourth

Special Collections

Barbara Wilson had married Grant Kerr immediately after he graduated from Harvard Medical and Dental Schools. He had then accepted an internship and residency in paediatric oral surgery at John Hopkins, and three years later they had moved to Los Angeles where Grant joined a paediatrics practice. He had become wealthy beyond reason.

It was, no doubt, in large part his love for children that had also led him to an equally strong love for children's literature. He had collected a number of children's authors for years before finally discovering Lewis Carroll. He had sold all of his earlier collections to Justin Thriller in New York, for a substantial profit, and used the money to begin building what was to become one of the world's greatest private Lewis Carroll collections.

Babs, as all of her friends called her, didn't share Grant's love of either *Alice* or Lewis Carroll, but tolerated it simply because the books and society acquaintances seemed to make him so happy. In the beginning, at least, if they made Grant happy they made her happy. However, images of the Rev.

Charles Dodgson photographing little nude girls were too much for her more modern, though otherwise liberal, sensibilities. She was amazed that the world was so willing to overlook his behaviour simply because he had written the *Alice* books.

Things had gradually turned for the worst with the founding of the California Chapter of the American Lewis Carroll Society. Naturally enough, Grant had been a founding member, and he had held every one of the society's offices, except Treasurer, at least once. The society often met in their palatial Brentwood mansion, But just because one had the facilities to entertain forty guests, didn't mean that one had to enjoy the meetings, which she usually found excruciatingly boring. Silly papers about whether or not Queen Victoria or Mark Twain was the true author of *Alice in Wonderland*, or elaborate analyses of the printing variations of the tails of mice, were more than she could stand, and she usually left shortly after the meetings got started.

Over the years Grant had become so obsessed with Carroll that he had developed full-blown bibliomania. It was not an uncommon neurosis in California, where people seemed to have the necessary money to invest in all sorts of expensive things, from antique automobiles to the old clothing of movie stars. Most people could hardly afford $15,000 for an Appleton *Alice* or $30,000 for an original Dodgson photographic print of a young girl dressed up like Little Red Riding Hood; but Grant could, and often did. The halls of their mansion had fifteen framed Dodgson photographs, all fitted with little dark green velvet curtains, which served to block the harmful rays of light, which would tend to fade the antique prints. She felt it was absurd to live with so many pictures that you couldn't even see unless you pulled back a curtain. Somehow it always reminded her of Dodgson hiding behind the dark curtain of his tripod mounted camera, peering through the lens at upside-down little nude girls.

Babs also gradually began to resent the enormous amount of money he spent on his omnivorous collecting, but even more the time he spent with his books, and meeting the Society's endless demands. She felt like she had gradually lost her husband to some ghostly and beautiful virtual Victorian mistress.

Pinkman and Jinks arrived promptly at 7:00 at the Kerr's Brentwood mansion. Babs had been expecting them and met them at the door. "Good evening, gentlemen. I assume that you're from the Fresno Police Department?"

"Yes. My name is Detective Pinkman; this is my partner Detective Jinks." Jinks nodded at her.

"I'm Barbara Wilson-Kerr. Please, come in," she said, opening the door wide and stepping back to let them in.

They stepped into a spacious foyer that seemed cold enough to keep meat from spoiling. Pinkman's first thought was to wonder how anyone could possibly afford the electricity bill; he was glad that he had on a sports jacket. The foyer was graced by an elegantly abstract Brancusi bronze bust, perched atop a polished black marble pedestal on one wall and an Andy Warhol portrait of Marilyn Monroe opposite. Marilyn was flanked by two small-framed pictures, which were covered by dark green curtains. Pinkman wanted to go over and peek to see what they were hiding, but resisted the impulse.

"I'm afraid that Grant is delayed. He phoned a few minutes ago and said that he was on his way, but would be about fifteen minutes late. That's typical for doctors, you know; there's always some crisis or other."

"That's not a problem," Pinkman assured her.

"Good. Please come and sit down." She led the way into a huge living room with no fewer than five sectional sofas arranged around several coffee tables. Huge potted plants decorated the room, and large abstract paintings adorned the walls. "Would either you care for a glass of wine or a cup of coffee while you wait?"

"No thank you." Pinkman said, afraid that he might spill it on the white carpet. Jinks also declined. They all sat down, opposite each other.

"I assume that you're here to talk with Grant about these terrible murders," Barbara said, trying to make conversation.

"Yes. We're hopeful that your husband will be able to help us in our investigation. "

"I don't see how he possibly could."

"Oh, he's been very helpful already," Pinkman assured her. "As you probably know from all of the press, the murders and bombings are connected to Lewis Carroll."

"It's just terrible!" she said. "Some crazy person out these killing these harmless people just because they happen to like *Alice in Wonderland.*"

"Actually, the connection seems to be with *The Hunting of the Snark*, not *Alice*," Pinkman responded.

"Whatever. Do you have any suspects?"

"Well, I suppose everyone in the American Lewis Carroll Society could be considered a suspect."

"Even Grant?" she asked, her face expressing shocked disbelief at such a possibility.

"We're not actively investigating your husband. Actually, he called us, and wanted to talk."

"Well, I can assure you that Grant is not a serial killer!"

"Of course not. We have no reason to think that your husband is a serial killer," Pinkman assured her. "Quite the contrary, he's been very helpful and cooperative. I was just talking in generalities."

She smiled weakly.

"Oh! Here's Grant now," she exclaimed, as Grant Kerr walked into the room. "I'm terribly sorry to be late. It was unavoidable, I'm afraid. A teenage boy wasn't wearing his seatbelt and tried to remove the windshield with his front teeth."

Pinkman and Jinks stood up. "It's no problem at all," Pinkman assured him. "We've enjoyed a nice conversation with your wife."

"Please, be seated," Dr. Kerr said, gesturing at the couch they had just gotten up from.

"You'll please excuse me," Babs said. "I'm late for my karate class. It's been nice talking with you, gentlemen." She smiled and left the room.

"Your wife takes karate?" Jinks asked, surprised that a middle-aged woman would be doing that.

"She's a bit of an orientalist and very athletic. She also practices yoga and Thai Chi, and does Japanese flower arranging and brush painting. She's quite talented; very clever with her hands."

Pinkman tried to imagine her shattering cinder blocks with her bare hands, but couldn't. "What did you want to talk to us about?" he asked, changing the subject. "As you can imagine," Dr. Kerr replied, "these terrible bombings and murders have had a very negative impact on our California Chapter of the American Lewis Carroll Society."

"I'm sure they don't help," Pinkman agreed.

"To put it mildly! Over half of our members have quit out of fear that they might be one of the killer's next targets. Most collectors have put their *Snarks* up for auction on e-Bay or have offered them to antiquarian booksellers; they're available for a song. Our next meeting is at UCLA and the university has had to beef up security because of us."

"That would seem to be prudent, under the circumstances," Pinkman said. "I imagine that their insurers probably put up a fuss about it."

"Exactly. I suppose I can't blame them."

"What did you want to talk to us about?" Pinkman asked.

"How close are you to catching this maniac?" he asked.

"All we have at the moment is a rather obtuse theory."

"Which is?"

"I'm afraid I can't discuss that. It might jeopardize our investigation."

"Of course; I understand. I shouldn't have even asked. It's just that if the police don't catch this person soon the California Chapter will dissolve out of fear. That would be a great tragedy. It's taken many years and a great deal of work to get it established."

"Yes, sir. I'm sure that it has. I can assure you that we are doing everything we know to do; and it's not just the Fresno Police. LAPD has a task force, as does the FBI and ATF. Some of the best investigative minds in the country are involved. I'm sure it's just a matter of time until the perpetrator is caught."

"Is there anything I can do to speed up that process?" Kerr asked.

"I can't think of anything right now."

"I was wondering if there might be some way to set a trap for the killer," Kerr said.

"Like what?" Jinks asked.

"Oh, I don't know; perhaps at a chapter meeting, or something."

"I don't think that would be too good of an idea. It would put those in attendance at great risk. But we'll keep that in mind, if something makes sense. Thank you for offering. "

"Not at all. I desperately want you to apprehend this guy!"

"Are you also dumping your own *Snark* collection?" Jinks asked.

"Oh, no! I'd never do that! You'd have to pry them out of my cold, dead fingers," he said as a joke, then laughed. "Quite the contrary, actually; I've been buying most of the copies that are coming onto the market. It's a once in a lifetime opportunity."

"How many editions have you got now?" Pinkman asked.

"I'm not sure; something over six hundred."

"Can we see them?" Jinks asked.

"Of course! I'm always happy to show my collection. It's back this way." He got up, and Pinkman and Jinks followed.

"I'll have to turn off the alarm and fire protection systems. It'll just take a moment." He left, retreating into a hallway, and then returning shortly.

"The library has a rather sophisticated burglar alarm system, and a Halon fire suppression system. In the event of a fire the room is automatically flooded with an inert gas to smother combustion by depleting the oxygen."

"Wouldn't that kill you if you were in the library?"

"Of course. You only have about ten or fifteen seconds to get out of the room when a fire alarm sounds."

"That seems a bit risky," Jinks said.

"It's a necessary precaution. The books are not only valuable, but many items are unique and irreplaceable. It would be completely unacceptable to have them go up in smoke."

"What if the fire just comes through the walls from somewhere outside the room?"

"The library has eight-hour fire walls," Dr. Kerr replied. "That's not too likely."

They went inside. The room was window-less, perhaps twenty-five foot square. The air was cool and dry. Lighting was indirect and subdued. Three walls were covered, floor to ceiling, with bookcases, all completely full. Rows of lower bookcases filled the middle of the room, like those in a public library. There was a desk, with a PC and a lamp, and several adjacent filing cabinets. A large glass case, that reminded Pinkman of the trophy case outside a university gymnasium, covered the fourth wall; it was filled with figurines, dolls, and a wild assortment of *Alice* ephemera: wristwatches, jewellery, dishes, glasses, etc. Stacks of books sat on most of the available floor space between the bookcases.

"I'm going to have to expand the room. As you can see, I'm running out of space."

"This must be the largest Lewis Carroll collection in the world," Pinkman said.

"I doubt it, but without doubt it's one of the largest," Kerr said. "Most of the *Snarks* are over this way," he said, stepping over and around stacks of books. Pinkman and Jinks followed.

The collection was impressive. "We've seen the *Snark* collections owned by Poole and Cleaver. They were quite small compared to this," Pinkman said. "Aren't you afraid that this collection makes you a prime target for the killer?"

"Oh, I'm sure he wouldn't want to kill me. Why would he want to? I'm nice to everyone."

"As far as I know, Poole and Schwartz were nice to everyone, too. I don't think that absolves you of the risk."

"Did you ever see Clapham's collection?" Kerr asked.

"No one's been able to locate it. He must have it hidden away somewhere; perhaps under another name. He was very secretive. Who knows? It may never surface."

"That would be a pity!" said Kerr. "A very big pity! I'd like very much to acquire it from his estate."

"Well, thank you for showing us your collection. It's quite impressive," Pinkman said. "Unless you have something else, I think we'll be driving on back to Fresno."

"No, no; I don't have anything else in mind."

As they were leaving Jinks bent over and looked at one of the stacks of books on the floor. They were all various editions of *The Hunting of the Snark*.

They said good night and left.

"That was very strange," Pinkman said.

"One thing's for sure; the guy sure has lots of money!"

"That's an understatement. His book collection must be worth millions."

"I wouldn't be surprised. But that pales in comparison to his house."

"I'd guess at least fifteen million."

"It seems to me that we have to start thinking of Dr. Kerr as a suspect," Pinkman said.

"Yeah, I agree. He has the money to do anything he wants. Did you notice that those stacks of books on the floor were all editions of the *Snark?*"

"No, but I'm not surprised. This whole situation makes it very easy to acquire them cheaply and in huge numbers."

"Are you thinking that he might be perpetrating the murders as a way of acquiring the books?"

"It's a possibility."

"A bit extreme, but the same thought occurred to me."

"Yeah, and besides, the guy's a bibliomaniac. Who knows what he's capable of doing in order to get his hands on more books?"

"What'd you think of his wife, Barbara?"

"I wouldn't want to meet her in a dark alley!" They both laughed.

The next morning Cox came by their desks with the morning newspaper. "You guys see this?" he asked, tossing it to Pinkman.

"You seem to have taken on a newspaper route," Jinks told him. "The Department not paying you enough?"

"Just trying to be helpful," Cox said, grinning. Pinkman looked at page three:

SERIAL KILLER STILL AT LARGE

FBI Contacting Carrollians in Hunt for "Boojum" Snark

Washington, DC (UPI) - An FBI spokesman confirmed today that FBI and ATF agents have begun interviewing all present and past members of the American Lewis Carroll Society (ALCS) in a desperate nationwide hunt for the serial killer, dubbed by the press as the "Boojum" Snark. Members of the literary society are outraged that they have come under suspicion. Parents of school children who are members are particularly upset, protesting that the interviews are upsetting their children, whose grades have begun to suffer.

Well over half of the current ALCS members have panicked and cancelled their memberships.

Fred Poole, the killer's first victim, is still recovering from his wounds that cost him an eye and a finger. "I've sold my collection," Mr. Poole told UPI yesterday. "I'm not willing to die over some silly children's books."

Mr. Poole evidently isn't alone. E-Bay on-line auction has hundreds of editions of *The Hunting of the Snark* listed, as collectors dump their holdings of Lewis Carroll's nonsense poem out of fear of becoming the "Boojum" Snark's next victim.

Rob Duckworth, current President of the ALCS, spoke to UPI by phone from his home in Maryland. "The Society wishes to offer its condolences to the families of the victims. We hope and pray that this dastardly killer is caught and brought to justice with all speed." He denies rumours that the ALCS plans to disband. "Our next quarterly meeting at the Harry Ransom Humanities Research Center (HRHRC) at the University of Texas at Austin (UTA) will go ahead as planned, and we hope that everyone will attend."

UTA Police spokesman Jim Baca confirmed to UPI that extraordinary security precautions would be in place for the upcoming Austin meeting. "We plan to shoot Snarks on sight," he joked. "Anyone entering the building the day of the meeting will have to pass through a metal detector and we will have a bomb sniffing dog on hand."

Two of the serial killer's victims, Alison Cooksley of Fresno and George Clapham of Los Angeles, died in separate attacks earlier this year.

"Dr. Kerr's worst fears," Pinkman said.

"Or fondest hopes," Jinks said; "could go either way."

Babs was literally hot blooded, her body temperature normally hovering a few degrees above normal. Anyone else would have thought they were suffering from a fever.

Because of this physiological oddity she was invariably uncomfortable with the room temperature. She set the thermostat for the house low enough to be just bearable, though most people found it much too cold. She also found it impossible to sleep unless the room temperature was somewhere below fifty degrees; even then, she often slept nude or with only a sheet as a cover. They had installed an industrial five-ton air conditioning unit just for her large four-room bedroom suite, and she ran it hard. She even took cold showers. Grant didn't normally go into her frigid suite, and on the rare occasion when he did he usually pulled on a sweater. He sometimes felt that she ran it so cold just to drive him away.

One of the reasons he had married her was that he loved her hot skin; it made sex all the more exciting when it was easy to imagine that she had warmed to his touch, even though that had almost nothing to do with it. However, in spite of her Latin body temperature, her libido had cooled and since it was close to Valentine's Day he had decided to try to put some spark back into their love life. He had bought her an expensive piece of antique Japanese calligraphy, but had also been shopping the Internet for very sexy lingerie that he would like to see her in, though he realized that it was problematic as to whether or not he could get her to wear it. He was hoping that the calligraphy would warm her to the idea. All he needed was to confirm her bra size.

Babs was out for the afternoon, so he pulled on a sweater and went into her suite. It was so cold in her bedroom that he was amazed that he couldn't see his breath. He went into one of her walk-in closets, which felt like cold storage, and started opening drawers until he found one with bras in it. As he was fumbling around with the bras he noticed the comer of a manila envelope beneath them, and out of curiosity took it out to see what was in it.

He opened the envelope and pulled out a large book, which he immediately recognized as a copy of the Catalpa Press edition of *The Hunting of the Snark*. "What's this!" he exclaimed in his mind. "What an amazing thing to find in her lingerie drawer! Oh, I get it. She's been buying Valentine presents too! She probably doesn't know that I already have at least thirty copies of this one. Still, it's a very sweet thought!" He smiled and slipped it back inside the envelope without looking at the very familiar book and put it back where he had found it. He checked the tag on a few bras, then closed the drawer and left her suite.

Fit V
The Snark Club

Fit the Fifth

The Snark Club

Babs opened the lingerie drawer where she kept the Catalapa Press edition of *The Hunting of the Snark.* Something immediately didn't look quite right to her; she had the impression that someone had been rummaging through the drawer. She looked closely, but finally decided that it had probably just been her maid, Maria, and put it out of her mind.

She took the book out of its manila envelope and laid it on the thick carpet. She pulled out its crazy first chapter, which stretched the length of the closet. She had scrawled the surnames of ten members of the California Chapter across the faces in the illustration with a red Magic Marker: Clapham on the Bellman; Schwartz on the Boots; Barnett on the Maker of Bonnets and Hoods; Jurist on the Barrister; Imhoff on the Broker; Poole on the Billiard-marker; Constantinescu on the Banker; Castor on the Beaver; Cooksley on the Baker; and, Cleaver on the Butcher. In addition, the faces of both the Billiard-marker and the Baker had bold black X's across their faces. She didn't have anything personal against any of them;

she had simply selected them because of their names or occupations.

She got down on her knees and slashed a large X across the face of the Bellman with a ballpoint pen, wielding it like a dagger and puncturing the thick paper in the process. "You should have followed the Baker's advice and procured your own second-hand dagger-proof coat!" she said, as if the little man in the illustration could hear her. She stood up and studied the long nonsensical boat for a few minutes, trying to decide how to kill the next crewman. She folded the chapter back up, then returned the book to its hiding place beneath the stack of expensive bras, many decorated with lace so delicate that the Beaver could have made it.

Julia Castor was a great Carroll enthusiast, though she much preferred *Alice* to *Snarks*. Nonetheless, she was one of the founding members of the secretive Snark Club, and hadn't missed one of its annual meetings in thirty years. The exclusive club always met in a private dining room at the Hotel del Coronado in San Diego for a seafood dinner.

It was a pleasant drive from L. A. to San Diego, where the weather was invariably nicer; and there was typically less smog, though she could remember twice when it had been just as bad as L. A. The dinner was always at 8:00 p.m., but she went early and checked into the hotel by 4:00, just ahead of the heaviest rush-hour traffic. That gave her plenty of time for a nice walk around the bougainvillea bedecked hotel grounds, and a cocktail before dinner.

She timed herself to arrive at the meeting exactly at 8:00 and found the other seven remaining members of the club already there. She went round and greeted them all. Their mood was subdued, even a bit sombre, in light of recent events that had cost the lives of two of their long-time crew, Alison Cooksley and George Clapham.

The Bellman, a title held by Roger Bellamy ever since the founding of the club, rang an antique hand bell that had once been used aboard ship by the captain of a four-masted schooner. He always started the meeting this way. The crewmembers took their places at the sound, sitting wherever they liked. Membership in the Snark Club was strictly limited to ten members, and in the event one of them died or resigned, the remaining crew would elect a replacement, who would be contacted, sworn to secrecy and invited to join. No one had ever declined his or her invitation. Each member was assigned the name of one of the crew, which he or she retained for life or until they resigned, though no one had ever resigned. Julia held The Snark Club's position of Baker.

The table was set with three forks, but no spoon or knife, as befitted their Snarkian quest. As soon as they were seated the waiters came in with *Gambas at Ajillo* as their first course. The air was soon filled with the strong aroma of garlic. This was followed by a snapper *Bourride*, then *Kalamarakia Tiganita me Skothalia*. Now there really was a strong smell of garlic in the air! Next came *Cozze Arrosto*, with exceptionally large mussels, and finally *Latte alla Grotta*. A waiter brought in cognac and Kamal Biswas magically produced a box of $50 Cuban cigars that he had smuggled in from a recent trip to Montreal (where he had searched diligently for French *Alices*), and passed them around. Julia lit up with the rest of them. The cigar smoke finally overwhelmed the piercing smell of garlic.

The Bellman stood up to speak. He was dressed in his traditional costume that made him look very much like Henry Holiday's illustration of the character. He produced a prized miniature edition of *The Hunting of the Snark*, which had been custom bound in alligator in the 1920s, which he opened and read from:

"We should all of us grieve, as you well may believe,
If you never were met with again—
But surely, my man, when the voyage began,
You might have suggested it then?

"It's excessively awkward to mention it now—
As I think I've already remarked."
And the man they called "Hi!" replied, with a sigh,
"I informed you the day we embarked.

"You may charge me with murder—"

"I know that all of you share my great sadness at the tragic demise of our Butcher, Alison Cooksley, and our Beaver, George Clapham, taken from our midst by a cowardly murderer. We can only hope that the police will apprehend this monster quickly, and that none of us will become his next victim. He's as deadly as a Bandersnatch, and each of you must take special precautions for your own safety!"

The crew murmured.

"Since the first victim of the bomber wasn't one of our crew I assume that this psychopath hasn't somehow singled us out. However, the very fact that Alison and George were victims and that we are associated with the *Snark*, necessarily puts us all at high risk. You were all as courageous as the Baker in attending tonight. I'm just thankful that we have judiciously elected to keep our club's very existence a secret; that's probably our best protection. Even a second-hand dagger-proof coat is no match for a bomb!"

Dr. Kamal Biswas, the Club's Banker, interrupted the Bellman to say, "I can offer two excellent Policies, one Against Fire and one Against Damage from Hail."

Everyone laughed softly with relief at his small joke. Things were getting too grim and serious; these meetings were supposed to be fun.

"So, the first order of business is to nominate a replacement Butcher and a Beaver," the Bellman continued with his speech, looking grand, as always.

Julia stood up. "Captain, I nominate Wanda Kerley to be the Beaver. It would certainly be nice to keep another female on board, if at all possible. I'm not at all sure how safe a lone woman might be on a deserted isle with the likes of this crew."

Everyone giggled. Julius Imhoff, the Broker, stood up and said, "I'd like to remind you that Mr. Dodgson had the good sense to keep women off of the ship." He grinned. "We just made an exception for you and Alison, because you're such good cooks, and we get tired of eating nothing but bridecake."

Julia smiled back at him, then continued, "Wanda Kerley is a great Carrollian and Snarkist. And you're right; she makes excellent cheesecake." Having said this she started to sit down, but stood right back up. "Did I tell you that she makes excellent cheesecake?" She then sat down, only to pop up again. "Some of you might like to keep in mind when you're casting your ballots that Wanda makes excellent cheesecake!"

The Broker stood back up and said, "In spite of the fact that it's been established beyond any doubt that Wanda Kerley makes excellent cheesecake, I'd like to nominate Dr. Grant Kerr as the Beaver. This makes perfect sense, since he's a Canadian immigrant. As is well known, the beaver is his native country's national symbol and no one has ever been as busy as he has. Why, he's held every office in the California Chapter of the Society except one, some of them twice and one even thrice. He can recite *The Hunting of the Sn*ark from memory and even knows the first stanza backwards, something that I certainly can't do. He has also composed dozens of very funny limericks that involve Snarks. He has a pet Boojum Tree in his sunroom. I'm happy to report that he eats with a fork and frequently uses soap. His only drawbacks are that he's quite bald and not very furry, like a beaver should be; his tail is quite flat, however."

Everyone clapped and laughed, and the Captain tingled his bell. "Speaking of limericks," he said:

"A Butcher once took up his cleaver,
And decided to murder the Beaver,
The Beaver took flight,
And was soon out of sight,
So the Butcher wasn't able to eat her."

The crewmen laughed and the Bellman took a little bow. The Banker stood up. "Have you heard this one?" he asked:

"There once was a troublesome Snark,
Who frightened the crew as a lark;
It hid in a chasm,
Screamed like a phantasm,
Till the crew sailed away in their barque."

"Are there any other limericks or nominations?" asked the Bellman. The Broker stood up. "I can offer this one," he said.

"The Broker packed his pipe for a smoke,
But he found that his lighter was broke.
  He cried in despair;
  His grief rent the air,
Till a Snark lit him up with a stroke."

The Banker stood back up. Everyone was expecting another limerick, but instead he said, "I'd like to nominate Marcus Bernstein to be the Butcher. He may not have a pet Boojum Tree, but he does know everything that's printable about Henry Holiday, and he's presently writing a very boring biography of him. He has a beautifully framed map that is a perfect and absolute blank hung in the kitchen over his breakfast table. He has a collection of fossilized teeth, which he swears proves the existence of the Bandersnatch. Like any self-respecting butcher, he's a carnivore. In short, he'd be a perfect Butcher."

Again there was a round of applause and laughter

"Are there any further nominations?" the Bellman asked. He waited a moment, but none were forthcoming.

"Very well. Since there is only one nomination for the Butcher, we shall invite Marcus Bernstein to join us in that role. For the position of Beaver, we will cast secret ballots." Before passing out small strips of paper and pencils for the crew to mark their choice, he recited:

"The method employed I would gladly explain,
  While I have it so clear in my head,
If I had but the time and you had but the brain—
  But much yet remains to be said."

Everyone laughed. "Please mark your ballots and pass them up to me. We would normally have the Beaver and Butcher tally the votes and check the sums, but they are, after all, sadly departed, and in fact the very reason for this election." He tingled his bell three times in their memory.

The crewmen voted, and passed their ballots to the Captain. "There are five votes for Dr. Kerr and only two for Wanda Kerley," he announced after he had counted them. "Obviously not all of you are fond of cheesecake! Since there was not a tie I will not cast a vote. We will invite Marcus Bernstein to join us. In the unlikely event that he declines we will invite Wanda Kerley." He tingled his bell three times. "What I tell you three times is true," he said, and repeated the results of the vote two more times to make it official, as required by the Club's bylaws.

Having finished the business portion of the meeting, which they tried to limit severely as a matter of principle, it was time for reading the poem. This privilege passed from crewmember to crewmember on a simple rotation basis. It was to have been the Beaver's turn, but since no one present knew how to channel her this passed automatically to the Broker. He stood up and read the poem from beginning to end with great emotion. When he had finished they applauded, and had another cognac.

A keepsake was produced for each meeting, strictly limited to an edition of ten copies. This keepsake was typically a printing of a quote from or a specially commissioned illustration for *The Snark.* The only legal way to obtain any of these keepsakes was to be a member of the club or to inherit them from a member, since the crewmen were sworn to never place them on sale unless the club was disbanded, which no one could envision ever happening. Responsibility for producing the keepsake was also rotated through the crew, and each member strove to produce something of lasting beauty.

The keepsake for the evening was the Baker's responsibility, and Julia Castor stood up to make the presentation to the crew. She had brought only seven copies, having left her own at home and destroyed the copies that would have been given to the Butcher and Beaver. She passed them round like the Bellman serving out grog. The keepsake was a small cardboard mechanical device, printed in full colour and manufactured by hand by a craftsman in Venice. It showed the Baker perched on top of a crag, wildly waving his arms. A message in a small, framed window at the bottom said, "'It's a Snark!" When the scene was rotated by means of a wheel, the Baker rotated with it and softly and silently vanished, while the message in the framed window at the bottom simultaneously changed to, "It's a Boo—"

Everyone seemed to be thrilled with the keepsake, and they gave Julia a round of applause. She beamed in their approval. It was late and the crewmen said their good-byes and most retired to their rooms. A few went down to the bar for more grog.

Julia entered her room and took off her shoes, which were killing her. She was sure that she smelled like cigars and decided to take a shower and wash her hair before going to bed. As she was searching through her suitcase for a nightgown she failed to see a figure dressed entirely in black slip out from behind the curtains and approach her from behind. The killer stabbed her viciously in her left kidney and the pain was so severe that she could not even cry out. She crumpled to the floor. Her assailant calmly left the room, dropping the knife in plain view. Julia managed to crawl to the bedside phone and call the front desk, but bled to death before Security arrived.

Fit VI
Valentine's Day

FIT THE SIXTH

Valentine's Day

News of Julia Castor's murder screamed across the nation's headlines like the voice of a Jubjub. Pinkman first heard the shrill news on CNN when he got out of bed to go to work. He picked up a copy of the Fresno newspaper and a cup of coffee at a GO Mart on the way to the Station. He read the front-page article as he sat behind his car in the parking lot, drinking his java.

> **"BOOJUM SNARK" STRIKES AGAIN AT DEL CORONADO**
>
> **Woman Stabbed in the Back after Attending Secret "Snark Club" Meeting**
>
> San Diego (UPI) - SDPD report the murder of Los Angeles attorney Julia Castor. She was discovered dead in her hotel room late last night by hotel security at the historic Hotel del Coronado, in the same room once used by Tony Curtis during the filming of *Some Like it Hot.*
>
> She had been stabbed in the back on returning to her room after attending a meeting of the secretive 'Snark Club', of which she was a long-time member.

SDPD homicide detectives and FBI agents are continuing to interview the remaining seven members of the club who were in attendance. All are citizens of Los Angeles and members of the American Lewis Carroll Society (ALCS).

The FBI has confirmed that the killer left a message, which is a quote from Lewis Carroll's now-infamous nonsense poem, *The Hunting of the Snark*. This links the Castor murder to three other attacks earlier this year, two of which were also fatal.

Fresno resident Fred Poole narrowly survived a letter bomb, while Alison Cooksley, also of Fresno, died in her shower from a bomb hidden in a free sample bottle of shampoo. George Clapham of Los Angeles was murdered with a shovel.

UPI contacted Dr. Grant Kerr, President of the California Chapter of the ALCS, to find out more about The Snark Club. "I've heard rumours of The Snark Club's existence for many years, but I'd never seen any real proof. Until last night's murder I had no idea what they did, or when or where they met." When asked why the club would be secret he said, "I can't imagine."

All of the club's members are also members of the California Chapter of the ALCS. The Snark Club's President, Roger Bellamy, held a press conference this morning to vigorously deny rumours of orgies and Satanic worship at the Snark Club's past meetings.

Other members of the once-secret Snark Club are: K. Biswas, J. Imhoff, J. Moldenhauer, R. Loder, D. Hink, and P. Gent.

LAPD, SDPD, ATF, and FBI all seemed to be completely 'snarked" by the case, and are appealing to the public to come forward if they have any information that might help lead to the arrest of the killer.

The Justice Department has offered a $1 million reward for information leading to the killer's arrest and conviction.

Pinkman finished his coffee and drove to work. His partner was already there, reading the newspaper that Detective Cox had given him. “You see this?” Jinks asked Pinkman, holding up the newspaper.

“Yes. I picked up a copy from a newsstand. Have you requested a copy of the San Diego case report?”

“Yes. I'm expecting it over the fax any minute.”

Pinkman glanced at his desk and noticed that someone had placed a thimble on it. “Did you get a thimble, too?” he asked Jinks.

“No, they left me a bar of soap.” He held it up. It was from The Holiday Inn.

Just then they heard the fax and Jinks retrieved the report. He read the highlights aloud. “She bled to death from a stab wound to the left kidney. The murder weapon, a fish filleting knife with a thin blade, was dropped at the scene and recovered. There were no fingerprints. The engraved message on a strip of stainless steel reads: ‘A second-hand dagger-proof coat.’”

“Big surprise!” Pinkman said, interrupting him.

“The silly Snark Club appears to be innocent. Ten people meet once a year for seafood, cognac and illegal Cuban cigars, then read the poem to each other. Each member is named after a crewmember in the poem. Julia Castor was the Baker.”

“These people are nuts!”

“I suppose they must just like each other and use it as an excuse to get together. I can't see that it's any worse than a ball game and pizza afterwards.”

“No, I suppose not. But when people go to a ball game they don't usually end up knifing each other.”

“Not usually; but it happens. Anyway, there's nothing here to indicate the killer was a member of the Club. However, half of their alibis can't be verified, since they said they simply went to bed. They were all staying at the hotel for the evening, since they tend to drink heavily at their meetings. There's a list in the case report of names of all of the members and their honorary Club titles. I did a comparison with our own list and there are significant differences. Here take a look." Jinks handed Pinkman a sheet of paper. "I put an 'X' by the victims. Poole is the only one not on both lists. I also listed Dr. Kerr, since we agreed that he is a suspect."

Crewman	*Suspect List*	*Snark Club*
Baker	Cooksley ×	Castor ×
Boots	Schwartz	Moldenhauer
Bonnets	Barnett	Loder
Beaver	Castor ×	Clapham ×
Broker	Imhoff	Imhoff
Billiard	Poole ×	Hink
Bellman	Clapham ×	Bellamy
Banker	Trocan	Biswas
Barrister	Jurist	Gant
Butcher	Cleaver	Cooksley ×
	Kerr	

"I suppose there's no reason why the lists should be identical. Perhaps all this tells us is that the killer might not be a member of The Snark Club. If he was just killing off members of the Club then why would Poole have been his first victim?"

"Makes sense. Okay, if that's true then we can probably take Imhoff off our list of suspects. He's the only one on both lists."

"I forgot to tell you. Zabrodski's coming in to see us again."

He had no sooner said this than Zabrodski walked in. "Can I talk with you two somewhere in private?

"Sure," Pinkman said, and got up to lead the way to an empty interrogation room.

"I assume that you've seen the list of members of The Snark Club?" Zabrodski asked.

Pinkman and Jinks nodded.

"You know anything about them that we should know?"

"I can't think of anything. I assume you and the FBI are doing background checks on all of them."

"Yeah, that in progress. It will be a few weeks before they're complete."

"I'd suggest that you put Schwartz, Barnett, Imhoff, Trocan, Jurist, Cleaver, and Kerr under surveillance or provide protection," Pinkman said. "In our opinion one of them is highly likely to be the next victim."

"You have any basis for that?"

"Just our old list, which you"ve seen. So far all four victims were on the list. I'd bet serious money that the next one will be too."

"Let me know if you find out anything which might indicate which one is most likely, will you?" He had begun to daydream about the huge reward for finding the killer and how he would spend it; and it wouldn't be on old books, either.

"Will do," Pinkman assured him, though he didn't really mean it. He didn't want to share a million-dollar reward with anyone other than Jinks.

Agent Zabrodski left.

"Who do you think the next victim will be? You got any hunches?" Pinkman asked Jinks.

"I'd guess Schwartz, just because the Boots is the second crewman mentioned in the poem. He's already killed the first one."

"That's as good as any, I suppose. It's too bad we don't have the resources to put round-the-clock surveillance on her."

"Yeah, it might save her life."

*   *   *   *
*   *   *
*   *   *   *

Babs was seated on one of the couches in the living room, reading Lynne Truss's *Tennyson's Gift*. Every few minutes she would laugh hysterically. "This is the funniest book I've ever read!" she told Grant as he walked in carrying two packages, one very large one, and the other large enough for a sweater.

"You just like it because it's so hard on Dodgson," Grant said. "I didn't find it nearly so amusing."

"You wouldn't. That's because you idolize him," she said. "He's like a god to you."

"He's not a god to me," Grant objected. "Just because I like and collect his books doesn't mean that I worship him."

"Of course you do. You built that enormous shrine to him in there," she said, pointing to the library, "and you've filled it with his holy scriptures. You have more of his *Wonderland Bibles* in there than the Gideons have the real thing in hotel rooms. Every day you go in there and sacrifice your time and money, like a priest."

"That's a bit harsh!"

"Harsh? You even helped found the California mission for the mother church, the American Lewis Carroll Society! You've made hundreds of converts."

He decided to try to change the subject. "It's Valentine's Day," he said, giving her as warm a smile as he could after her abuse.

"I know."

"I have some presents."

"Why? Do you want me to be your little valentine, Grant?"

"Well, yes, I guess you could put it that way. After all, we are married." He moved the large, heavy package over to her with some effort. It was wrapped in a bright red foil and tied with a white ribbon. He propped up the package while she unwrapped it.

"It's gorgeous!" she said, with sincerity. He smiled broadly. He knew she would like it.

"Who is the calligrapher?" she asked.

"Hiro Yoshizawa."

"When was it done?"

"Sometime in the seventeenth century. The date's a little uncertain."

"Do you know the translation?"

"Not accurately. It's very stylized and difficult to decipher. They told me that the only words that are recognizable with certainty are 'plum', 'lips' and 'moon'. I guess you'll have to make up your own poem that includes those words."

"Thank you, Grant. It's very beautiful."

"You're welcome," he said, then sat there looking at her as if he expected her to give him something.

"What is it grant?"

"Well, I was sort of hoping that you might have a little something for me," he said, expecting her to produce the book he had discovered in her lingerie drawer.

"Why would you think that?" she said. "Frankly, I wasn't expecting anything from you, and I didn't get anything for you. Sorry, Grant. I didn't think you knew I existed."

Grant gave her a puzzled, hurt look.

It suddenly clicked in Babs' mind that it had been Grant messing around in her lingerie. "He's found the *Snark* and thinks it's a present for him!" she thought. "I wonder if he's looked at it!" She decided to change the subject.

"What's in the other package, Grant?"

He hesitated, then handed it to her without saying anything.

She opened it and pulled out a very scanty two-piece pink leather and chains outfit. "You've got to be kidding!" she said.

"Why?" He was very disappointed by the tone of her voice. "You would be beautiful in it."

"There's no way I'm putting that thing on!" she said with finality and tossed it and the box in his lap. She got up and stomped towards the hallway, leaving Grant sitting on the couch with his mouth open and propping up the calligraphy. The lingerie fell on the carpet. "Find yourself a whore if you like that sort of thing!" she snarled at him as she went through the door towards her frigid suite. She locked the door and went straight to the closet to retrieve the book. She wasn't sure if he had looked at the first chapter or not, and there was no way to know. She put on latex gloves and tore out the first chapter, then stuffed it into a large handbag. She got in her Alpha Romeo and drove to a seedy part of town, then up and down a few alleys until she found an appropriate dumpster. She drove up next to it and tossed the handbag with the Snark chapter into it, then drove away.

She hadn't noticed Nizar Gulam, watching her from behind another dumpster. Nizar was always interested in anything anyone threw away, since this was basically how he made a living, such as it was. It struck him very odd that an attractive, well-dressed woman, driving an Alpha Romeo, would throw a handbag into a dumpster. He noted her license plate number, and scratched it on the side of the dumpster with a pocketknife, so he wouldn't forget it. If she was throwing away stolen property there might be a reward for information. When she had turned at the street and was out of sight he scrambled into the dumpster and retrieved the handbag.

He opened the handbag and pulled out the folded chapter, took a quick look and dropped it to the pavement. He then went through the bag carefully, looking for money or drugs. There was nothing. He ripped out the lining, but still found nothing. In frustration he threw the handbag back into the dumpster and walked away. However, after he'd gone a short distance he decided that perhaps he should take a closer look at the paper. He went back and opened it out onto the filthy paving. He read the first verse slowly, struggling with the words, and saying them aloud: "*Just the place for a Snark! the Bellman cried as he landed his crew with care; supporting each man on the top of the tide by a finger entwined in his hair.*" He paused after the struggle. "Sounds like nonsense!" he said, which of course it was, and gave up trying to read it, since it just wasn't worth the effort. He folded it back up and stuffed it inside the plastic bag he always carried with him for empty aluminium cans.

Fit VII
The Hunting

Fit the Seventh

The Hunting

Grant drove downtown to the Farrell Building, an ugly 1950s office tower with twenty-three floors, of which about half were empty and for lease. People weren't exactly lined up wanting to move in. He parked his BMW across the street in a high-priced parking structure, hoping that it would be less likely to be stolen or stripped. He took the elevator to the tenth floor where a private investigator named Świątkiewicz had a small office. The PI shared the floor with a number of small businesses, including a not very successful dentist, a starving lawyer and a Korean urologist. The hallway was hot and stuffy and smelled like garlic.

He found Świątkiewicz's office and went in without knocking. The office was bleakly furnished with three worn-out upholstered chairs that looked like dentist office rejects, an end table with a ugly lamp, and a stack of old *Sports Illustrated* magazines. An attractive young receptionist sat behind an old grey metal desk, reading a Harlequin romance. There was a cheap tan four-drawer filing cabinet with a large dent in the top drawer behind her, and a PC on her otherwise empty desk.

She put down her paperback and smiled at Grant. "May I help you?"

"I have an appointment. My name is Dr. Grant Kerr."

"Oh, yes! Mr. Swat is expecting you."

"Mr. Swat?"

"Oh, that's what everyone calls him. No one except his family and ex-wife can pronounce his name, and the ex-wife usually refers to him as something much ruder."

Grant smiled. "You're sure he won't mind me calling him Swat?"

"I'm sure of it! That's what they called him when he played football. Just a moment; I'll tell him you're here." She got up and went into an inside office, then reappeared momentarily. "He'll see you now, Dr. Kerr."

Grant went in. Swat stood up then shook Grant's hand over the top of his bare desk. "He's either very neat or needs work," Grant thought.

"Pecheniuk Świątkiewicz," he said; "but you can call me Swat if you like. I realize that practically no one in this country can pronounce my name, much less spell it." Swat had played for the Rams for two years as a defensive lineman before he tore up his knee; he was a very large man, and still in formidable shape. He was dressed in dark slacks and a cream coloured Polo shirt, and looked more like a bouncer than a detective.

"It's nice to meet you. Your receptionist had already mentioned that I should call you Swat."

"Good. What can I do for you, Mr. Kerr?"

"I assume that you've heard about the so-called "Boojum" Snark murders?"

"Of course; it's been in the news for months. I'm all read up on them."

"I'm President of the California Chapter of the American Lewis Carroll Society. All of the victims have been members of our Society. We're concerned that more of our members may also be targets of this psychopath. We need to do everything we can to stop him. "

"I understand that there's a task force of about a hundred officers from a dozen police forces and Federal agencies trying to do just that," Swat said.

"Trying is the operative word. So far they have been completely ineffectual. Our members are quitting out of fear."

"Can't say that I blame any of them," Swat allowed.

"No; you're quite right. At this rate we will soon cease to exist. And I'm getting a bit nervous myself. All of those who have been attacked have been collectors of Carroll's *The Hunting of the Snark*. My own collection is probably larger than all of theirs put together. Actually, I'm surprised I wasn't his first victim."

"Why do you say 'his'?" Swat asked. "Are you certain it's a man?"

"Well, no. I just assumed that it was. After all, the murders have been bombings and assaults. You don't normally think of a woman being capable of doing such things."

"A woman shot Linen in the head at close range," Swat said.

"Really? I had never heard that. I see what you mean."

"What do you think that I might do that the police aren't already doing?"

"I'm not sure, exactly. Perhaps there's some rumour on the street. The bomber had to get explosives from somewhere. Perhaps you could find out from whom. Perhaps there is an accomplice. I'd just like for you to snoop around; see if you can come up with anything. "

"Do you want a body guard?"

"I hadn't really considered that, but I suppose that might be a wise precaution."

"My fee is $400 a day plus expenses if the job takes me out of town. I can drive you around, stay with you at work, and even live in your home if you want. Or I can just stake out your house and watch for anything suspicious. If there is someone that you suspect might be the killer I can try to find him or her and watch where they go and what they do."

"I don't have any suspects in mind. I can't imagine who could be doing these things."

"Do you want a body guard?" he asked again.

"Yes; that would be smart, I think. When could you start that?"

"Tonight. I could drop by about 7:00. I'll need your address and phone number."

"Okay." Grant took out a business card and handed it to him. "We live in Brentwood."

"I know the area. I'll be there. You might warn your wife, if you have one. I wouldn't want to scare her by showing up unannounced."

"Right; I'll do that. Thank you. See you this evening."

Swat nodded, and shook Grant's hand. "Please leave a check for $5,000 as a retainer with Mary Anne as you leave."

Grant nodded and went back out to the reception area, where wrote out the check. He felt a bit better.

When he went to collect his car he found that his transmission had been stolen.

When he complained to the attendant, a balding Chinese man with bad teeth, he shrugged his shoulders and pointed to a sign, saying, "No responsible for stolen! You pay $7 parking! You no pay, I call police!"

Grant paid him, then used his cell phone to call for a wrecker and a cab.

When Grant finally got home later that evening, driving a rental car, he went looking for Babs to tell her that Swat would be arriving that evening. She was locked in her icebox.

"Babs?" he yelled through the door.

"Go away!" she yelled back at him.

He knew better than to argue when she had that bitchy tone of voice, and went to the library. If Swat scared her, too bad; he'd tried.

An hour later Babs came out of her suite and went down to the library to see if Grant was still there. She peeked in the door and saw him typing away at the PC in the dim light. She pulled on a pair of latex gloves and eased the door closed. She locked it with her key, then went down the hallway and unlocked the closet where the alarm system control panel was located. She punched in the passkey to activate the fire suppression system and manually triggered it.

A shrill alarm went off immediately and she went back to her suite and locked herself in. She took several strong sedatives and crawled into bed. When the firemen arrived she wanted to be sure that they found her asleep.

Inside the library Grant reacted immediately to the alarm, realizing that he only had seconds to respond. He jerked open the bottom drawer of his desk and pulled out a small fresh air mask with an attached compressed air cylinder and managed to put it on just as the Halon system activated and began flooding the room. He had fifteen minutes capacity on the mask.

He rushed to the door and found it locked. He momentarily panicked, then remembered the spare key he had in his desk. He retrieved it and escaped into the hallway, then closed and locked the door behind him to prevent Halon from flooding the rest of the house or anyone going in, which might be fatal. He took off the mask and went outside to wait at the front door for the fire trucks to arrive.

Two trucks and a rescue van arrived about ten minutes later with lights on, and horns and sirens blaring. He explained that the system had been accidentally tripped and that there was in fact no fire. They wanted to go inside and check until he explained that the Halon system had flooded the library and it was too hazardous to enter the room. They left and he went back inside to start the ventilation system that would clear out the Halon.

Grant went to Bab's suite to check on her. When she didn't respond to his knocks he let himself in using his master key. He found her sound asleep, and he left her alone. It never occurred to him that she had tried to kill him.

*　*　*　*
*　*　*
*　*　*　*

A few days after Nizar Gulam found the incriminating chapter in the dumpster he came across a used bookstore on his daily rounds of searching for aluminium cans. In spite of its pretentious name, Catcher in the Rye Antiquarian Books was nothing more than a junk bookstore, specializing in paperbacks and abused girlie magazines. The owner, Rodeny Bryer, had chosen the name because *Catcher in the Rye* was the only piece of genuine literature that he'd ever read from cover to cover. The shop's walls were lined with shelves knocked together from 1x12 lumber, filled with well-read and dog-eared romance, mystery and sci-fi novels, and a few Penguins and other mass market classics. The only antiquarian book in the shop was an old worn-out copy of *The Wizard of Oz*, which Rodney imagined to be worth hundreds of dollars. Nizar went in and looked around. The old books smelled almost as bad as he did. The only customer in the shop was a balding man who looked to be in his sixties. He was wearing an old flannel shirt and baggy pants, and was flipping quickly through an old *Playboy*. Nizar went up to the counter.

"What do you want?" snarled Rodney. He was smoking and the effort of talking caused him to cough violently, as if trying to expectorate a piece of his lung. Rodney didn't like street people coming into his shop, since they invariably wanted a hand-out and never bought anything.

Nizar dug around beneath the cans in his plastic bag until he found the folded chapter. "You interested in this?" he asked hopefully, placing it on the counter. It had become rather heavily stained and damp from the cola and beer that had leaked from some of the cans.

Rodney opened it up with the end of a pencil, as carefully as he might poke at a landmine, not wanting to touch the filthy thing. He recognized the poem, though he had never seen this particular set of illustrations. "It's from *The Hunting of the Snark*," he said. "It's a children's book for adults. I think Lewis Carroll wrote it; or maybe it was Edward Lear; I can't really remember. Why'd you rip out of the book and mark all over it? It's nothing but a piece of garbage now!"

Nizar wasn't encouraged by this assessment. "I didn't rip it out or mark it up. That's how I found it."

"Where'd you find it?"

"In a dumpster. I figured it might be worth something."

"Not to me."

"Not even five bucks?"

"You've got to be kidding!"

Nizar put it back into his plastic trash bag, and then turned to leave. The old guy looking at the *Playboy* made a strange noise and both Rodney and Nizar turned to look at him, half expecting to see him collapse from a heart attack.

Suddenly Rodney's neurons fired and he recalled reading about the Boojum Snark murders. He also remembered that there was a huge reward involved for information leading to an arrest and conviction, though he couldn't recall the exact amount. "Hey!" he yelled.

The customer in the back froze, as if he had been caught ripping out the centrefold, and Nizar stopped with his hand on the doorknob. Nizar asked, “Me”

“Yeah, you. Come back here a minute.” Rodney motioned to him.

Nizar walked back to the counter and the customer resumed his furtive thumbing. “Yeah?”

“Tell you what; there’s a woman comes in here sometimes looking for Lewis Carroll stuff. She might be interested in that piece of garbage. I’ll give you a buck for it on a gamble that I can sell it to her. That’s the best I can do.”

Nizar hesitated. He had hoped for much more. Still, a dollar was better than nothing. He pulled it back out of the bag and handed it to him across the counter.

When he had gone, Rodney called the FBI. After several transfers he connected to the agent in charge of the case. “Arnold Schlichenmayer. May I help you?”

“I understand there’s a reward for information leading to the arrest and conviction of the Snark bomber,” Rodney said. The customer in the back stopped looking at the magazine when he heard this and Rodney noticed.

“Just a minute,” Rodney told Schlichenmayer; “I got to deal with a customer. “Hey you! Since you ain’t buyin’ nothin, get your butt outta here!” The old man frowned, crammed the magazine back onto a self and shuffled out with a glare. “Sorry about that,” he said into the phone. “Guys come in here and act like it’s a damn public library. I’m goin’ to have to start bagging things up in plastic. As I was askin’, is there a reward?”

“Yes. The Justice Department is offering a reward of one-million dollars.”

This was bigger than he had remembered. “I may have something for you.”

“What is it?”

"It's a chapter torn out of a copy of *The Hunting of the Snark*. It's got names written across the faces of the characters in the poem. Four of them are victims."

"How do you know?"

"I checked their names against a newspaper article; it's public knowledge."

"Can you bring it in?"

"No. I run a bookshop. I don't have anyone to watch it for me."

"What's your name and address? I'll drop by and see you this afternoon."

"Rodney Bryer. My shop's called Catcher in the Rye Antiquarian Books." He gave him the address.

"Please don't handle the paper; there may be fingerprints of interest on it. Place it in a plastic bag and keep it in a safe place until I get there."

"Okay. When will you be by?"

"Within the hour. Thank you for calling."

"Right."

They rang off.

Schlichenmayer picked up a technician on his way out, and they rushed over to Catcher in the Rye Antiquarian Books. They went in and identified themselves. "Let's see what you've got," he told Rodney.

Rodney pulled a plastic bag out from under the counter and handed it to him.

The technician put on gloves and opened it up. They looked it over briefly and Schlichenmayer said, "Bag it up," at which the technician took a large plastic Ziploc bag out of a small case he had brought with him and inserted it. He then labelled it with a marker.

Schlichenmayer wrote out a receipt and handed it to Rodney. "We need your fingerprints," he said; "so we can figure out which fingerprints on that paper are yours. You ever been fingerprinted?"

"Yeah. A few times. "

"By whom?"

"LAPD."

"Okay. We can get them from there. No need to get a new set from you. Do you have any outstanding warrants?"

"I don't know; maybe a traffic warrant. Why?"

"I'd go take care of that if I were you. You may end up in the limelight if this is significant. You could find yourself in jail."

"Yeah. Okay, I'll do that."

"Where did you get this?"

"A guy came in off the street and offered it to me for five bucks. I gave him a dollar. Just remember that it's my property now."

"If it's what it looks like you won't be seeing it again, since it will go into evidence. If you're lucky, there may be a chunk of the reward coming to you. If it turns out to be nothing we will return it to you."

"What do you mean by "a chunk" of the reward? Why wouldn't I get all of it?"

"You might. But then maybe the guy who found it might get some of that reward as well. A judge would have to decide. Do you know this street person's name?"

"No idea. I never saw him before he came in here today."

"Can you describe him?"

"Dirty and smelly."

"That describes at least a third of L. A. What else?"

"Thirtyish; shoulder length black hair, with some grey in it. He's shorter than me. Rough looking, from living on the street; gaunt. No beard, but not clean-shaven either. He was wearing an old Raiders tee shirt, jeans and sneakers."

"Any distinguishing marks? Tattoos? That sort of thing. "

Rodney thought for a moment. “You mean other than the fact that he’s blind in one eye?”

Schlichenmayer rolled his eyes. “Now, don’t you think that it might be of some importance when describing someone to say that he was blind in one eye? What else? Did he have both of his hands and feet?”

Rodney was offended. “Yeah, he had both hands and feet.”

“Both ears?”

“Yeah.”

“Schlichenmayer handed him a card with his phone number. “Call me if you see him again. Try to get a name if you can.” Rodney took the card and studied it.

“Okay, but I doubt I’ll see him. He doesn’t look like the type that reads a lot.”

“Oh, I don’t know; he obviously collects Victorian poetry.” They turned to leave. “We’ll be in touch.”

They left.

Rodney started thinking about having to share the million dollar reward with some street person, and decided that he didn’t much like that idea. He put the pistol he kept under the counter in his jacket pocket, closed his shop and went looking for him. He figured he had to be within walking distance, though that might still be a rather large area.

Fit VIII
The Vanishing

Fit the Eighth

The Vanishing

Babs woke up about four hours after the incident in the library, still groggy from the sedative. She lay there for another fifteen minutes until her mind began to clear. She got up and washed her face with cold water, then went out into the hallway and down to the library, which was empty. She went into the living room looking for Grant and was startled to find Swat sitting on one of the sofas, watching TV.

He stood up when he heard her come in. "Who the hell are you?" she demanded.

"Pecheniuk Świątkiewicz. I'm a private investigator. Your husband hired me today to look after him."

"Where is he?"

"He went to the kitchen for a beer."

Grant walked in, interrupting their conversation. "Oh, you're awake!" he said to her. "You missed all of the excitement."

"What excitement?"

"Someone tried to kill me a few hours ago."

"They did what!"

"Tried to kill me. Locked the door to the library and tripped the fire suppression system."

"How did you escape? Did Arnold Schwarzenegger here help you?"

"It's Pecheniuk Świątkiewicz," the PI corrected her.

"Whatever," she said. "I'll just yell, 'Arnold,' if I need you; which I don't foresee."

"Swat wasn't here yet," Grant explained.

"Squat?" she said.

"Not 'Squat'; it's 'Swat'. It's Mr. Świątkiewicz's nickname."

"As in SWAT Team?"

"I suppose. Actually, as it happened, I was able to save myself. I had taken the precaution of placing a fresh air mask in the bottom desk drawer. When I heard the alarm go off I put it on. Luckily, I also had a spare key in the desk, so 1 was able to let myself out."

"Why would anyone want to kill you?"

"For the same reason the Snark's been killing the others, I suppose."

"Is Arnold here spending the night? I need to know whether to lock my door at night." She glared at Swat, who just stood there impassive and impervious to her insults. After several years in the NFL trenches he didn't intimidate easily.

"Yes, he'll be staying here for a while. After the incident this afternoon I don't want him too far away."

"How was the killer able to trip the system?" she asked.

"That's an interesting question, Babs. The police wanted to know the same thing. They were here earlier, and said that it had to be someone who knew the passkey number. That narrows it down a bit."

"Not really," she said. "It's written down on a piece of paper stuck on the refrigerator door with a magnet. Anyone who's been in the kitchen over the past few months could have seen it."

"You have it posted on the refrigerator?" Grant asked in shocked disbelief.

"Just in case I forget it."

Grant shook his head. "Millions of dollars' worth of books in there, guarded by a sophisticated alarm system, and you put the passkey number on the fridge?"

She shrugged. "Well, excuuuuse me!"

"It's okay, Babs; don't get upset! We can reset the alarm to a new number. But please, don't post it in plain view!"

"Why didn't you wake me when all of this was going on?" she demanded.

"I tried to, but you were out cold. I couldn't rouse you. Everything was all right, so I just let you sleep."

"I may have overdone it with the sedative," she said. "I had a bad headache and wanted to go right to sleep. Well, I'm glad you're okay," she lied. "I'm going out for sushi. I'm hungry." She turned and left the room for her suite.

Grant turned to Swat and said, "She's a pistol!"

"I can see that. Strange; she didn't seem all that upset, though. Most wives would have been all over you, patting your hand and carrying on."

"Not Babs; not her style."

Schlichenmayer received the lab report on the torn out chapter provided by Rodney Bryer several days later. They had identified the chapter as having been from the Catalpa Press, London edition of *The Hunting of the Snark*. There were quite a number of fingerprints. The book had been well read. The only prints that were identifiable were Rodney Bryer's and those belonging to a petty criminal named Nizar

Gulam who was homeless and living somewhere in L.A. Mug shots taken by LAPD following his previous arrests were attached. Gulam's lengthy rap sheet was also attached; it was primarily for vagrancy, shoplifting and petty theft; he had spent time in the L. A. County Jail on several occasions. Stains on the paper were identified as Pepsi Cola, beer and dog urine; there were no detectable human bodily fluids. Marks-A-Lot felt pens had been used to write names across the faces, and all of these names were also listed on the membership rolls of both the American Lewis Carroll Society and its California Chapter. They included all of the known victims of the so-called "Boojum" Snark killer.

Schlichenmayer issued an arrest warrant for Nizar Gulam and sent copies to all agencies and police departments working on the case. His old mug shots were distributed to local new organizations and would be on the front page of local and many national newspapers and TV newscasts the next day, along with cautionary notes that he should be considered armed and extremely dangerous.

Świątkiewicz was one of many people in L. A. who recognized him immediately when they saw his face broadcast on the local nightly news. Swat got in his car and raced downtown to prowl the alleys and see if he could find him before the FBI, LAPD or someone else picked him up. There was a million-dollar reward involved and Swat wanted to find out what Nizar knew about the murders before the police did.

It took him less than an hour to find him, crouched behind a dumpster eating the remains of someone's Chinese dinner out of a Styrofoam container.

"You're in big trouble, Nizar," he said as he reached down and easily lifted him into an upright position. Nizar dropped the remains of the beef in black bean sauce.

"Swat!" he said, recognizing him from a few unpleasant past encounters. "Why's that? I ain't done nothin'!"

"That's not what the FBI thinks. You ought to read the papers once in a while. Your ugly mug's on the front page of practically every newspaper in the country; you've even made CNN."

"Why?" he asked, completely dumbfounded.

"For some reason they seem to think you're the "Boojum" Snark serial killer."

"Who? Me?"

"Yeah, you."

"I've never killed nothin' in my life!" he protested.

"Yeah, I know. And you don't have the brains or the strength, either."

"Why would they think I'm the serial killer?"

"I haven't any idea," he said truthfully. "We're going for a little ride, Nizar," he continued, then picked him up as easily as he would a child and carried him to his car. He stuffed him into the passenger seat, and buckled him in. "You try to get out and I'll break your back," he said with genuine menace.

Nizar believed him, and wasn't about to try anything that foolish.

"Every cop in L. A. is out scouring around in alleys and under rocks looking for you. We need somewhere a little more private to try and jog your memory."

Swat drove to the top level of a multi-level car park. It was empty since no one wanted the sun to fade the paint on his car.

"Now you need to start thinking real hard," Swat said. "What do you know about snarks?"

"What's a snark?"

"Oh, it's a scary little monster in a fairy tale."

"I don't read fairy tales."

"I'm sure you don't read much of anything." He reached over and took Nizar's left hand, then casually broke his index finger, as easily as snapping a pencil. Nizar screamed in agony at the worst pain he had ever felt in his life. Swat looked at him as murderously as a Bandersnatch contemplating a Banker for dinner. "Your memory any better yet?" he asked.

Nizar shook his head, tears and snot streaming down his face. He gingerly held his left hand with his right, and rocked back and forth on the car seat in a vain effort to ease the throbbing pain in his already swollen finger.

"You got nine more fingers to help fix that lousy memory of yours."

Nizar screamed again, just at the thought. He started thinking desperately about anything that he had ever heard of snarks.

Swat reached over and took Nizar's right index finger, prepared to break it next.

"Wait!" Nizar screamed. "I just thought of something!"

"I'm waiting; but, as you know, I'm not a real patient man."

"I watched this lady throw a handbag into a dumpster about a week ago. I crawled into the dumpster and got it. All it had in it was some pages tom out of a book."

"What's that got to do with snarks?"

"I took it over to a used bookstore and sold it for a buck. The guy told me it was torn out of a book about hunting snarks."

"What did these pages look like?"

"It was real weird; all folded up, like an accordion. I stretched it out and it was maybe twenty feet long. There was this long, goofy-looking boat, with cartoons of men with big heads looking over the railing. Someone had wrote names across their faces with a marker. Some of them had a big X drawn across their face, too. And there was a long poem written down the whole thing. I read the first verse, but it sounded like some sort of nonsense, so I didn't bother to read the whole thing. I think I remember somethin' about a hotel bellman holding up some guy by his hair; somethin" stupid like that."

"Why would anyone give you a dollar for that?"

"The guy said he had a customer that liked this stuff and he thought he could sell it to her."

"The lady who threw it in the dumpster; what'd she look like?"

"She looked like a movie star. Dark brown hair. I didn't see her real good, though, 'cause she didn't get out of the car; she just threw it in the dumpster from her window."

"What was she driving?"

"A late model light blue Alpha Romeo; real nice."

"What's the license number?"

"I didn't notice," he lied and looked away.

Swat was still holding his right index finger. He broke it and Nizar screamed again, in excruciating pain. "Now, Nizar, you must think I'm real stupid. You think I'm stupid, Nizar?"

Nizar shook his head. "No; no. 1 know you ain't stupid."

"Now 1 know that if you saw something like that happen that you'd memorize that plate number; might be worth something. Right now it might be worth your life."

"I didn't memorize it. I scratched it on the side of the dumpster, 'cause I knew I'd forget it."

"Okay. We're going to go find it. You'd better hope someone hasn't taken that dumpster anywhere." He reached into his jacket and retrieved a set of handcuffs. He attached one to Nizar's left wrist and the other to an eyebolt that he had installed beneath the dash for such a purpose. "You do anything silly, like try to wave at a cop, and I'm going to put a bullet in your liver," he said. "No further warnings. Got it?" He opened his jacket so that Nizar could see the pistol he had in a shoulder holster.

"I'm not going to do anything like that," Nizar assured him, through teeth clenched in pain.

"I hope not, for your sake." He started the SUV and they drove out of the parking structure. Swat paid the attendant.

"Now exactly where is that dumpster you vandalized?" he said as he turned onto the street.

"I don't know the address. I'll just have to give you directions. Take a left at the next comer and then go about six blocks. Turn into the alley next to a Greek restaurant named Mykonos."

"I see your memory's improving. Who'd you sell the page to?"

"The owner of a bookshop called Catcher in the Rye Antiquarian Books. I don't know his name. He's a real jerk. I think he has lung cancer or TB; serves him right."

Swat turned in at the alley at the Mykonos restaurant.

"Stop here," Nizar said. "She threw it in that dumpster over there," he said, pointing with his chin. It hurt too much to point with his throbbing hands.

Swat got out and went around to the passenger side and uncuffed him. "Show me where you scratched the plate number."

Nizar led him to another dumpster about fifty feet away. "It's here," he said, pointing at it with his elbow, and grimacing from the pain caused by the movement.

Swat looked at it, and wrote it down. "Get back in the car."

Nizar reluctantly climbed back in. Swat buckled him back in and reattached the cuffs.

Swat took the freeways for over a hundred miles out into the desert towards Vegas, then turned north on a ranch road with a cattle guard. Nizar sat very still, trying not to move or bump his hands. He needed to urinate, but knew that he'd never be able to get his pants unzipped, so he decided to try and hold it. Eventually the pain in his bladder distracted him from the pain in his broken fingers. They drove another thirty miles, before turning up a dry arroyo, Swat driving the SUV on the hard creek bed. He stopped and got Nizar out. Nizar started to plead for his life, well aware that he was in a very serious situation. Swat ignored him and without so much as a goodbye, reached over and broke his skinny neck, as easily as one might wring the frail neck of a Jub-jub.

He removed the cuffs from Nizar's wrists and backed the SUV out to the road, then turned it around and parked it. He retrieved a Polaroid from the back seat and removed his boots. He cut off a sagebrush branch with a pocketknife, then hiked with the camera and branch to Nizar's body, where he took two photos of him. He then systematically obliterated the tire tracks and his own footprints, using the branch like a broom, walking backwards all the way back to the SUV. He got in and swept away his last footprints, closed the door and then drove away, tossing out the branch after he had gone another mile.

Once back in L. A., Swat stopped by his office and got on the Internet to track down the owner of the license plate. Just as he had expected, it was registered to Dr. Grant Kerr. Swat had seen Babs driving a blue Alpha Romeo and was sure it was her that Nizar had seen.

He went to a coin-operated car wash and methodically cleaned the SUV, including the undercarriage, wheel wells and other recesses where any dirt might have lodged. He wiped down the front seat and dash areas to remove any trace of fingerprints and bodily fluids such as tears or mucus and then vacuumed up every thread and hair. Satisfied that the car was clean enough to withstand a FBI search he went to a tire dealership and bought four new tires with a radically different tread pattern and had them mounted. He had them put the spares in the back, explaining that he wanted to keep them for off-roading. But, later that night he drove out Highway 1 until he was at an appropriate cliff and tossed the old tires into the ocean. He drove back to L. A. and went to a coin operated Laundromat where he washed all of his clothing with excess soap and very hot water, then dried them. He dropped them off in the first Salvation Army container he encountered, along with the shoes he had worn that day. Having finished his clean-up he drove to the Kerr's Brentwood mansion and rang the doorbell. Babs answered.

"Oh, it's you," she said, with as much disappointment in the tone of her voice as she could manage.

"Is the doctor in?" he asked.

"The doctor is definitely out," she said sarcastically.

"Good. It's you I wanted to talk to anyway." He pushed his way in and closed the door.

"About what?"

"The time has come, the Walrus said, to speak of many things," he said. "Of bombs, and death, and whether snarks have wings."

"What's that supposed to mean?" she snarled, not the least amused.

"I suppose you've seen the mug shots of a street person named Nizar Gulam. They've been on the front page and on TV. The FBI and LAPD have been searching for him. "

"Yes, I've seen them. What about them?"

"You might not be aware that Gulam witnessed you throw a handbag into a dumpster about a week ago. He had the good sense to write down your license plate number. He dug your bag out of the dumpster and inside it he found some pages that had been torn out of a copy of *The Hunting of the Snark*. He sold that to the owner of a second-hand bookstore, who in tum gave it to the FBI, hoping for the big reward that's been posted for information leading to the arrest and conviction of the same serial killer who tried to kill your husband in the library."

This was big news to Babs. She knew the police were searching for Gulam, but didn't know why, and was stunned to learn that the FBI now had the pages that she had tried to dispose of. "I knew I should have burned them," she thought, trying not to panic.

"And exactly who is this serial killer?" she asked, waiting to see if he really knew as much as he seemed to imply that he did.

"You're probably the only one who knows for sure. I figure that you're the killer. But another possibility is that you have an accomplice; perhaps a lover that you got to do it for you. Or even a hired killer; they're not hard to find in L. A."

"Why would I want to kill all of these people?"

"My guess is that you just got tired of your husband, and want his money. You've set out to kill him and throw suspicion on some mystical psychopath to cover your tracks."

"What do you want?" she asked.

"I can collect a million by turning you and Nizar over to the FBI. You'll go to prison. Now I realize that California doesn't like to execute women; but, at the very least, you'd spend the rest of your life waiting on death row. I think a better arrangement would be for you to give me two million instead."

"You would just continue to blackmail me, even if I agreed to the two million. After you spent that, you'd want another million, then another. And besides, Gulam could always turn me in."

"Here's my proposition. You give me the two million and I kill Nizar. I'll give you a photo to prove it and then tell the police where to find his body. You'll see it in the newspapers. They'll think he was the "Boojum" Snark killer and close the case. You'll have the photo of Nizar's body, with my fingerprints on it. If I ever try to blackmail you again you can turn that into the police and I'll go to death row for Nizar's murder, so I wouldn't dare. If you try to blackmail me to get your two million back I'll turn the tape recording of this conversation over to the police and give another copy to your husband. I would imagine that your husband would then either divorce you, or have you killed, even if the police don't do anything."

"What tape recording?,

He opened his jacket to reveal a pocketsize recorder, which was running. She glared at him.

"Deal?"

She thought for a moment, but couldn't see any way out of it. He was too big and strong to take the recording away from him, even if she did have a black belt in karate. He probably did too. "Deal," she finally said. "It will take a little while to get the money."

"How long? I'm not a patient man."

"Two full working days. I'll have to sell some stock."

"Okay. I want the money in old bills; nothing bigger than a hundred."

"It might take an extra day to come up with that many old bills."

"Okay, I'll give you three days." He opened the door and left.

"You might want to go out and buy yourself a second-hand dagger-proof coat," she said to him through the closed door.

Three days later Swat showed up at the Kerr mansion and rang the doorbell. Babs answered and let him in without saying anything, then closed it behind them.

"Do you have the photo?" she asked.

He didn't answer, but went in and searched the house to be sure there wasn't anyone hiding somewhere to eavesdrop. He came back to the foyer and took her by the wrist into a guest bathroom and turned on the faucets, just in case she had hidden a micro-cam or a tape recorder somewhere.

"Where's the money?"

"In my suite. I'll go and get it."

"I'll go with you," he said and pulled out his pistol, which he pointed at her. He followed her into her suite and into one of her huge walk-in closets.

"It's like the damn North Pole in here!" he remarked, glad that he'd worn a jacket. "No wonder you've got such a cold heart!"

She ignored him and bent down and opened an aluminium case sitting on the floor. "There's a million in used bills."

"What are you talking about? The deal was two million!"

"I'll give you the other million when I have proof that Gulam is dead."

He reached into a coat pocket and produced the Polaroid of Nizar, which he handed to her.

She stared at the photo. "This doesn't prove anything. You two could have faked this."

"You'll know tomorrow, when you see the newspaper headlines."

"Okay. Come back at 9:00 a.m. Grant will be gone to the office. If everything is as you say I'll give you the other million."

He picked up the suitcase and turned to leave."9:00 a.m. sharp. If there's anything funny happening I'll kill you."

"I'm not a fool; everything will be in order. I already have the money; it's just in a safe place."

He motioned to her with his pistol for her to lead the way out of the house. She shut and locked the door after him.

Babs put the photo in an envelope and went immediately to a small bank in Orange, where she had a safe deposit box that only she knew about, and put it in the box.

She was up early the next morning to look at the newspaper.

"BOOJUM" SNARK SERIAL KILLER'S BODY FOUND IN NEVADA DESERT

Well Known Street-Person Nizar Gulam Dead from Broken Neck

Los Angeles (UPI) - The FBI has announced the discovery of the body of Nizar Gulam. He had been tortured and murdered. Mr. Gulam had been the subject of a massive police search following a tip that he might somehow be involved in the string of so-called "Boojum" Snark serial murders.

The grisly discovery followed an anonymous telephone tip to the hotline set up for seeking information from the public. The caller gave the body's location. The caller made no claim for any of the million-dollar reward that had been posted by the Justice Department.

The tip that led to Mr. Gulam's arrest warrant was provided by Rodney Bryer, owner of Catcher in the Rye Antiquarian Books in downtown L.A. Bryer had purchased some pages tom from an old edition of Lewis Carroll's notorious nonsense poem *The Hunting of the Snark* from Nizar Gulam, who claimed to have found them in a dumpster. Fingerprints on these pages led police to issue a warrant for Gulam's arrest.

Police remain puzzled why Gulam would have sold the pages rather than destroy them if he was the "Boojum" Snark serial killer. One theory is that he may have wanted to get caught, perhaps out of remorse for his crimes, or to stop him before he committed the next murder, unable to control the compulsion to do so himself.

The pages apparently have the names of the past victims written on them, as well as the names of what appear to be planned future victims. Police have refused to reveal who these future targets were.

The FBI and Nevada police have opened a homicide investigation into Nizar Gulam's murder.

> Whoever killed Gulam methodically removed all traces of their footprints and tire tracks from the scene of the murder.
>
> Casts have been taken from thirty different tire treads on the adjacent dirt road. Most have been identified as belonging to various ranch vehicles in the area.
>
> Why Gulam was tortured also remains a mystery. The index fingers on both of his hands had been broken,

The lengthy article continued with a description of the past murders and attack attributed the "Boojum" Snark, as well as a photograph of Nizar Gulam. It was the same face in the Polaroid photo that Swat had given her and Babs breathed a sigh of relief. But what Babs didn't realize was that the fingerprints that were obvious on the image were not Swat's, but those of a random drunk that Swat had found passed out in an alley. It had been simple enough to press the unconscious man's hand on the photo.

At 9:00 a.m. sharp the doorbell rang. Babs went to the door carrying the suitcase that contained the other million dollars. She opened the door and handed him the case without saying anything, then closed the door. Swat returned to his car and counted the money.

Babs went immediately down to the basement and retrieved an explosive device she had made for use on one of the Carrollians and put it in the trunk of her car. That evening she made an excuse about going to a movie and went out, but made her way to Swat's office building instead. The building was open, as there was no money to pay for a receptionist or guard. She took the stairs to the tenth floor and broke into Swat's office. There was no alarm system since there was nothing in the office worth stealing. Inside she affixed the explosive to the underside of the swivel chair behind Swat's desk, along with a pressure sensitive trigger. She left, again by the stairs.

Babs was up again early the next morning to see if there had been a reported explosion, but there hadn't been. She had to wait for the evening edition for that bit of news.

RECEPTIONIST AT LOCAL P. I. FIRM KILLED IN EXPLOSION

Los Angeles (UPI) - Mary Anne Little, receptionist for a private investigation firm owned by former Rams lineman Pecheniuk 'Swat' Świątkiewicz, was killed today by a bomb placed under her employer's desk chair.

She was killed instantly by the powerful blast, evidently intended for Mr. Świątkiewicz.

No motive for the murder is known. However, it has been learned by UPI that Dr. Grant Kerr had recently employed Mr. Świątkiewicz as a bodyguard. Dr. Kerr, who is President of the California Chapter of the American Lewis Carroll Society, had apparently feared for his life because of the recent "Boojum" Snark murders.

Police had previously reported that the "Boojum Snark" murders had been solved with the discovery of the body of Nizar Gulam in the Nevada desert. LAPD spokesperson Nanoo Shepard told reporters today that they have reopened the case, and are focussing their attention on Rodney Breyer, owner of Catcher in the Rye Antiquarian Books.

Rodney Bryer provided the FBI with information that led police to issue an arrest warrant for Nizar Gulam. He has submitted a claim to the Justice Department for the one million dollar reward leading to the capture of the "Boojum" Snark serial killer.

Babs fought back the panic that tried to take her. She realized that Swat would be sure to seek revenge, if not for his secretary's death, then because he would realize that she had tried to kill him. "With my luck Mary Anne was probably his niece," Babs said aloud to herself. "What was she doing sitting in his damn chair?"

Babs went to the bank and retrieved the photo Swat had given her of Nizar Gulam's corpse. She bought a box of plain white envelopes, a BIC ballpoint pen and a ream of standard Xerox computer paper from an Office Depot, and took everything back home again. She went into her suite and put on latex gloves, then carefully wiped off any of her own fingerprints from around the edges and back of the Polaroid photo, using fingernail polish remover. Writing with her left hand to disguise her own handwriting, she addressed one of the envelopes to the FBI's Los Angeles branch office using the BIC ballpoint pen. She also wrote out a note that said simply: "GULAM KILLER PRINTS ON PHOTO." She folded the paper, put the note inside the envelope with the photo.

Having completed this task she gathered up the remaining paper, the ballpoint pen, the box of envelopes, and the book of postage stamps, and put them all in a plastic bag. She drove to the main post office in Hollywood and dropped the letter in an outside drop box. She then drove to a McDonald's restaurant and dumped the contents of the plastic bag into an outside trash can, then went inside to the Ladies Room, where she deposited the latex gloves in the paper towel waste bin.

She returned home and went back to her suite, where she got her pistol from her bedside table. After checking to be sure that it was loaded, she put the pistol in her purse. She packed a small suitcase, including a black jogging suit, a black ski mask, and black running shoes. She then went to the basement, where she retrieved two other explosive devices, some wire leads with alligator clips, a roll of duct tape, and a few simple hand tools, and put them all into a backpack. She drove out to the L. A. Airport and parked her Alpha Romeo in the long-term parking, then rented a midsize from Hertz.

She drove downtown, checked into the Marriott then drove over to Swat's office tower and parked on the roof of the parking structure across the street, where she could watch the building's entrance, to see if Swat would either show up or leave.

Three hours later she saw Swat enter the building. Babs got back in her car and exited, then parked on the street and waited twenty minutes until Swat left to get in his car, which he had parked on the street. She tailed his black Toyota, holding back a block or more so that he wouldn't get suspicious. They drove across town to a middleclass suburb in east L. A., pulled into the driveway of a small house and went inside. Babs drove by and noted the house number, then drove back to the Marriott.

After midnight she dressed in her black jogging suit and put the ski mask in her purse, then took the stairs down to the basement car parking level. She drove back out to Swat's neighbourhood and parked four blocks down the street from his house. She got the backpack with the bomb and tools out of the trunk and jogged casually along the quiet street. She ducked into Swat's driveway, then quickly slid under his Toyota. It took her only ten minutes to attach the bomb under the driver's seat and wire it to the ignition. Her task completed she slid back out from under the car and casually jogged back to her car, taking a roundabout route. She then drove back to the Marriott and went to bed.

The next morning she got out of bed when she heard room service slide the morning paper under her door. She opened and read the article on the bottom right of the front page.

FORMER RAM "SWAT" DIES IN EAST L. A. CAR BOMBING

Los Angeles (UPI) - Local Private Investigator and former Rams lineman Pecheniuk 'Swat' Świątkiewicz was killed this

> morning when a car bomb ripped through his automobile in his driveway.
>
> The bomb set the car on fire and his body was burned beyond recognition. Police were able to identify the body through dental records, even though Świątkiewicz had lost most of his front teeth while playing football.
>
> This morning's bombing falls on the heels of a failed attempt on his life yesterday at his office, in which his secretary, Mary Anne Little, was killed when she inadvertently triggered a bomb mounted under the seat of his desk chair.
>
> Police are continuing to investigate whether Mr. Świątkiewicz and Ms. Little's deaths are related to the unsolved murder of Nizar Gulam, whom the police at one time believed to be "Boojum" Snark serial killer. Gulam's body was recently discovered in the Nevada desert. He had been tortured and died from a broken neck.

The article was continued on page two, giving a summary of the "Boojum" Snark killings, and a history of Swat's brief NFL football career. Babs threw the newspaper in the trashcan and went down for breakfast.

A few days later, when the FBI received Babs' letter with Gulam's photograph, they went into frantic action. The fingerprints were quickly identified as belonging to Yerani Dolash from LAPD records. He had been arrested innumerable times for drunkenness and vagrancy. A police search of the filthy streets and alleys of downtown L. A.'s tenderloin district had finally located his corpse inside a large cardboard box. His neck had been broken. Homicide opened a case, and the subsequent investigation revealed that Dolash had been in the LAPD drunk tank the night of Nizar Gulam's murder. His death was subsequently reported in the newspaper as a simple crime statistic, with no reference to any possible connection to the "Boojum" Snark murders.

A week after Swat's murder Grant Kerr received an envelope from an attorney, who said that he represented Mr. Świątkiewicz's estate. Inside was a numbered key to a footlocker at a private country club, along with the club's address. The letter said that Mr. Świątkiewicz's will had stipulated that he was to receive the key to this locker in the event of his death. Inside the locker there would be an envelope addressed to him. "Curiouser and curiouser!" Grant said aloud.

That evening Grant drove out to the country club and eventually located the locker. Inside he found, hidden beneath Swat's dirty golf clothes, a plain manila envelope with his name written across it. He removed the envelope, closed and locked the door, then dropped the key off at the member's counter. He went out to his car and opened the envelope. Inside was the other Polaroid of Nizar Gulam's corpse and a pocketsize cassette player/recorder. Grant thought he recognized Gulam's photo from mug shots he had seen in the newspapers. He pushed the play button on the cassette recorder and listened to the entire conversation between Babs and Swat. He rewound the tape and listened to it again two more times, before he believed what he had heard.

He sat in silence for the next twenty minutes, contemplating what he had heard.

He dropped the photograph and recorder back into the envelope and drove home. He went immediately to Babs' bedroom suite and opened the door without knocking. She was in bed, wearing a robe, reading a mystery novel.

"Didn't you ever hear of knocking?" she asked.

He ignored her. "I have something I'd like for you to hear."

"What? A new Lawrence Welk collection?"

He took the cassette recorder out, turned up the volume and pushed the play button. Babs' eyes went narrow as she listened.

"What have you got to say?" Grant demanded after it had played it through. He pulled out the photo that Swat had sent, along with the tape and held it up so she could see it.

She said nothing and just continued to stare coldly at him. "I'm calling the police," he said.

Babs reached under her pillow and produced her pistol, which she aimed at Grant's chest. "I don't think so. You're going to do exactly what 1 tell you to do or I'll kill you! Come on; we're going out onto the patio. Bring that stuff with you." She said this with such menace that Grant didn't resist, terrified at the gun pointing directly at him and realizing that he was confronted with a psychopathic killer. He hadn't imagined her being armed, and didn't even know that she owned a gun. She marched him outside to the grill.

"Take out the cassette and put it in that empty tin can, along with the photo," she demanded, pointing at a coffee can with the pistol. Grant fumbled with the recorder, but finally managed to get the cassette out, quite shaken by his predicament. "Now pour charcoal lighter in it." He fumbled with the plastic lid on the can. "I can never get these dang things open," he said. "Twist and lift! Twist and lift!" he thought. He finally succeeded, and soaked the cassette and Polaroid.

"Not set it alight!" she demanded.

"I don't have a match. You know I don't smoke."

"You're bloody hopeless!" she said.

"Where's a snark when you need one?" he thought.

She fished around in her robe pocket and produced a book of matches, which she tossed to him. He didn't manage to catch them, and had to bend over to pick them up.

"Clumsy idiot!" she said. He finally managed to set the contents aflame. "Now sit down on that chair." She motioned to a plastic lawn chair. Grant sat. They waited silently as the cassette and photo burned. Finally satisfied that the evidence was destroyed, she lowered the pistol. "I want a divorce," she said.

"I wouldn't think of contesting it."

"I'll be reasonable; I'll settle for sixty per cent of everything you have."

"Seems perfectly fair to me."

"You will have your book collection appraised and you can either pay me sixty per cent of the appraisal or have it auctioned and I will take sixty per cent of that. You can keep the house as long as you pay me sixty per cent of that appraisal as well. You'll move into a hotel until I find a place I like and move my things out. I want the Brancusi."

Grant nodded. "That will be fine. No problem."

"You have an hour to pack your bags and get out."

"I'll probably only need about twenty minutes; I'm a quick packer."

"Since when?"

Two months after their divorce was finalized Grant moved back into the Brentwood mansion. He was happy to be rid of Babs, even though she had exacted a very high financial price. He had been forced to re-mortgage the house. But he wouldn't really miss the money; he could always earn more than he knew what to do with in his lucrative profession. And best of all, he still had his precious books and the Dodgson photographs. He had auctioned all of the paintings at Sotheby's.

He had bought a sailboat, which he had named *The Boojum* as a sort of joke. He kept it moored down in Long Beach, and had become quite good at sailing it, even venturing out into the open Pacific when the winds weren't too strong.

The following February following his divorce he drove down to Long Beach for a cruise, and made his way to where *The Boojum* was docked. He went aboard and put his key in the lock to go into the small cabin below deck, only to find that it was already unlocked. He eased the door open and peered inside, half-expecting to see some beach bum asleep on his bunk. He was surprised to see instead a large black book. He went over to the bunk and picked it up, surprised to find that it was a copy of the Catalpa Press *Snark*. He opened it up and found to his dismay that some idiot had ripped out the entire first chapter, ruining the copy. There was a large bookmark inserted near the back, and he opened it to find that someone had drawn a large heart with a red pen next to the last stanza of the poem:

In the midst of the word he was trying to say,
In the midst of his laughter and glee,
He had softly and suddenly vanished away—
For the Snark WAS *a Boojum, you see.*

He dropped the book and rushed to get off of the boat. Babs, who was sitting on the deck of her powerboat tied up not far away, had been watching *The Boojum* intently through a pair of binoculars. She smiled as she saw the panic on George's face as he clambered back up onto the deck. When she pushed a button on the small transmitter she held in her hand the boat exploded in an enormous fireball. Acting the part of an innocent bystander, she screamed and dove to the deck of her boat.

After the debris had settled she eased herself up to look at what little remained. Boats on both sides of where *The Boojum* had been floating moments before were in flames. Thick black smoke billowed up from burning diesel and gasoline floating on the water.

"Happy Valentine, Grant," she said, and smiled that gorgeous smile of hers. She was wearing a pink leather micro-bikini for the occasion. Grant would have liked it.

Also available from Evertype

Sources

Alice's Adventures in Wonderland: The Evertype definitive edition, by Lewis Carroll, 2016

Alice's Adventures in Wonderland, illus. June Lornie, 2013

Alice's Adventures in Wonderland, illus. Mathew Staunton, 2015

Alice's Adventures in Wonderland, illus. Harry Furniss, 2016

Alice's Adventures in Wonderland, illus. J. Michael Rolen, 2017

Through the Looking-Glass and What Alice Found There, by Lewis Carroll, 2009

The Nursery "Alice", by Lewis Carroll, 2015

Alice's Adventures under Ground, by Lewis Carroll, 2009

The Hunting of the Snark, by Lewis Carroll, 2010

Sequels

A New Alice in the Old Wonderland, by Anna Matlack Richards, 2009

New Adventures of Alice, by John Rae, 2010

Alice Through the Needle's Eye, by Gilbert Adair, 2012

Wonderland Revisited and the Games Alice Played There, by Keith Sheppard, 2009

Alice and the Boy who Slew the Jabberwock, by Allan William Parkes, 2016

Alice and the Missing Chapter, New chapters by fourteen authors, edited by Michael Everson, 2024

Spelling

Alice's Adventures in Wonderland, Retold in words of one Syllable by Mrs J. C. Gorham, 2010

𐐈𐑊𐐮𐑅'𐑆 𐐈𐐼𐑂𐐯𐑌𐐽𐐲𐑉𐑆 𐐮𐑌 𐐎𐐲𐑌𐐼𐐲𐑉𐑊𐐰𐑌𐐼 (Alis'z Advenchurz in Wundurland), *Alice* printed in the Deseret Alphabet, 2014

𐐜 𐐐𐐲𐑌𐐻𐐮𐑍 𐐲𐑂 𐑄 𐐝𐑌𐐫𐑉𐐿 (Dh Hunting uv dh Snark), *The Hunting of the Snark* printed in the Deseret Alphabet, 2016

Also available from Evertype

(Thru dh Lüking-Glas and Hwut Alis Fawnd Dher), *Looking-Glass* printed in the Deseret Alphabet, 2016

Alice's Adventures in Wonderland, *Alice* printed in Dyslexic-Friendly fonts, 2015

Through the Looking-Glass and What Alice Found There, *Looking-Glass* printed in Dyslexic-Friendly fonts, 2020

Alice's Adventures in a Dyslexic Wonderland, *Alice* printed in a font that simulates Dyslexia, 2015

(Ælɪsɛz Ædvɛ́ntʃuɹz ɪn Wʌ́nduɹlænd), *Alice* printed in the Ewellic Alphabet, 2013

'Ælɪsɪz Əd'ventʃəz ɪn 'Wʌndəˌlænd, *Alice* printed in the International Phonetic Alphabet, 2014

Alis'z Advnčrz in Wundland, *Alice* printed in the Nspel orthography, 2015

Alice printed in the Nyctographic Square Alphabet, 2011

The Hunting of the Snark printed in the Nyctographic Square Alphabet, 2024

Alice's Adventures in Wonderland, *Alice* printed in Pitman New Era Shorthand, forthcoming

Alice's Adventures in Wonderland, *Alice* printed in QR Codes, 2018

(Alɪs'əz ədventjuːrz ɪn Wʌndərlænd), *Alice* printed in the Shaw Alphabet, 2013

ALISIZ ADVENCƎRZ IN WUNDRLAND, *Alice* printed in the Unifon Alphabet, 2014

(Aliz kalandjai Csodaországban), The Hungarian *Alice* printed in Old Hungarian script, tr. Anikó Szilágyi, 2016

Scholarship

Elucidating Alice: A Textual Commentary on *Alice's Adventures in Wonderland*, by Selwyn Goodacre, 2015

Reflecting Alice: A Textual Commentary on *Through the Looking-Glass*, by Selwyn Goodacre, 2021.

Engaging the Snark: A Textual Commentary on *The Hunting of the Snark*, by Selwyn Goodacre, 2024.

Behind the Looking-Glass: Reflections on the Myth of Lewis Carroll, by Sherry L. Ackerman, 2012

Selections from the Lewis Carroll Collection of Victoria J. Sewell, compiled by Byron W. Sewell, 2014

SOCIAL COMMENTARY

Clara in Blunderland, by Caroline Lewis, 2010

Lost in Blunderland: The further adventures of Clara, by Caroline Lewis, 2010

John Bull's Adventures in the Fiscal Wonderland, by Charles Geake, 2010

The Westminster Alice, by H. H. Munro (Saki), 2017

Alice in Blunderland: An Iridescent Dream, by John Kendrick Bangs, 2010

SIMULATIONS

Davy and the Goblin, by Charles Edward Carryl, 2010

The Admiral's Caravan, by Charles Edward Carryl, 2010

Gladys in Grammarland, by Audrey Mayhew Allen, 2010

Alice's Adventures in Pictureland, by Florence Adèle Evans, 2011

Folly in Fairyland, by Carolyn Wells, 2016

Rollo in Emblemland, by J. K. Bangs & C. R. Macauley, 2010

Phyllis in Piskie-land, by J. Henry Harris, 2012

Alice in Beeland, by Lillian Elizabeth Roy, 2012

Eileen's Adventures in Wordland, by Zillah K. Macdonald, 2010

Alice and the Time Machine, by Victor Fet, 2016

Алиса и Машина Времени (Alisa i Mashina Vremeni), *Alice and the Time Machine* in Russian, tr. Victor Fet, 2016

SEWELLIANA

Sun-hee's Adventures Under the Land of Morning Calm, by Victoria J. Sewell & Byron W. Sewell, 2016

선희의 조용한 아침의 나라 모험기 (Seonhuiui Joyonghan Achim-ui Nala Moheomgi), *Sun-hee* in Korean, tr. Miyeong Kang, forthcoming

Alix's Adventures in Wonderland: Lewis Carroll's Nightmare, by Byron W. Sewell, 2011

Áloþk's Adventures in Goatland, by Byron W. Sewell, 2011

Alice's Bad Hair Day in Wonderland, by Byron W. Sewell, 2013

The Carrollian Tales of Inspector Spectre, by Byron W. Sewell, 2011

The Annotated Alice in Nurseryland, by Byron W. Sewell, 2016

The Haunting of the Snarkasbord, by Alison Tannenbaum, Byron W. Sewell, Charlie Lovett, & August A. Imholtz, Jr, 2012

The Millennium Snark Trilogy, by Byron W. Sewell, 2024

Snarkmaster, by Byron W. Sewell, 2012

In the Boojum Forest, by Byron W. Sewell, 2014

Murder by Boojum, by Byron W. Sewell, 2014

Close Encounters of the Snarkian Kind, by Byron W. Sewell, 2016

TRANSLATIONS

Кайкалдыҥ Јеринде Алисала болгон учуралдар (Kaykaldıñ Cerinde Alisala bolgon uçuraldar), *Alice* in Altai, tr. Küler Tepukov, 2016

Alice's Adventures in An Appalachian Wonderland, *Alice* in Appalachian English, tr. Byron & Victoria Sewell, 2012

Սնարքի Որսը (Snarḱi Orsě), *The Hunting of the Snark* in Eastern Armenian, tr. Alexander Kalantaryan & Artak Kalantaryan, forthcoming

Ալիս Հրաշալիքներու Աշխարհին Մէջ (Alis Hrashaliḱneru Ashkharhin Mēch), *Alice* in Western Armenian, tr. Yervant Gobelean, forthcoming

Patimatli ali Alice tu Văsilia ti Ciudii, *Alice* in Aromanian, tr. Mariana Bara, 2015

Also available from **Evertype**

Әлисәнең Сәйерстандағы мажаралары (Älisäneñ Säyerstandağı majaraları), *Alice* in Bashkir, tr. Güzäl Sitdykova, 2017

Алесіны прыгоды ў Цудазем'і (Alesiny pryhody u Tsudazem'i), *Alice* in Belarusian, tr. Max Ščur, 2016

На тым баку Люстра і што там напаткала Алесю (Na tym baku Liustra i shto tam napatkala Alesiu), *Looking-Glass* in Belarusian, tr. Max Ščur, 2016

Снаркаловы (Snarkalovy), *The Hunting of the Snark* in Belarusian, tr. Max Ščur, forthcoming

Troioù-kaer Alis e Vro ar Marzhoù, *Alice* in Breton, tr. Herve Kerrain, forthcoming

Crystal's Adventures in A Cockney Wonderland, *Alice* in Cockney Rhyming Slang, tr. Charlie Lovett, 2015

Aventurs Alys in Pow an Anethow, *Alice* in Cornish, tr. Nicholas Williams, 2015

Aventurs Alys in Pow an Anethow Dyllans Dywyêthek Kernowek-Sowsnek, *Alice* in Cornish, bilingual edition, tr. Nicholas Williams, 2021

Alice's Ventures in Wunderland, *Alice* in Cornu-English, tr. Alan M. Kent, 2015

Maries Hændelser i Vidunderlandet, *Alice* in Danish, tr. D.G., forthcoming

آلیس در سرزمین عجایب (Âlis dar Sarzamin-e Ajâyeb), *Alice* in Dari, tr. Rahman Arman, 2015

Äventyrą̈ Alice i Underlandą̈, *Alice* in Elfdalian, tr. Inga-Britt Petersson, 2022

La Aventuroj de Alicio en Mirlando, *Alice* in Esperanto, tr. E. L. Kearney (1910), 2009

La Aventuroj de Alico en Mirlando, *Alice* in Esperanto, tr. Donald Broadribb, 2012

Trans la Spegulo kaj kion Alico trovis tie, *Looking-Glass* in Esperanto, tr. Donald Broadribb, 2012

Les Aventures d'Alice au pays des merveilles, *Alice* in French, tr. Henri Bué, 2015

ALSO AVAILABLE FROM **EVERTYPE**

Les Aventures d'Alice au pays des merveilles, *Alice* in French, tr. Henri Bué, illus. Mathew Staunton, 2015

De aventoeren fan Alice yn Wûnderlân, *Alice* in West Frisian, tr. Tiny Mulder, 2024

ელისის თავგადასავალი საოცრებათა ქვეყანაში (Elisis t'avgadasavali saoc'rebat'a k'veqanaši), *Alice* in Georgian, tr. Giorgi Gokieli, 2016

Alice's Abenteuer im Wunderland, *Alice* in German, tr. Antonie Zimmermann, 2010

Die Lissel ehr Erlebnisse im Wunnerland, *Alice* in Palantine German, tr. Franz Schlosser, 2013

Der Alice ihre Obmteier im Wunderlaund, *Alice* in Viennese German, tr. Hans Werner Sokop, 2012

Balþos Gadedeis Aþalhaidais in Sildaleikalanda, *Alice* in Gothic, tr. David Alexander Carlton, 2015

Nā Hana Kupanaha a ʻĀleka ma ka ʻĀina Kamahaʻo, *Alice* in Hawaiian, tr. R. Keao NeSmith, 2017

Nā Hana Kupanaha a ʻĀleka ma ka ʻĀina Kamahaʻo Kope ʻōlelo Hawaiʻi–ʻōlelo Pelekānia, *Alice* in Hawaiian, bilingual edition, tr. R. Keao NeSmith, 2022

Ma Loko o ke Aniani Kū a me ka Mea i Loaʻa iā ʻĀleka ma Laila, *Looking-Glass* in Hawaiian, tr. R. Keao NeSmith, 2017

Aliz kalandjai Csodaországban, *Alice* in Hungarian, tr. Anikó Szilágyi, 2013

Ævintýri Lísu í Undralandi, *Alice* in Icelandic, tr. Þórarinn Eldjárn, 2013

L'Aventuri di Alicia en Marvelia, *Alice* in Ido, tr. Gonçalo Neves, 2020

Le Aventuras de Alice in le Pais del Meravilias, *Alice* in Interlingua, tr. Rodrigo Guerra, 2020

Eachtra Eibhlíse i dTír na nIontas, *Alice* in Irish, tr. Pádraig Ó Cadhla (1922), 2015

Eachtraí Eilíse i dTír na nIontas, *Alice* in Irish, tr. Nicholas Williams, 2007

Eachtraí Eilíse i dTír na nIontas: Eagrán Dátheangach Gaeilge–Béarla, *Alice* in Irish, bilingual edition, tr. tr. Nicholas Williams, 2022

Also available from Evertype

Lastall den Scáthán agus a bhFuair Eilís Ann Roimpi,
Looking-Glass in Irish, tr. Nicholas Williams, 2009

Le Avventure di Alice nel Paese delle Meraviglie,
Alice in Italian, tr. Teodorico Pietrocòla Rossetti, 2010

Alis Advencha ina Wandalan,
Alice in Jamaican Creole, tr. Tamirand Nnena De Lisser, 2016

L's Aventuthes d'Alice en Émèrvil'lie,
Alice in Jèrriais, tr. Geraint Williams, 2012

L'Travèrs du Mitheux et chein qu'Alice y dêmuchit,
Looking-Glass in Jèrriais, tr. Geraint Williams, 2012

Алисэ Телъыджэщӏым зэрыщыӏар (Alisė Tel″ydzhėshchḣym zėryshchyḣar), *Alice* in Kabardian, tr. Murat Temyr & Murat Brat, 2020

Алиса Къужур Дунияны Къыдырады (Alisa Qujur Duniyanı Qıdıradı), *Alice* in Karachay-Balkar, tr. Magomet Gekki, 2019

Әлисәнің ғажайып елдегі басынан кешкендері (Älïsäniñ ğajayıp eldegi basınan keşkenderi), *Alice* in Kazakh, tr. Fatima Moldashova, 2016

Алисаның Хайхастар Чирінзер чорығы (Alïsanıñ Hayhastar Çïrinzer çorığı), *Alice* in Khakas, tr. Maria Çertykova, 2017

Алисакӧд Шемӧсмуын лоӧмторъяс (Alisaköd Šemösmuyn loömtor″ias),
Alice in Komi-Zyrian, tr. Evgenii Tsypanov & Elena Eltsova, 2018

Алисанын Кызыктар Өлкөсүндөгү укмуштуу окуялары
(Alisanın Kızıktar Ölkösündögü ukmuştuu okuyaları),
Alice in Kyrgyz, tr. Aida Egemberdieva, 2016

Las Aventuras de Alisia en el Paiz de las Maraviyas,
Alice in Ladino, tr. Avner Perez, 2016

לאס אב׳ינטוראס די אליסייה אין איל פאאיס די לאס מאראב׳ילייאס
(Las Aventuras de Alisia en el Paiz de las Maraviyas),
Alice in Ladino, tr. Avner Perez, 2016

Alisis pīdzeivuojumi Breinumu zemē,
Alice in Latgalian, tr. Evika Muizniece, 2015

Alicia in Terrā Mīrābilī, *Alice* in Latin, tr. Clive Harcourt Carruthers, 2018

Alicia in Terrā Mīrābilī: Ēditiō Bilinguis Latīna et Anglica,
Alice in Latin, bilingual edition, tr. Clive Harcourt Carruthers, 2021

Also available from **Evertype**

Aliciae per Speculum Trānsitus (Quaeque Ibi Invēnit), *Looking-Glass* in Latin, tr. Clive Harcourt Carruthers, forthcoming

Alisa-ney Aventuras in Divalanda, *Alice* in Lingua de Planeta (Lidepla), tr. Anastasia Lysenko & Dmitry Ivanov, 2014

La aventuras de Alisia en la pais de mervelias, *Alice* in Lingua Franca Nova, tr. Simon Davies, 2012

Alice ęhr Ȩventüürn in't Wunnerland, *Alice* in Low German, tr. Reinhard F. Hahn, 2010

Contoyrtyssyn Ealish ayns Çheer ny Yindyssyn, *Alice* in Manx, tr. Brian Stowell, 2010

Ko Ngā Takahanga i a Ārihi i Te Ao Mīharo, *Alice* in Māori, tr. Tom Roa, 2015

Dee Erlăwnisse von Alice em Wundalaund, *Alice* in Mennonite Low German, tr. Jack Thiessen, 2012

Auanturiou adelis en Bro an Marthou, *Alice* in Middle Breton, tr. Herve Le Bihan & Herve Kerrain, forthcoming

The Aventures of Alys in Wondyr Lond, *Alice* in Middle English, tr. Brian S. Lee, 2013

Þurh þe Loking-Glas and What Alys Founde Þere, *Looking-Glass* in Middle English, tr. Brian S. Lee, forthcoming

L'Avventure d'Alice 'int' 'o Paese d' 'e Maraveglie, *Alice* in Neapolitan, tr. Roberto D'Ajello, 2016

Attravierzo 'o specchio e cchello c'Alice ce truvaie, *Looking-Glass* in Neapolitan, tr. Roberto D'Ajello, 2019

L'Aventuros de Alis in Marvoland, *Alice* in Neo, tr. Ralph Midgley, 2013

Elises Eventyr i Undernes Land: den første norske *Alice*: Elise's Adventures in the Land of Wonders: the first Norwegian *Alice*, *Alice* in Norwegian, ed. & tr. Anne Kristin Lande, 2022

Alice sine opplevingar i Eventyrlandet, *Alice* in Nynorsk, tr. Sigrun Anny Røssbø, 2020 OUT OF PRINT

Æðelgýðe Ellendǽda on Wundorlande, *Alice* in Old English, tr. Peter S. Baker, 2015

Also available from **Evertype**

La geste d'Aalis el Païs de Merveilles,
Alice in Old French, tr. May Plouzeau, 2017

Alitjilu Palyantja Tjuta Ngura Tjukurmankuntjala (Alitji's Adventures in Dreamland), *Alice* in Pitjantjatjara, tr. Nancy Sheppard, forthcoming

Alitji's Adventures in Dreamland: An Aboriginal tale inspired by *Alice's Adventures in Wonderland*, adapted by Nancy Sheppard, forthcoming

Alice Contada aos Mais Pequenos,
The Nursery "Alice" in Portuguese, tr., Rogério Miguel Puga, 2015

Aventurile lui Alice în Țara Minunilor,
Alice in Romanian, tr., Claudia E. Stoian, 2020

Aventurile Alisei în Țara Minunilor,
Alice in Bessarabian Romanian, tr., Tatiana Sima, forthcoming

Сыр Алиса Попэя кэ Чюдэнгири Пхув (Sir Alisa Popeja ke Čudengiri Phuv), *Alice* in North Russian Romani, tr. Viktor Shapoval, 2018

Соня въ царствѣ дива (Sonia v tsarstvie diva): Sonja in a Kingdom of Wonder, *Alice* in facsimile of the 1879 first Russian translation, 2013

Соня в царстве дива (Sonia v tsarstve diva),
An edition of the first Russian *Alice* in modern orthography, 2017

Приключения Алисы в Стране Чудес (Prikliucheniia Alisy v Strane Chudes), *Alice* in Russian, tr. Yury Nesterenko, 2018

Приключения Алисы в Стране Чудес (Prikliucheniia Alisy v Strane Chudes), *Alice* in Russian, bilingual edition, tr. Yury Nesterenko, 2022

Приключения Алисы в Стране Чудес (Prikliucheniia Alisy v Strane Chudes), *Alice* in Russian, tr. Nina Demurova, 2020

Алиса в Стране Чудес (Alisa v Strane Chudes), *Alice* in Russian, tr. A. Daktil' (Anatolii Frenkel'), 2022

Охота на Снарка (Okhota na Snarka),
The Hunting of the Snark in Russian, tr. Victor Fet, 2016

Ia Aventures as Alice in Daumsenland,
Alice in Sambahsa, tr. Olivier Simon, 2013

Ocolo id Specule ed Quo Alice Trohv Ter,
Looking-Glass in Sambahsa, tr. Olivier Simon, 2016

Also available from **Evertype**

ʻO Tāfaoga a ʻĀlise i le Nuʻu o Mea Ofoofogia,
Alice in Samoan, tr. Luafata Simanu-Klutz, 2013

Eachdraidh Ealasaid ann an Tìr nan Iongantas,
Alice in Scottish Gaelic, tr. Moray Watson, 2012

Alice's Adventchers in Wunderland,
Alice in Scouse, tr. Marvin R. Sumner, 2015

Mbalango wa Alice eTikweni ra Swihlamariso,
Alice in Shangani, tr. Peniah Mabaso & Steyn Khesani Madlome, 2015

Ahlice's Aveenturs in Wunderlaant,
Alice in Border Scots, tr. Cameron Halfpenny, 2015

Alice's Mishanters in e Land o Farlies,
Alice in Caithness Scots, tr. Catherine Byrne, 2014

Alice's Advenchers in Wunnerlaund,
Alice in Fife Scots, tr. Tom Hubbard, 2024

Alice's Adventirs in Wunnerlaun,
Alice in Glaswegian Scots, tr. Thomas Clark, 2014

Ailice's Anters in Ferlielann,
Alice in North-East Scots (Doric), tr. Derrick McClure, 2012

Throwe the Keekin-Gless an Fit Ailice's Funn There,
Looking-Glass in North-East Scots (Doric), tr. Derrick McClure, 2021

Alice's Adventirs in Wonderlaand,
Alice in Shetland Scots, tr. Laureen Johnson, 2012

Ailice's Àventurs in Wunnerland,
Alice in Southeast Central Scots, tr. Sandy Fleemin, 2011

Ailis's Anterins i the Laun o Ferlies,
Alice in Synthetic Scots, tr. Andrew McCallum, 2013

Alice's Carrànts in Wunnerlan,
Alice in Ulster Scots, tr. Anne Morrison-Smyth, 2013

Alison's Jants in Ferlieland,
Alice in West-Central Scots, tr. James Andrew Begg, 2014

Alice muNyika yeMashiripiti,
Alice in Shona, tr. Shumirai Nyota & Tsitsi Nyoni, 2015

Алисаның қайғаллығ Черинде полған чоруқтары (Alisanıñ qayğallıġ Çerinde polğan çoruqtarı), *Alice* in Shor, tr. Liubov′ Arbaçakova, 2017

Alicia's Adventuras en Wonderlandia, *Alice* in Spanglish, tr. Ilan Stavans, 2021

Alis bu Cëlmo dac Cojube w dat Tantelat, *Alice* in Ṣurayt, tr. Jan Beṯ-Ṣawoce, 2015

Alisi Ndani ya Nchi ya Ajabu, *Alice* in Swahili, tr. Ida Hadjuvayanis, 2015

Alices Äventyr i Sagolandet, *Alice* in Swedish, tr. Emily Nonnen, 2010

'Alisi 'i he Fonua 'o e Fakaofo', *Alice* in Tongan, tr. Siutāula Cocker & Telesia Kalavite, 2014

De Aventure Alisu in Mirviziland, *Alice* in Uropi, tr. Bertrand Carette & Joël Landais, 2018

Ventürs jiela Lälid in Stunalän, *Alice* in Volapük, tr. Ralph Midgley, forthcoming

Lès-avirètes da Alice ô payis dès mèrvèyes, *Alice* in Walloon, tr. Jean-Luc Fauconnier, 2012

Lès paskéyes d'Alice è payis dès mèrvèyes, *Alice* in Central Walloon, tr. Bernard Louis, 2017

Anturiaethau Alys yng Ngwlad Hud, *Alice* in Welsh, tr. Selyf Roberts, 2010

I Avventur de Alìs ind el Paes di Meravili, *Alice* in Western Lombard, tr. GianPietro Gallinelli, 2015

U-Alisi Kwilizwe Lemimangaliso, *Alice* in Xhosa, tr. Mhlobo Jadezweni, forthcoming

Di Avantures fun Alis in Vunderland, *Alice* in Yiddish, tr. Joan Braman, 2015

Alises Avantures in Vunderland, *Alice* in Yiddish, tr. Adina Bar-El, 2018

אַליסעס אַוואַנטורעס אין וווּנדערלאַנד (Alises Avantures in Vunderland), *Alice* in Yiddish, tr. Adina Bar-El, 2018

Insumansumane Zika-Alice, *Alice* in Zimbabwean Ndebele, tr. Dion Nkomo, 2015

U-Alice Ezweni Lezimanga, *Alice* in Zulu, tr. Bhekinkosi Ntuli, 2014

www.ingramcontent.com/pod-product-compliance
Lightning Source LLC
Chambersburg PA
CBHW032042050726
47590CB00001B/99